Con

CW01501683

PART I: BOROUGH MARKET

1	The Stage	3
2	A Gateway	7
3	Mrs Kirkham's	13
4	Carotting the Comté	17

PART II: LIFE BEFORE CHEESE

5	The Presenter's Tale	25
6	1924 versus 2019	33
7	Raclette for One	38
8	The Munster Mash	45
9	What Else Can a Radio Presenter Do?	53
10	The Ottolenghi Audition	58
11	Picking Myself Up	72
12	The Answer Lies in Borough Market	77

PART III: APPRENTICESHIP

13	The Cheese Talk	87
14	East Dulwich and the Cheesemonger Avengers	95
15	First Shift	104
16	Did You Just Lick Your Fingers?	111
17	A Brief Introduction to the Art of the Squeegee	118
18	No Maure Like This, Please	129
19	Knackered	133
20	Like French Kissing a Sheep	142

Contents

21	'I think we should move into the fridge'	153
22	The Morning After	177
23	A Clean Slate	188
24	Michael, What Have You Done?	196
25	Christmas Eve	202
26	A Cheesesome Threesome	210

PART IV: BI-CONTINENTAL

27	Back to the Microphone	217
28	Cheese in a Time of Corona	223
29	Decision Time	235

PART V: CHEESEMONGER'S CHOICE

30	Changes	241
31	We Close at 5	249
32	New Cheese on the Block	257
33	Tier Four	261
34	Good Friday	275
35	Tying the Knot	286
36	Cheese Daemons	298

Acknowledgements	309

The Cheese Cure

MICHAEL FINNERTY

The Cheese Cure

How Comté and Camembert fed my soul

MUDLARK

Mudlark
HarperCollins*Publishers*
1 London Bridge Street
London SE1 9GF

www.harpercollins.co.uk

HarperCollins*Publishers*
Macken House, 39/40 Mayor Street Upper
Dublin 1, D01 C9W8, Ireland

First published by Mudlark 2025

1 3 5 7 9 10 8 6 4 2

A catalogue record of this book is available from the British Library

ISBN 978-0-00-874944-6

Printed and bound in the UK using 100% renewable electricity at CPI
Group (UK) Ltd

For the cheesemongers

Part I
Borough Market

1
The Stage

OPENING THE STALL ALWAYS begins with the shutters, a metal curtain that grinds and clatters as it rises. Behind it, polished surfaces shine eerily in the grey light. The smell is a bleach-like clean. There's something slightly sinister to the market before sunrise. It's a stage without the lights or the actors, the decor in shadows.

All around Borough Market at this hour, there are stirrings, the beginnings of a determined, pre-dawn buzz in the air as traders arrive to start the day. In the distance, a floor sweeping machine, the echo of foldable tables falling to the concrete floor, chains being unlocked and released, the occasional audible groan or grunt from someone lifting something heavy.

In our row, there is only one stall that's illuminated. It sells Italian cured meats and cheeses: Mozzarella, Burrata, Stracciatella, ham that begins to melt as soon as you place it on your tongue, but they're all packed away now. At this hour, the only visible harbinger of the day to come is the meat slicer, waiting.

You need to make a little effort in order to flick on the lights in our stall. They're controlled by a socket near the floor. I place my bag down, reach across a table and stretch to turn it on, then pop my head next door to say hello. It's Francis, their cheesemonger. If you were to look up stock photos of a solitary lighthouse operator, you might see someone exactly like him: navy blue beanie, dark cable-wool jumper, grey hair and long grey beard, specs, gravelly voice. As it happens, Francis was a solitary lighthouse operator for many years.

'Morning, Francis. All well?'

'Morning, Michael. It's early.'

Maybe you've only seen the market when it's packed with foodies on a summer afternoon, laughter and delight in the air. You could set a rom-com at the market. At this early hour, you'd be forgiven for thinking you'd stepped into a thriller, horror story or gritty drama. As it happens, the market has acted as the setting for each of the above.

That the face of the market changes so radically from night to day, from winter to spring, from rain to sun, is not just down to the elements and the passage of time, of course. It's the hard graft from all of us, the people who work here, and all those who came before us.

On this site for a thousand years, a food market has stood – beneath the bell tower of Southwark Cathedral, at the foot of London Bridge, on the banks of River Thames – in a state of permanent renewal and transformation, feeding the city. When I first laid eyes on it, it was a wholesale market primarily and I knew nothing about it, except that it was big and beautiful and already casting its spell over me, as it has so many others.

Brie de Meaux

'Je viens de découvrir l'un des mets les plus délicieux qui soient.'

– Charlemagne, reputedly, after his first bite of Brie de Meaux in 774 AD at the Reuil-en-Brie Abbey. Loose translation: 'This cheese is banging.'

Origin: Born in the Brie region, east of Paris, it dates back to the seventh century. The recipe originates from the monks of Jouarre Abbey, 20km outside the town of Meaux. It became a favourite of European royals and the aristocracy. A raw milk cheese, it is now protected by both an Appellation d'Origine Contrôlée (AOC) and Appellation d'Origine Protégée (AOP) designation.

Presentation: About 36cm across and weighing in at around 3kg, it is more often oval, not round, and features a downy, white rind – referred to as a bloomy rind – due to the mould and yeast that bloom on its surface. Depending on how ripe it is, the paste can be chalky in the centre, or oozing. The cliché is that the French prefer the former, the British the latter.

How to serve: A gooey wedge of Brie is a beautiful thing on a cheeseboard; smaller slices on little toasts work as an apéro. It's popular in sandwiches, some like it melted, and others fancy it alongside fruit, such as cranberries. It's versatile, an absolute classic French cheese. Beware imitations – supermarket Brie abounds, but these are not Brie de Meaux and sometimes they are more texture than taste. For pairings, the classic is a glass of Champagne, otherwise choose something with a good acidity. Beer is a great choice, anything from a stout to a blonde ale to a pilsner.

Fun fact: In the sixteenth century, Margaret of Valois, popularly known as La Reine Margot, is said to have kept her husband Henri of Navarre, later 'Good King Henry' of France, from visiting his mistress, Gabrielle d'Estrées, by offering him Brie on toast.

2
A Gateway

ONE OF THE MOST exciting things about being a cheesemonger is discovery. Your own discovery of new cheeses is one thing, but I'm talking here about the customer's. It's a thrill to introduce people to good cheese, to watch them as they taste something they've never tried before and, if you're lucky, fall in love with it.

Sharing the joys of discovery means treating regulars to new products; it's the excitement of a newly arrived batch of an old favourite cheese, and one of the biggest highs of all is to watch a newbie as their whole world gets rocked.

If the newbie in question is open-minded and curious, that's fun, but there's a special thrill involved in converting a sceptic. Sceptics are easy to spot. You can see from their body language that they're wary of anything too exotic. Arms are often crossed, and they'll be half a step back from our display of cheeses at Borough Market. They're here because they were brought along by someone else. Often, it's a couple.

'Oh, he only likes strong Cheddar,' says the cheese-loving girlfriend as you offer a sample to her beau. He is shaking his head.

'That's a shame. What about goat's cheese?' I ask.

'I don't like it,' he announces matter-of-factly.

'Why don't you like it?'

'It's just not for me. Can't stand the taste.'

'When was the last time you had it?'

'Dunno. Years ago, I guess.'

'Supermarket goat's cheese?'

'Probably.'

'Okay, hang on a minute.'

I reach for a block of ash rind goat's cheese called Tomme de Chambrouze. It's a cheese that has ups and downs. Each wheel is from the same cheesemaker, and she is something of an eccentric, based in the Beaujolais area. We are currently on a considerable up with this cheese. The wheel we have open has an intensely white paste – it's slightly firmer than most goat's cheeses, with an alluring citrus and pepper vibe. Some nice acidity makes it feel bright on the tongue. It does not taste like supermarket goat's cheese.

I look him in the eye and speak earnestly. 'Right, so you may not like goat's cheese, and I respect that may be the case. What worries me is that you maybe had a not-great cheese years ago that was sitting on a supermarket shelf for weeks, entombed in plastic, and now you can't get past it, like a mental block, and I'm just not sure that's a great place to be in life. What do you say? Can we give this a go? It's limited exposure. One taste.'

'Try it!' says his girlfriend. She is invested now.

He does.

You can pretty much tell instantly once the cheese gets put in someone's mouth which way a thing is going to go. For instance, some people just don't like goat's milk. Is it something about the farmy sweetness? Who knows. In this case, he's poker-faced at first, but there is no spitting out, and the tell – no frown. Sure, he's cautious at first, leaving it on the tip of his tongue so it can be expelled immediately, if necessary, but that's not happening. I think we're in for the win.

A couple of moments later, you can see his tongue move a bit. The cheese has made it past the second barrier, back further into the mouth where other taste centres are being recruited. His head begins to nod, only slightly at first. Then I'm getting eye contact. We're there.

'All right.' A proper, full nod. 'Not bad. You got me. What's that cheese called, then?'

These are the moments you live for when you're wearing the apron. I wish I had a special button under the table to produce an orchestral flourish or a firework. A cowbell hangs from the ceiling, but we have agreed only to ring that when a monger cuts a piece of cheese precisely to a requested measure.

So much of it is in the approach but also, of course, the cheese! You have to know how far you can go. That gooey piece of Sainte-Maure that's currently sharply goat-forward, that would have sent him running for the hills. Things have to look and feel safe.

I have my own set of gateway cheeses that I go to for sceptics. These are cheeses that have enough character to ensnare, but present low risk. They are not overly smelly, there's no bonkers mould or bacteria growth. The Tomme de Chambrouze is often a winner, Tomme de Savoie for semi-soft cow's milk, Fourme d'Ambert for the blues, the big Alpine Comté and Gruyère, of course. No matter how wary people are, if the door opens just a crack to try something new, the right non-threatening cheese can be the ticket. That guy standing half a step back from our stall? That was me, once, before a whole world of cheese love opened up to me. For me, the gateway cheese was, wait for it: La Vache Qui Rit, paired with apple sauce.

As a secondary school student, I lived in France for the better part of a year with my exchange host family in a mid-sized city, Saint-Étienne. They would bring out a platter of cheeses without fail every midday and evening meal. The cheeses struck me as exotic at the time, strange and foreign to my palate, at once off-putting and intriguing. When I tell this story to them now, they laugh. My host family thinks their cheeseboards of the 1980s were unadventurous to say the least, mostly popular, branded, store-bought cheeses.

To me, they were a wonder. I grew up in Canada with industrially produced blocks of bright orange cheese wrapped in heavy plastic, individually wrapped slices for hamburgers and Cheez Whiz. These French cheeses were all shapes, smells, sizes and colours. Some of them weren't even cow's milk. At first, I didn't dare to eat them. They were just too out there, and I thought I might gag.

I stuck a toe in the water by taking a triangle of La Vache Qui Rit and eating it alongside some *purée de pomme*, unsweetened apple sauce. The two together were delicious and allowed me to overcome my reticence. Beyond seemed a big step, though.

Weeks went by. Hunger dictated that I would venture further into the daily cheeseboard. Our family had eight mouths to feed, the parents, the five children and me. Often there was a cousin or a family friend to boot. I soon began to understand that food was not in unlimited supply, and the way the French ate; the main course was a much smaller portion than in Canada, so seconds were rare and fought over.

If you didn't have a bit of each course, you were going to leave the table hungry. So it was yes to that leek soup, to the salad of tomato and red onion and to the platter of cheeses that came near the end of dinner. Things I suspected I would not like suddenly became more appetising through necessity. A food paradigm was shifting.

As with just about everything I tasted that year for the first time – different types of fish, foie gras, Dijon mustard, oysters, smoked salmon, pâté, endives, certain types of salad leaves, even rice salad – cheese was a revelation. Once I opened my mind, my tastebuds followed.

The cheeses, as it turns out, were awesome, and I moved from taking little, experimental bits of them alongside plenty of baguette in case I couldn't stomach the taste or smell, to healthy chunks and wedges that I ate with enthusiasm, no bread. I was a convert. Those were times of happy discovery, my initial entry into the world of cheese.

Tomme de Savoie

'Le fromage, ça se partage, mais si en plus c'est de la Tomme de Savoie, alors là, on festoie!'

– From the Tomme de Savoie IGP website, this wee verse rhymes in French, but not in English: 'Cheese is for sharing, but if it's Tomme de Savoie, then it's for celebrating!'

Origin: Hails from the heart of the French Alps, the Maurienne and Tarentaise Valleys. In the time of the Duchy of Savoie, from the sixteenth century, it became a staple on farmhouse tables, served at every meal.

Presentation: They vary, typically a chubby-looking wheel, around 20cm in diameter and weighing about 1.5kg.

How to serve: Eat the rind, give it to children, place a chunky wedge on your cheeseboard and watch it disappear. It can pair with fruit paste or even a high-fruit jam, but if you have a good one, there's no need. An excellent breakfast cheese. A lighter red such as a Gamay or Pinot Noir will work nicely; for whites, lean towards something aromatic.

Fun fact: People often will ask, 'What is a tomme, anyway?' and the fact is, many cheeses are labelled as a tomme but have little in common. They tend to be from the mountains, France, Switzerland or Italy, they are mostly uncooked curd cheese and have a natural rind. You'll find goat's, sheep's, and cow's milk tommes. A tomme can also refer to a family of cheeses that are lightly matured. In Roman times, soft cheeses coming from Lozère and Gévaudan were called *toumo* in patois. There are so many different varieties, the word *tomme* might as well mean cheese.

3
Mrs Kirkham's

THERE IS A LARGE DANDY of a man, a customer, an Englishman who wears extravagant, countryside outfits with splashes of London colour. His hair is long and unruly. He has a full beard, ginger and grey. Often, he wears a hat adorned by a feather. He shops at Borough Market, and he loves Mrs Kirkham's Lancashire, a crumbly, buttery, cow's milk cheese that we stock. We are known for our French and Swiss cheeses, so not a lot of people come to us for it and, to be honest, we carry it there mostly for him. It's a lot of pressure vying for his approbation.

When he declares the Lancashire to be 'Marvellous!' the whole stand feels marvellous by extension. Customers smile and buy more cheese, and cheesemongers feel a flush of pride. The energy boost can last an hour.

'Yes, very good that is! Give me a large cut from that piece, will you, Squire?'

If he's particularly taken by our wheel of Lancashire, he'll sometimes add, with a wink and a grin: 'I shall take one more cheese as well. Cheesemonger's choice!'

Lancashire is a deceptively fussy cheese for a sturdy Northerner. It dries out easily when unwrapped, it can take on an overstated acidity, has a proclivity to mould over on its cut face, develops blue veins, and can tip over into sour.

'This is about to go off,' he will sometimes say. We are in an open-air market but hearing those words sucks all the oxygen out of it anyway.

'You may be right about that, I'm afraid,' meaning he is right about that. 'It's the only wheel I have but what if I give it a good trim?'

I remove about a centimetre from the face of the piece and try again.

'No. This needs to be eaten in the next three days and no longer. I shall have a piece, not as big as usual,' he says, for all to hear. I catch myself flinching in sympathy with the Lancashire because, truth be told, I'd been verging similarly towards sour and dried out for a while.

Fast forward to a different day altogether and even from the back of the stall, I can tell he's just pulled up, call it a sudden shift in energy.

'How's your Lancashire today, Squire?'

'It's just come in! Let's find out together.'

'It's my lucky day,' he says, and he means it. Mine too because his timing is perfect.

Can a cheese glow? This one seems to be performing for us. I take my black-handled tasting knife and carve off two pieces, one for each of us. This Lancashire has depth and balance, a slight sweetness with a touch of sour that play off each other. There is a pleasant hint of acidity, a faint line of vanilla. The paste yields easily between the teeth; it has just the right degree of moisture.

He gives an ostentatious chew, and we lock eyes. 'Delightful. A hair on the young side, this is! Very good. I'll take a substantial piece of it, Squire.'

Most people when they taste 'the Kirkham's', as it's sometimes called, find it tastes nice, then purchase a slab and off they go. I mean, it's Lancashire, a gentle, often subtle cheese, not complicated like a Camembert or Époisses, both of which evolve rapidly and feature a more complex set of flavours. For him, though, it has a universe of meaning. One of the unexpected things about becoming a cheesemonger is that the more you learn about the cheeses, the more you learn about people.

Sure, a moister paste, a higher acidity, a sweetness that recalls vanilla are things we experience together as we taste, objective qualities. To what extent he finds those things pleasing will depend on his gustatory predispositions. But then there is a whole other realm, that of memories and associations, how certain tastes make us feel, where they transport us. When Lancashire tastes like this, I can tell it has taken him some place wonderful and personal that only he can ever visit. It's why he keeps coming back and why disappointing him is felt as a blow.

Today, it's brought him joy that I get to share a piece of.

Kirkham's Lancashire

'Around 1890, a Lancashire County Council employee named Joseph Gornall began visiting all the farms in Lancashire, observing the cheesemaking activity and giving practical advice on production and method. His aim was to standardise Lancashire cheese production across the county and create a formal recipe and method. In this, he succeeded and the recipe is basically the same as that used today.'

– Nigel White, *The Evolution of the British Cheese Industry*

∽

Origin: Lancashire cheesemaking, dating back to the twelfth century, was entirely located within a few kilometres of the Forest of Bowland, formerly Viking territory. Mrs Kirkham's Lancashire is one of only two farmhouse, raw milk Lancashires still in production.

Presentation: A wheel of Lancashire is impressive, weighing in at around 25kg and shaped like a squat barrel.

How to serve: Eat it straight off the cheeseboard, along with some bread or a cracker, with fruits, nuts or a chutney. It makes a superb cheese toastie. Pairs well with a pint of beer.

Fun fact: Each cheese is slathered in butter from the farm after being wrapped in cheesecloth.

4
Carotting the Comté

TASTING CHEESE IS PART ritual, part science, part art. It relies a lot on memory, and it gets personal. We'll be tasting a lot of cheese in these pages. Similarly to Lancashire, Comté is gentle, but there's more to it – don't tell our number one Kirkham's fan I said so. Comté is one of the big, Alpine cow's milk cheeses, a staple in kitchens across France. Wheels of Comté can measure the better part of a metre across and weigh close to forty kilograms. They are without question the heaviest and most awkward of the cheeses we have at our Borough Market stall and require strength, dexterity and familiarity to handle without injury. When we stack them one on top of the other on the display, people stop to take photos or just to ooh and aah. At its best, Comté is liltingly smooth, nutty and creamy. I've heard many people dub it heavenly.

Flat Comté, on the other hand, is a thing that happens, and when it does, it is very, very sad. Flat Comté has no brightness to the paste, the sweetness absent, the nuttiness muffled or stale. It can approach a sour onion flavour, or worse, it's just blah. You might even find yourself wondering, what is the point of this cheese?

On one late autumn afternoon, I decide to tell Manager Elle, after having worked a few shifts at our shop in East

Dulwich, that the Comté we are currently serving at Borough Market, where she is in charge, is not as good.

'What do you mean exactly?'

'I don't know, maybe it was just the novelty of working at a different site, but the Comté just tasted so much brighter.'

'The Comté is definitely flat. What can I do if I keep getting underwhelming wheels?'

I have hit a nerve.

'What about the returns?' I ask. Every Sunday, we send back to Cheese HQ our unsold pieces from wheels cut during the week so that they can be moved on quickly for wholesale. If a cut piece hangs around for more than a couple of weeks, it goes south. Essentially, what I am asking Elle here, irritatingly, is whether she remembered to return last week's cut pieces.

'I am returning it,' she says, turns on her heels and walks to the back of the stall.

I shouldn't have asked that. Can I blame a hangover from days working in live radio where a clock is running, meaning things are said more directly and too spontaneously? There again, I should have known she would take it personally. Elle is one of the best. Maturing cheese is a central part of her job so of course she is keeping track of the stock.

Elle hails from Swansea. She has a gentle charm that wins over the customers. Some of them come to chat with her for long minutes about the cheeses, about restaurants and food, theatre outings or just the weather. She has long chestnut hair that she keeps up while working, and a prominent pair of specs. She can surprise you with her simplicity, or with her complexity. She's genuinely fascinated with smaller, everyday developments around the market and in people's lives. Professionally, she's a proven problem-solver. She'll untie a tricky knot before you've even noticed it's there.

Sometimes, as she says, the wheel of Comté we receive is just flat. The problem is elsewhere but it becomes ours. On that same day, two different customers have a taste of our Comté, and follow it with a long pause, saying: 'I'll have the Gruyère, thanks.'

'And the Comté?'

'I don't fancy your Comté, I'm afraid. It has no spark,' says one. The other adds: 'It's like it's died inside.' You will occasionally get on-the-nose feedback like that at the stall and bristle. In the event, it is fair comment, so I smile, thank her, and ring up the Gruyère.

Later that same week, Owner Jon comes to Borough Market around midday and the subject turns towards the underwhelming Comté.

'Let's choose one then,' Jon says without skipping a beat. He is not arguing the point, even for a second. He goes to the back and pulls out an instrument known as a cheese iron. Some call it a tester, or even a trier. It looks like a cross between a ballpeen hammer and a corkscrew. In fact, the flatter end can also be used to give the wheels a knock. You can tell things about a wheel of cheese by the sound it makes. Our company features a cheese iron prominently in our logo, on the front of all our branded aprons.

The French call this instrument *une sonde*, which makes sense because it is used to probe the cheese. *Une sonde* is a probe. When you insert it diagonally into a wheel of Comté and give it a good twist, it will remove a smallish cylinder of cheese. The French call that a carrot. They will also call a cheese iron *une carotteuse,* something which draws out a carrot-shaped piece from a bigger whole. It's a word I love, partly because away from the language of cheese, the verb *carotter* has a more whimsical meaning. It indicates someone removing or taking away something, sometimes brazenly, from a secure place. It can also be used to say someone has been scammed or swindled.

Jon decides to iron all three of the wheels of Comté we are keeping in stock in our hard cheese cupboard at the market. There are dozens more at Cheese HQ, or The Arch as we call it. After handing us each a sample, he looks at me expectantly.

'I mean, it's pleasant enough but no more than that, a hint of sweetness.'

He says nothing as he turns it over in his mouth. Elle is also silent. Jon pauses, considers, then inserts the *carotte* of cheese back into the wheel to plug the hole he's made and moves to the second wheel.

'Yeah, that really is a bit flat,' says Elle immediately of the second. This time there is no pause, and Jon moves on to the third.

As I put this latest sample in my mouth, I have an instant, involuntary exclamation. 'Ohhh! This is smooth.' There is cheesy magic in the taste of the third wheel of Comté. You can read it on the face of all three of us. It has a solid combination: rich, nutty, with a sweet creaminess to round everything off. It's considerably different from the other two, like a couple of levels of taste better.

When you know cheese, you know when the Comté is flat. Cheesemongers spot signs of trouble early on because we're always looking for them. Do we know ourselves so well? Pressures build up in our daily lives; routines wear us down. It can all happen without us taking note. Then when the world begins to feel grey and bland, where do we find the courage to grasp the cheese iron and 'carotte' ourselves, to find out what's gone wrong and make a change?

Comté

'Comtois, rends-toi ! Nenni, ma foi!'

– Translates to 'Comtois, surrender! Not on your life!' and is the motto of the Franche-Comté region of France. Comté is emblematic of the region and its people hold it in great esteem.

Origin: The origins of Comté reach back to the thirteenth century, but Comté was only given as the name to the cheese around 1924. Its history is also the history of the people where it is made in the Franche-Comté. Throughout the years, there were heated disputes over methods of production. Comté was awarded its AOC designation in 1958.

Presentation: 50 to 70cm across, it weighs as much as 45kg – a big Alpine wheel of cheese. The height can vary between 8 and 13cm.

How to serve: A good Comté needs no accompaniment; it's delicious on its own. I like it slightly chilled, mountain temperature, giving it a firmer texture and more resistance between the teeth; when warm, it sweats and loses some of its appeal. Serve ideally with a mountain red like a Pinot Noir or a Savoyard white wine. Comté is a great melter and works in fondue, but also in cooking as a gratin. A favourite recipe – there are many – mixes it with rice and kale, baked.

Fun fact: Before the wheels leave the Franche-Comté, they are graded on a scale of 1 to 20. The best wheels are graded 15 points and higher and given a green band denoting Comté

Extra. There's a lot of room for variation between 15 and 20, meaning some wheels are notably better than others. Wheels that score 12 to 14 points are given a brown band. Wheels that score less than 12 are not sold as Comté.

Part II
Life Before Cheese

5

The Presenter's Tale

I AM A JOURNALIST BY TRAINING, with Canadian citizenship by birth and Irish citizenship through my father. For years, after graduating from university, I was a researcher, then a reporter, and finally one day arrived at the BBC World Service, at Bush House in London. In total, I ended up working at the BBC and the *Guardian* for fifteen years on either side of the Millennium. Thanks to the wise counsel and assistance of a colleague obsessed with the London property market, I stretched my life savings in 1999 and managed to grasp a rung of the ladder before prices really exploded, a cosy ex-council flat in Southwark, a stone's throw from Borough Tube station.

I thrived for many years in London, professionally and personally. It was a formative time for me. On a night out in 2002, I met the man I would make my life with, a beautiful, compassionate, eccentric and understanding Frenchman from the rocky coasts of Brittany.

During those London years, the BBC dispatched me to produce from Moscow to Paris, Washington to San Francisco. I covered summits and big events like the September 11th attacks, the introduction of Euro notes and coins, and the George W. Bush elections. My shift-work schedule meant that I could cultivate rich friendships and partake in London's millennial nightlife scene, a source of wonder and excitement for a boy originally from the Canadian prairie (I was born in a small town called Esterhazy, Saskatchewan).

In the late 2000s, I traded all of that in for an offer to return to Canada to present the daily radio morning programme for the Canadian Broadcasting Corporation (CBC) in Montreal. It was the realisation of a dream – my own show. As the years went by, the programme became known as innovative and successful. So far, so glamorous.

Here's the problem: the programme eventually ate my life. To help convey what that meant, let's start with the classic scene, which you may have seen in movies or on telly. We are in the bedroom; the blind is drawn and the lights are out. It's 3 a.m. on the clock, sometimes 2.45 a.m. There's a daily alarm calculus which has to do with the amount of prep left for the day's interviews, +/- the amount of news expected to occur when setting the alarm the night before, multiplied by the value of every extra minute of sleep.

Oh, and when I talk about setting the alarm, I should say alarms, because there are three, on two different devices, staggered by five-minute intervals. One of them is not a computer (you never know), and none of them depends on the electricity staying on.

Next, I remove my mouth guard. I was once in Westmount, an upmarket part of Montreal, doing 'streeters', where you stop people on the street to ask them a question to put on air. At the end of one interview, I asked a woman what she did for a living. She said she was a dentist. Then, as she walked away, she told me, 'You have nice teeth, but you grind them too much.'

Back to the dark. The alarms are positioned carefully so that to turn them all off, you need to get out of bed. It is, of course, pitch black, although occasionally you get some impressive moonlight. Proceeding down the hallway at home, sometimes I need to steady myself with a hand to the wall. I flip on the radio tuned to BBC Radio 4, where in London it is a civilised eight o'clock in the morning. It helps to reconnect me; allows me to pretend in a corner of my brain that this is all normal.

Every morning in the shower, I say the same words to myself after wetting my head and pointing my face into the warm spray: 'That feels better,' preceded by a big sigh. About six months earlier, it clicked to me that I make exactly the same sigh and say the same three words in the same way at the same point in my shower every working morning without fail.

My clothes are set out in the living room from the night before, every article. My lunch is sitting in the fridge, prepared, as well, the night before. I don't eat before going on air, and especially never within an hour of being on live, so there's no point in having 'breakfast', or is that a late-night snack? If I eat anything in that hour before going on air, I will burp sometimes, slightly under my breath in mid-sentence. I used to think people didn't notice. I fill a thermos with hot coffee.

On opening my building's front door in a Montreal winter, I am braced for an influx of snow and an icy wind, -15°C on the thermometer. Anything warmer feels spring-like and is worthy of inward celebration. You need to calculate the right amount of time to catch the bus but not wait too long in freezing conditions. There is one bus per hour at this time. Oh, and there is no such thing as sprinting for the bus on an ice- and snow-covered pavement, so you need to factor in road conditions.

The beauty of the Night Bus, aka the Vomit Comet, is that even though it most often does smell like someone's been sick, it is lightning fast and filled with a group of like-minded people. There is solidarity in the 4 a.m. bus. These are people whose alarms have gone off in the 3 a.m. hour. Most of them are counting on making the night bus connection at René-Levesque and St-Denis for the 747 bus that will take them to Pierre-Trudeau International Airport. I imagine they have jobs as security or baggage-handlers or maybe they run a de-icing machine for the six o'clock flights to Cuba.

There is comfort and an unspoken bond for this determined weary crew heading off as pioneers of the Montreal morning. Except on Monday mornings, when you tend to still have some straggling revellers aboard. Mostly, though, with my chauffeur-driven bus, I can sit back, take off my toque (a beanie-like hat, for Brits) and read through the morning news sources on my tablet. Every minute counts. I am reading in the way you do in order to be able to relay the information accurately and in detail, with attribution, on the air, in less than an hour. Let's call it uploading.

When I arrive at the office, I finally allow myself the morning's first coffee, unless I have forgotten to pack the thermos in my bag. When I forget, it is sadness, sometimes inconsolable. In that case, once in the office, I have to do a mad, middle-of-the-night scramble of the first-floor basement of La Maison de Radio-Canada searching for a brew. If I'm lucky, I'll find a plastic, hotel-style sachet of instant coffee at the back of a drawer behind some cutlery. Sometimes it's decaf, in which case the sadness reaches new depths.

I feel it's important to make one thing really clear. If I were writing this ten years ago, it would be a whole other wheel of Comté. It would be a story of the joys of live radio, the excitement of being among the first journalists awake in the city, the magic of the moment when the light goes red after a night of canned programming from around the world, the thrill of starting the day for thousands of people in the intimacy of their early morning.

It would be the story of working with a crew of brilliant, creative, resilient people, people who love storytelling and have a vision for a better city, a better world, people who lean on each other for motivation and support in high-pressure jobs.

It would be the story of the heartfelt connection with my audience, people who send me notes of encouragement, who smile at me in the street or stop me to talk, people who come to watch me at remote broadcasts, people who happily read my social media and like it, who depend on me to be their morning companion, to tell them what's new and important in the world, to reflect their concerns, to ground their days.

It would be the story of the high-wire act that is live radio, with me balancing everything: smart, funny, full of empathy, curious, inquisitive, agenda-setting, ready to interview a government minister or an administrator, the mayor, a doctor, a victim of crime or a company executive all at the drop of a hat, and being aware enough of their areas of expertise so that I can push them to answer candidly and accurately, without embarrassment or confusion.

Through it all, I need to be technically sharp enough to convey information like weather and school closures, all so that it ends at exactly one second before the top of the clock. And while on the air, I need to do all that as though it is effortless, plus have plenty of supportive energy to extend to my on-air colleagues and production team to help draw the best from them.

Five years earlier, this might have been the story of the drama of announcing the first victory of Donald Trump in a surprise US presidential election result, of conveying the sadness of the death of David Bowie and doing some justice to the legacy of his music. More recently, it could have been the story of being steady, calm and finding the right note of urgency, not alarm, as we came to grips with a virus that challenged all our assumptions about normal life.

I could write the story of having a front-row seat to modern history, and a relationship with all the big newsmakers in Montreal, from the Prime Minister, to the Premier, the Mayor, but also the man who jumped into the river to try to save two people from drowning in their cars, the woman who was struck and handcuffed for not speaking to Montreal police with what they thought was an appropriate tone, the Mohawk elder who faced down the Canadian army in 1990, the son who just lost his mother in a care home, the athlete who just won a gold medal, the filmmaker just awarded an Oscar.

This could have been a story about the excitement of processing the day's news and information in my second language, French, and then conveying it in English, sometimes live on air, of living in two cultures and understanding the mindset that comes with each, while trying to stand far enough apart from both to see clearly.

I could write the story of someone whose great privilege it was to be the city's CBC morning show presenter for thirteen years total. I could detail the stories that came with it, of politicians hanging up the phone on me or walking out of the studio angry, of conflicts with editors, frustrations navigating the CBC and its confluence of the news, public broadcasting and taxpayer mandate.

This is not that book. This is a book about the transformative power of mongering and cheese, how I began learning about its reach through history, its unique alchemy. Cheese fed my soul just as I was flagging.

Époisses

'Regarde-moi, voyons, sa rougeâtre patine; Vois les pleurs épaissis qui coulent sur ses flancs; Sent ce fumet subtil adoré des gourmands; Et convient que c'est là dessert de haute mine.'

– L'Abbé Charles Patriat, 1900, and part of his poem celebrating l'Époisse:

'Look at its blushing patina,
See the thickened tears that run down its flanks,
Inhale the subtle aroma that gourmands adore,
And agree this is the finest of desserts.'

Origin: This is one of the gastronomic prides of Burgundy, deriving its name from the town of Époisses. An iconic French cheese, it can be traced back to the sixteenth century. Napoleon was a fan. Documentation indicates that as early as the nineteenth century a set of production standards was formulated, and judging by the written descriptions, it seems closely to resemble today's version. An AOC was awarded in 1991.

Presentation: Like Camembert, Époisses is sold in a box and weighs around 250g. Larger wheels are also made, from which you might purchase a slice. When they are younger, they tend to be somewhat firmer, although still wonderfully unctuous. Their orangey-ochre coat darkens in hue as the cheeses age. They become hardcore with time: gooier, the taste and aroma get stronger.

How to serve: Remove it from the fridge in ample time for it to relax and soften. If you are serving it on plates, say with a salad or with some form of cracker or bread (spiced, raisin and/or nut breads work well), cut it when it's straight out of the fridge the way you would a cake. That way the wedges will come away more cleanly and begin to ooze on the plates. Know your audience. If they like big cheeses, go ahead and push their boundaries with a more mature wheel. However, Époisses doesn't have to be a big, manly cheese. When it's young and slightly chalky at the centre of the paste, it has an approachable, peanut-Marmite or bacon flavour that's hard for anyone not to enjoy. If you're serving it on a cheeseboard, keep in mind that it can dominate the others. For wine pairings, try a Gewürztraminer, a Gamay or a younger red. Beer goes well with Époisses, but the beers need to stand up to all that flavour, so think stout, porter, or stronger ales. A bitter cider will also pair up nicely. Few cheeses have as many recipes associated with them as Époisses: pasta, tarts, pastries, sauces, in combination with leeks, bacon, endive, mushrooms and potatoes: there is a world of possibilities.

Fun fact: There are all sorts of stories about how Époisses is not allowed on public transport in France because of its antisocial aroma. I wrote to the RATP, which runs the Paris Métro – not true. Use common sense with it (with any cheese) – don't leave it in a hot car. Customers have told me stories of placing one in checked luggage and things going disastrously wrong. I feel Époisses is one of those wonderful, ephemeral things in life. Buy it at the stage you like it, eat it as close to the same day as possible, remember it fondly thereafter.

6
1924 versus 2019

THERE IS A WOMAN who comes to the stall at Borough Market who is unusually tall, blonde-haired, well-spoken and forthright. She loves a cheese called 1924. She buys great hunks of it and seeks it out enthusiastically: 'I am looking for a large chunk of one of your blue cheeses. It's named after a year from the early twentieth century, but I have forgotten which one.'

'1924.'

'That's it!'

'Would you like to taste?'

'Should I? I know I want it. Go on then, why not?'

'I always recommend tasting so as not to be disappointed – especially with a cheese like 1924.'

I refer to this customer as 'Maybe Gwendoline Christie' because I have never had the courage to ask her if she is indeed Gwendoline Christie but goodness, she looks just like the sword-wielding Amazon from television's *Game of Thrones*. She is English, tall and impressive, with a shock of blonde hair.

She tastes the sample. Her eyes close. She is silent.

'Oh my God, yes,' she says, at first slowly. Then with some urgency: 'Yes, yes, yes. That's it. Cut me something impossibly large, please.'

'This much?'

'More!'

An acquaintance of the real Gwendoline Christie's knows Cheesemonger Fionnuala and works over at one of the wine shops, a charming Irishman. He once promised to ask her whether she had fallen for 1924. Knowing her, he says, it is a cheese you can well imagine her enjoying.

The name of the cheese is a reference to the year before Roquefort received its AOP status. AOP stands for *Appellation d'Origine Protégée*, which translates to Protected Designation of Origin. The peculiar, cheesy/in-crowd reference is this: in the year 1924, the world was on the cusp of designating Roquefort an AOP (1925). That meant in 1924, the strict AOP rules were not in place. These are rules dictating exactly how and where you can make Roquefort if you want to label it as such. So this cheese, the one Maybe GC adores, could have been/would have been called Roquefort in 1924. Fast forward to today – it contains cow's and sheep's milk, while Roquefort can now only be made with sheep's milk and only under certain conditions. That's the thing with AOPs, and that's how 1924 got its name.

It's the brainchild of a somewhat eccentric Franco-American named François Kerautret, an executive from a Seattle-based cheese importer who wanted to know 'what would happen if Roquefort and Stilton had a baby'.

I understand Maybe GC's obsession with 1924 at a deep and personal level. My infatuation with it began in the run-up to Christmas in my first year as a cheesemonger. A particularly popping batch arrived that surpassed its predecessors by so much that it was bordering on narcotic-grade.

Every note of it was heightened to the nth degree. It was cake-like, moist and crumbly and breathtakingly beautiful. Its rind was mottled – bumpy brown with the most peculiar neon yellow mould spots, almost as though someone had been playing with a yellow highlighter pen. When you cut into it, it collapsed slightly in on itself, such was the weight of the moist centre of the paste as the wire ran through it.

1924, as mentioned, is a blend of sheep's and cow's milk and that means you get a buttery and creamy texture together (Roquefort plus Stilton's 'baby'). En bouche, it's a full-spectrum umami headrush. It's salt-forward with a hint of pan-drippings as from a Sunday roast, but the thing that cuts through above all others is a rich mushroom-y flavour. Imagine the earthiest, most lip-smacking mushrooms you've ever tasted. That's what this cheese was packing. To top it all off, it had a singular line of sweetness reminiscent of an Oreo cookie. It was an absolute whammy of a cheese.

Once I had a taste, the sheer intensity of the flavours was such that my brain could not escape its call. It was a high, there's no other way of saying it. I would carry on my day performing other tasks but all the while a little voice in the back of my head kept repeating, 'Malty, creamy, mushroom-y goodness', until I gave in and ate some more. I began to understand Odysseus, tied to the mast of his ship while the Sirens called.

On that particular day, I had eaten so much of it that Cheesemonger Fionnuala finally turned to me mid-bite and exclaimed, 'Michael!' as if trying to snap me out of a trance. I was trying to look inconspicuous. Failing at it. She looked more than just alarmed. I think she was genuinely concerned for my well-being. 'Are you okay?'

I. Could. Not. Stop. Eating. This. Cheese.

By the evening, I developed a bad case of 1924 belly, a protrusion and a slight aching. It was still delicious, mind you.

It can be so difficult to recover after a fall like that.

Or not. 1924 is one of our most variable cheeses and you will get batches that are too salty for my tastes, slightly bitter and without that line of sweetness. Off-putting. Such are the mysteries of artisan cheese. That's why I was clear with Maybe Gwendoline Christie that she needed to taste before committing.

Likewise, journalism and live radio were for years akin to narcotic-grade 1924 to me. Clearly, something about them changed, or was it something about me?

1924

'What if Roquefort and Stilton had a baby?'

– François Kerautret, Breton transplanted to Seattle, cheese marketer and godfather of 1924.

Origin: The first prototypes were developed around 2012 based on a concept from Kerautret. Hervé Mons, Meilleur Ouvrier de France, took on the cheesemaking. It was not a sure thing, blending sheep's and cow's milk, tacking close to Roquefort and Stilton. The result exceeded expectations. It's pasteurised with injected blue moulds.

Presentation: The wheels weigh about 3kg and closely resemble Roquefort in shape, 20cm in diameter. They have a handsome, mottled, pock-marked rind: browns, whites and greys. Inside, the paste is both creamy and buttery thanks to the blend of cow's and sheep's milk, with stunning blue moulds.

How to serve: *Game of Thrones* cosplay: big hunks on crusty bread and lick your fingers! Great as a cheeseboard blue.

Most wheels have a heavenly sweetness, but not all, so if it's too salt-forward or you're getting bitter notes, complement it with wildflower honey. For a meal, it serves nicely with a spinach salad. A shame to use it as a cooking ingredient unless it's given pride of place, however, try adding it to cooked mushrooms alongside a steak. Pairings for a decadent blue cheese like this can include your favourite fortified or dessert wine. Top tip: try an ice cider for a truly sublime companion.

Fun fact: 1924 was originally intended for export to the US market, but the cheesemakers and the customers in France liked it so much they've kept it in Europe, while still allowing it across the Atlantic. It has ties to l'Auvergne, where it's produced, and Roanne, where it's matured, and it's wrapped in foil which displays Breton symbols in honour of Kerautret. Plus, the whole 1924/25 thing. You might think it suffers from an identity crisis, but it seems to know exactly what it is.

7
Raclette for One

AFTER SO MUCH EVERYDAY burden and routine in my role as breakfast show presenter, a monotone grey, a flatness, settles into the life I lead when I'm not on the air. Oddly, I don't seem to grasp it, and I don't really know why that is. The penny does finally drop, but not as you might expect.

I am focused on functioning above all, moving through the day. When long ago I did Myers-Briggs, I came out right on the line between extrovert and introvert. So when all that extrovert energy suddenly leaves the body mid-morning, the collapse into inward-looking fatigue is truly awesome. I go from wanting to talk to everyone to wanting to talk to no one.

On arrival home in this state, there are two imperatives: eating and sleeping. For the first, remember that I ate my 'lunch' at 8.30 a.m. after the show, so this is a second snack within about two and a half hours. Snack, who am I kidding? The problem with fatigue-eating is that you think it will cure the fatigue. It doesn't, so you keep eating.

As for the sleep imperative, a question: have you ever felt like attaching the adjective 'thirsty' to sleeping? For me, that is how I approach every late morning nap after the show, with a type of thirst I expect people crossing the desert might have. I want it so badly; it is the thing that has been driving me forward for the last three hours. Now here it is, hallelujah! I am back in my bed clothes, I am under the covers, my pillow is in just the right place, except that this kind of sleep deprivation is a kind that does not quench easily.

For this nap, I feel like I am at the top of a skyscraper or a cliff, looking down into sleep. It is a long, long way down. I know that when I finally do get there, it's going to be a glorious release, but getting from point A to point B means falling. Sometimes, it provokes actual fear in me and I cannot explain why.

Most days, I set my alarm to end this nap – I say most days because sometimes the fatigue is so deeply felt that I just want to live in that nap and I don't want the idea of an alarm to crush the joy of it. If I don't set the alarm, hours can go by and there is a risk, especially in winter, of not waking up until the sun is so low in the sky that basically the day has come to an end.

For years on a Friday, with no live programme on Saturday, I get to this nap a bit earlier. Then, I wake myself up around noon, get dressed quickly and head straight out the door and to the movies. What a day Friday is during those years, and what fun! Picking the film is something I do days if not weeks in advance. There are, of course, the blockbusters – I am a sucker for escapism – but I get as much, if not more pleasure from the January/February stable of weird and wonderful arty films. Subtitles? Not a problem.

What I want is to get absolutely lost in the film, and a matinée, bliss! I am awake! I time the whole thing so that I get there early and get the pick of the seats. I play along with the cinema pre-game show and because there's no one there usually, I am the winner!

When people do arrive, and sometimes after the lights go down, occasionally someone will end up sitting, if not directly beside me, then inside my 'zone', and in so doing will shatter my glorious, solitary bubble. I learn the only thing to do is to gather up my coat, mitts, scarf, drink and popcorn (large salted, no butter) and move to another seat, no matter where, as long as I have my zone back.

Bizarrely, it doesn't really matter whether the film is mediocre or excellent, because the escape is so complete that when the credits roll, I feel almost dizzy, like I'm getting off an amusement ride. I become an amateur film buff because of all the films I've seen, and I have so many loyalty points I start accumulating multiple free entries. Thirteen free films are my high-water mark.

One day as I'm sitting in the cinema and gathering up my things, thinking about what comes next in my day, what I need to buy before going home, what plans I have for the weekend, it dawns on me that this is the happiest moment of my week: this exact moment. This is the moment where I live the elation of having spent two hours in my alone zone in the dark, munching on hot popped corn in my own company, having travelled via the cinema to somewhere else entirely, watching someone else's life play out on a giant silver screen.

Cheesemonger Thomas tells the story of a French woman who, from time to time, visited the shop where he used to work, approached the cheese counter, chin held high, and pronounced, 'Raclette for one, please.' Thomas says those visits have stuck with him, years later, and that he still finds himself slightly unnerved by the recollection. Perhaps he worries she might be a harbinger of his own fate later in life. More likely, he can't fathom someone going through all the work involved in assembling the convivial ceremony that is a raclette meal, but for one person, to be consumed in solitude.

Now, when I think back to that day in the cinema, 'Raclette for one' inevitably pops into my head: my weekly, non-work joy was spent with a similar ceremony, but by myself in the cinema.

Preparing to leave the picture house on the day of my revelation, I also become suddenly aware that this is one of the only moments – okay the only moment – that I ever feel free of the mental and physical burdens of my job, and as sure as the lights going back on in the cinema, it is a fact: my next moment of liberation is now a full seven days away. And, like so many people all around the world, in all sorts of jobs – careers they worked so hard to find, careers their families made great sacrifices for, jobs taken by necessity, jobs that feel like (and maybe genuinely are) the only option – like so many people before me toiling day after day, I think: 'What exactly is the point?'

What I have to give is given every day at work with colleagues, but mostly when the microphone light goes on and I'm in communion with the audience. Afterwards, apart from the cinema, I am languishing, as flat as a disappointing wheel of Comté.

That stunned Friday-afternoon cinema session leads to an uncomfortable weekend for me. I start to get a pain in the pit of my stomach. I would say butterflies, but it feels more intense. I even feel I might be sick.

If my job as a well-paid, well-regarded radio presenter is robbing me of joy, what am I going to do about it, quit? Cue the anxious sick feeling. I am so proud of the show and where my presenting has arrived! It is my identity. Hell, my face is on billboards and on the side of CBC trucks. What would I do without the presenter's chair?

Beyond that, I have a mortgage on a beautiful new flat. There are so many things I am accustomed to: travel, restaurants, financial peace of mind.

That Saturday, I have a dream about a former CBC morning show presenter named Sheila and end up bolt upright in bed in a cold sweat. Sheila was into her sixties when I first met her at a training session with a group of other presenters, mostly younger. She was a bit of a legend – she WAS the Regina morning programme. She'd worked her way up from an intern through grit and talent.

We were asked to go around the table and present ourselves. I was excited about my role as the new presenter of the CBC morning show in Montreal, one of Canada's biggest, most vibrant cities, and I said so. When Sheila was next up to speak, I was looking forward to hearing wise words. Plus, I felt a special attachment because I was born in Saskatchewan, where her programme is broadcast live.

When she was introduced, there was an overlong pause and then she let out a big sigh. 'I've been hosting this show for more than twenty years now. Guess what? I know I should probably move on. It's time. I just don't know how. And I don't know what the hell else I can do. Anyone got any bright ideas? Can radio show hosts DO anything else?'

No one said anything. Dead silence. The moderator stepped in, finally: 'Good question, Sheila! Maybe we can come back to that topic later this week.'

We didn't.

I was taken aback by her candour and couldn't believe what she'd said. It was so direct. It was all I could do not to gasp. I remember thinking, in the way you sometimes contemplate death (yes, death – seriously): 'Oh well, I don't have to think about that for a long time.' This was about fifteen years ago. I was starting out on my presenter's journey, before the accumulated fatigue, before my Friday cinema outings began.

At that point, I had absolutely no intention of leaving the presenter's chair. My job thrilled me. The sacrifices I was making I would only much later identify with clarity. They seemed, at the time, part of the excitement of the package, at worst battle scars, not sacrifices at all. In fact, I was mystified at the thought that Sheila or anyone would want to leave the job. Part of me thought, 'Maybe there's something wrong with her.' But if I'm being honest, even in those heady days, there was another part of me, buried deep inside, that had the sinking feeling that Sheila's candid pronouncement was a prophecy.

Now, fresh from my cinema moment of clarity, a future without presenting seems suddenly to be calling out to me, exciting me and terrifying me in equal measure. Problem is, I cannot see anything on the other side of my CBC gig, nothing except rejection and anxiety. Rejection, anxiety and poverty, actually. I can think of no other purpose for my working life. I am convinced I've reached the top of the mountain and the only way is down. My lack of vision is that total.

Come to think of it, it was all a bit like a scary piece of washed rind cheese – Munster, Langres or Époisses – something that sends conflicting signals. Is it repulsive or is it delicious? If I overcome my reticence, will I get lost in its magic or end up retching?

Langres

*'First the aroma, a paste that smells of cowsheds and cows.
But not too much! Then there's the creaminess that makes
this cheese one of the jewels in France's gastronomic crown.'*

– 'From Paris', French delicatessen

Origin: AOC since 1991, Langres was first written about around the middle of the eighteenth century in Eastern France, but its history reaches back to the thirteenth century. It's considered the speciality of the Champagne-Ardenne region, where the market town of Langres is located.

Presentation: It's a stunner – bright ivory in the paste and a rind that has vivid orange notes. Its shape is also singular, including the traditional fontaine or divet in the centre and the wrinkles and puckers that make up its rind. This cheese is not for turning – one of the production stipulations is that they remain upright as they mature so the divet can reliably form. They are mostly 10cm in diameter and between 5 and 6cm high, weight 250 to 300g. There are also medium and large Langres, served by the slice or as a centrepiece for an event. Be careful, Langres becomes strong as it ages and the aroma also gets powerful.

How to serve: Their otherworldly appearance will enliven any cheeseboard, not to mention their taste (all that *fromunda*! – see below). Crusty bread is a must: most Langres are soft and creamy, so slathering them over bread is a treat. Many Langres connoisseurs feel the perfect pairing is a glass of Champagne; some even pour it into the centre. For other pairings, try wines that hail from the same area, red burgundies for example. Marc de Bourgogne is also recommended – Langres are washed with it as they mature.

Fun fact: A bit of fire can transform your Langres experience. Set it alight with Marc de Bourgogne or a Christmas plum brandy or the alcohol of your choice, poured into the fontaine in the centre, and make an occasion of it.

8
The Munster Mash

AT BOROUGH MARKET, CHEESEMONGER Fionnuala will tell how her boyfriend's love of Alsace in Eastern France has led to their holidaying there from time to time. It's not on many of the lists of Top 10 must-visit regions in Europe, but this part of Eastern France, along the Upper Rhine across from Germany, is known for its cheese, meat and wine. Nuala and Henry are lovers of good food and drink.

The story, however, doesn't start out with a declaration of love. Nuala tells instead of an Alsatian hotel where descending into the breakfast room, she and Henry were struck by a pungent tang, the kind that makes your nose wrinkle involuntarily. They took it to be body odour.

As they came down the stairs, Nuala and Henry looked with deep suspicion at the bleary-eyed patrons of the hotel, quietly sipping their cups of tea and coffee. Who forgot to wash this morning?

Imagine their surprise, relief even, when they discovered that the forward aroma hanging in the air over their petits-déjeuner was being emitted by a local speciality cheese, Munster. Several wheels of it were sitting proudly in the centre of the breakfast buffet and people had been tucking in with gusto.

They soon followed suit. I've heard this story several times because Nuala tells it to some customers as she recommends

Munster for them to try. She tries to seduce me with Munster from time to time, suggesting I try it along with her as we set out the display.

'Pass, thanks.'

Munster has caught me off guard several times at the cheese stall in Borough. It's not a cheese we sell a lot of, although it has committed fans. At Christmas, sales ramp up considerably, and so Owner Jon and Cheesemonger Nuala put about half a dozen wheels of Munster on a shelf behind the display to entice people making their Christmas cheeseboards. The wheels are pretty, a light orangey-yellow colour with an ivory paste, about fifteen centimetres in diameter.

Munster has such an assertive aroma and it comes at you with such a rush that it can have a strange effect. Sometimes, when the Munster has been put out unwrapped without me realising, I can spend half an hour trying to determine who has forgotten to brush their teeth to the point of having such noticeable halitosis. Terrible to have your faith in colleagues shaken like that.

'Oh! Never mind, it's the Munster,' I say to myself after the penny drops, trying to laugh it off. In truth, it can be unsettling.

As Munster is matured, the cheesemakers give each wheel a wash, twice a week, by hand, in a tepid brine. That's why it, and other similarly matured cheeses, fall into the category 'washed rind'. Munster is a softer cheese, sometimes even spreadable.

If you're looking for an explanation as to why washed-rind cheeses smell like some of the lesser attended-to nooks and crannies of our bodies, or like used socks, it's due to bacteria, specifically *Brevibacterium linens*, or *Brevibacterium aurantiacum*. There is some debate. In any case, they're harmless and live also on our skin, with a particular fondness for feet.

They also thrive on washed-rind cheeses because they like the environment there: moist and salty with low acidity. There's a subset of cheese aficionados who refer to washed-rind cheeses as 'stinky cheese', although I don't condone the term. I take it personally on behalf of the cheese. Sometimes, I will even lean into the Munster after someone has called it stinky, and say just under my breath, 'Don't listen to them.'

Fairly regularly, people will come to the stall specifically asking after 'stinky cheese'. I'm puzzled by the fascination to this day. I mean, check the dictionary for yourselves, but stink means strong and unpleasant, rank even. There again, people also queue up for the London Dungeon just around the corner. Maybe there's a connection, an appeal to wanting to be 'grossed out', a thing we used to say as kids.

We are at the cheese stall in Borough, Cheesemonger Molly and I, when a father rolls up with his pre-teen son in tow.

'What's your stinkiest cheese?' asks Dad, with an air of nervous excitement.

I can hear Molly mutter something under her breath and step to the side.

These are early days in my cheesemongering, so I wouldn't say I'm disdainful towards stink questers at this point, but instinctively wary, protective of the cheeses as always.

'What do you mean, exactly?' I ask, narrowing my eyes somewhat.

'I want my son to try something really smelly.'

I decide to ask straight out, 'Is this some sort of coming-of-age ritual you're engaged in?'

Molly's eyes become as big as saucers and she slides discreetly to the back counter, still in earshot. I've said it too bluntly, clearly, and there is some discomfort now. Thing is, though, as Molly confirms to me afterwards and I learn over time, some sort of strange dare does exist, treating washed-rind cheeses like they're part of a freak show. For the cheesemongers, not only is it off-putting but it's time-wasting: they are unlikely to buy any cheese.

The father looks part confused, part taken aback by my question. Before too much time goes by with them not answering, I try to paper over the awkward moment and gamely suggest they try some Munster since I have some on the tasting board anyway, a fact I've been unable to ignore for the past hour.

'Phwoar, yeah!' says Dad. 'This really stinks.'

He puts the taster on his finger under his son's nose. The son laughs, but I hear some anxiety creeping in. He is starting to look a little concerned.

'Come on, taste it! What's the worst that can happen?' goads his father.

Well, the worst that can happen is that he can start to gag, spit it out, or even vomit, and I know it's not a nice place to go in your head, but the question of what exactly will happen is hanging in the air as the boy is shaking his head 'no', but Dad is insisting.

In the end, the boy reluctantly tries, his face scrunches up, and he bursts out with a loud, 'Ewwww!'

Ritual endured, the father says thanks and off they go on their way, having shared some father-son bonding, but buying no cheese, as expected.

'I can't believe you said that to them.' Molly is the calmest cheesemonger I know, but she was fascinated by the whole exchange and her eyes are twinkling talking about it.

'I wasn't trying to be rude. It's genuine curiosity. I mean seriously, what is it about assertive odours? Do some people – mostly men, let's be honest – think they're stronger or more attractive if they can endure them, enjoy them or produce them?'

'Such a good question.' Molly's a recent university graduate and does a lot of thinking about gender. 'I think so, yeah. It happens all the time, men asking for the stinkiest cheese.' She shakes her head. 'I don't have much time for it.'

Molly once told me that if she's working with male cheesemongers and sales are sluggish, looking like we won't meet the day's target, she'll slip a word in the ear of one of them to say the other is beating him in sales. 'Works every time,' she laughs. Sales go up. Come to think of it, that trick works on me, too.

'Do you like Munster?' I ask her.

'I do, and especially when it's got a lightly sausage-y creaminess. Sometimes I get some fruity notes from it. It's pretty gentle, despite the smell.'

'I get that. Lots of customers say that, too, but for some reason, I don't find it gentle. There's something going on in the upper registers of it, like a pungent mustard almost. It catches at the back of my mouth, something involuntary. During my job interview, I had to stop myself gagging when they asked me to taste it.'

'Really?'

'Yeah, I mean I hid the gagging. I think. It went okay. I talked about the Munster film on our website instead.'

'Wrapping Munster first thing in the morning can be a challenge.'

You can say that again. Later in my cheesemongering career, during a lunch break, I pen the lyrics of a song called 'The Munster Wrap', sung to the tune of the Hallowe'en classic, 'The Monster Mash':

> *I was working at the stall, early one morning*
> *When my eyes beheld an eerie warning*
> *For my Munster from its slab, began to ooze*

From the cheesemongers, came a chorus of boos!
CHORUS
(He did the wrap) I did the Munster wrap
(The Munster wrap) It caused a cheeseshop flap
(He did the wrap) It smelled like crap
(He did the wrap) I did the Munster wrap

I feel a bit bad for playing into the whole House of Horrors thing. Truth is, there is something wonderfully mystical about washed-rind cheese, a before and after. The barrier to trying it can be high, but the reward in flavour immense.

One day in the pre-pandemic summer, when tourists from around the world flocked to Borough Market as they do now, an American couple who adored cheese came to the stand and we tasted through a whole bunch of the stock. They were loving it.

At one point, after tasting another washed-rind cheese, Langres, the fellow looked at his wife and said, 'Now that's got some major *fromunda*.'

Me: 'Wait, what did you just say?'

Him: 'That cheese has got *fromunda*. It's a word we invented. From + Under. *Fromunda*.'

'From under where?'

They burst out laughing. 'I don't know, from under the covers, from under your clothes. You name it!'

I immediately loved the word and adopted it. Maybe that craving for *fromunda*, funk essentially, is because washed-rind cheese smells of life, animal and raw. It is connecting to us at some primal level. I wonder whether in a world of digital cleanliness, of smartphones, careers, and using your cognitive mind all day long, we yearn for reminders of the physical, that we aren't just thoughts and ideas but also smells and tastes. Maybe this even helps to explain stink questers.

After a few weeks on the job, I take home half a Langres, a cheese that put me off at first because of its *fromunda*. I have it for dinner at home, alone, with a glass of Pinot Noir and I love it. It is something about the boozy, farmy, animal taste of it, combined with the creamy paste. A switch is thrown in my brain.

Munster

'Devinez ce que j'ai mangé! – Du Munster? – Non, une pêche!'

– *La Zizanie*, film (1978). Have a look online for this hilarious scene from the French comedy *La Zizanie*. At a party, a woman approaches a man on the dance floor. 'Guess what I've just eaten!' She exhales; he recoils at her bad breath. 'Ugh, Munster??' She doesn't get it, 'No, a peach!'

Origin: Monks who emigrated to the Vosges from Ireland and Scotland began producing it in the seventh century so as not to waste milk and to help feed the community. The name 'Munster' is derived from the word 'monastery', and there is a town of the same name. It became popular in the sixteenth century and has since been designated AOC and AOP.

Presentation: Handsome, flat wheels about 15cm in diameter and a few centimetres high, Munster has an ochre/ivory rind that is tacky to the touch. More mature wheels will present with a dry, cracked rind, still with appeal. Sometimes the paste is spreadable. Eat the rind.

How to serve: With bread or crackers. A quarter Munster on the
cheeseboard will ensure your selection doesn't bore, but
beware, the aroma may not be alluring for some. In France,
they will occasionally eat it with cumin or caraway seeds. In
Alsace, it is often served alongside sautéd or baked potato
and a salad, making a whole meal. Tartiflette is usually made
with Reblochon, but if you want to kick it up a few notches,
try substituting with Munster. For a wine pairing, go with an
Alsatian like Gewürztraminer.

Fun fact: There is an American cheese that goes by the same
name, though often spelled Muenster. It isn't washed-rind, so
it's a poor imitation and has none of the complexity of
Munster AOC/AOP. It has its own virtues, no doubt, but I've
met Americans who buy Munster thinking it will be the same
or very close, and then are met with a surprise.

9

What Else Can a Radio Presenter Do?

O NCE THIS THOUGHT APPEARS in my brain: 'I could take a sabbatical from my radio presenter job – not quit – hedge my bets and everything will be okay!', it spreads like cat fur mould in a box of Crottins de Chavignol. I need to make a change, and I need to be less tired to see what it is. The woman who oversees CBC Montreal at the time is a friend, and when I set up a meeting to discuss all of this with her, I am nervous, as you might imagine. She listens as I explain to her what I've begun to recognise about the way things are going in my life. I need to try to figure this out, I tell her.

A few days later, she taps me on the shoulder at work and asks to see me again. A six-month sabbatical is a go. I am elated, light-headed, even. Then, there it is again: that empty feeling in the pit of my stomach, not to the point of feeling unwell, but to the point of feeling unsteady.

This whole period has an out-of-body feel to it. I have shifted in a matter of weeks from being unable to envisage leaving the microphone, to seeing the way paved ahead of me. The notice period on my little London flat is coming up for the tenants. I decide to go there. I miss my friends from my days as a journalist. I love London. Maybe the city will hold the answers.

What am I going to do for six months in London? I'll start by catching up with old friends! I'll go to museums! I'll wander around London! Read fiction! I'll clean the flat after the tenants leave! I have ideas, but even as I hear myself rattling them off, I can tell they aren't substantial. There is also the whole money issue. I can maybe scrape by, but it's London.

As the date of departure approaches, I begin to entertain, partly through necessity, the low-risk idea of working temporarily. Definitely not in journalism, that is not the point. It can be nothing that will suck the life out of my sabbatical; rather, it needs to be something that might add to the experience. The idea slowly begins to enthuse me. It also raises again the uncomfortable Sheila question: what else can a radio presenter even do?

Then I remember something. There is a parlour game two friends of mine from Boston once told me about that addresses this. Rainey's a successful museum curator and Graham's a talented radio producer and trainer – classic Brahmins, people who are always seeing the big picture, spotting trends and identifying challenges to overcome.

Over dinner one night, they throw on the table the story of one of Rainey's cousins, whose job is in the realm of disaster preparedness, preparing for the possibility of a collapse of our modern-day systems. It's something codenamed 'The Long Emergency', after the book by James Kunstler where he examines how the confluence of the oil production peak, climate change, viruses, water scarcity, warfare and economic instability could lead to us all having to live in much smaller communities where we protect ourselves first and foremost and find we are cut off from the globalised world. Before Donald Trump, the Coronavirus and the attack on Ukraine, it seemed more amusing, like a game.

The exercise here is to take a group of people and score them on their usefulness to the community during The Long Emergency. Rainey's cousin knows how to build a combustion engine. Another cousin's wife is an emergency-room doctor. Rainey knows how to make and stitch clothing. Graham jokes that as a radio producer, he is going to have to hope that his manual labour will be enough to prevent him from being cannibalised.

I am not good at manual labour. Mostly, I just don't want to do it. In this game, I am coming up short.

What useful thing can a radio show host do after the boss pulls him aside to say, 'Sorry, we prefer another voice at this stage'? What survival skills do I possess when you consider it took three sessions of remedial training for me to learn how to place a contact lens in my eye?

Honestly, I can't come up with the answer. One of the skills Rainey says I possess is making people feel spoiled and looked after. We can agree, this is not going to make you an invaluable part of a post-apocalyptic village, but in the thriving modern capital that is London? She is persuasive. Maybe she is on to something.

Morbier

'Le Morbier est un fromage qui plaît. Tout le monde mange du Morbier.'

– Hervé Poulet, Syndicat Interprofessionnel du Morbier, boasts how 'Morbier is a crowd pleaser – everyone eats Morbier'.

∽

Origin: The first recorded evidence of Morbier dates to 1795; however, it wasn't until 100 years later that a traditional recipe emerged from peasant farmers in the Franche-Comté region. In the 1960s, production of Morbier was spread throughout France after a group of students from dairy school in Poligny fell for its charms and began making it back in their towns of origin, leading to the term 'délocalisation'. It now has both its AOC and AOP with all the accompanying rules, and has been firmly re-localised in the place of its birth.

Presentation: Wheels of Morbier vary considerably, but can be impressively plump, as much as 8cm high, 40cm across and weighing 5 to 8kg. Morbier has an orangey-beige rind, but its most distinctive characteristic is the line of dark ash that runs through the middle of its golden or ivory paste.

How to serve: A slice of Morbier is a natural on a cheeseboard – people are drawn to that smart line of ash. It's a cheese that benefits from being out of the fridge for a time, allowing for the paste to lose its bouncy, elastic quality and instead almost melt in the mouth. This is what you can reasonably call a mild, washed-rind cheese, which is to say it has some nice funk to it, proper farminess, while being approachable for any lover of artisan cheese. I find it buttery. On a recent reading of *Kitchen Confidential*, I was taken aback to see Anthony Bourdain refer to it as a 'daring' choice for a cheeseboard that would 'make your fingers smell for a week'. I can't agree, but maybe that is more a reflection of how far our familiarity with cheese has grown in the Anglophone world since the year 2000. Morbier works well at breakfast or brunch. Farmier notes will come more readily to the fore at room temperature and with age. Apples and walnuts are a great complement. It's an outstanding melter. Try it as an open-faced toastie on a thick piece of country bread, allowing it to display its handsome stripe. Use it instead of, or alongside Raclette.

White wine from the Jura will pair nicely. Try a Savignin grape. Some swear by Gewürztraminer. For reds, a Pinot Noir or a Gamay will do the trick.

Fun fact: People who are unfamiliar with French cheeses often confuse Morbier for a blue cheese, due to the line of ash which they mistake for blue mould, but it's more a sibling to Comté than to Roquefort. When farmers had leftover milk that would normally go towards a wheel of Comté, they would start a wheel of Morbier with the evening milk. Ash 'from the bottom of the cauldron' would cover and protect it, then curds from the morning milking would be added on top. Nowadays, vegetable ash is used and the signature line of ash is for aesthetic purposes above all.

10
The Ottolenghi Audition

I BECOME INTRIGUED BY THE idea of working in a restaurant owned by Yotam Ottolenghi, beloved creator of food that is bright, fresh, healthy and bursting with flavourful surprises, all inspired by his Middle Eastern roots. His food features vegetables, herbs and spices some of which I've never heard of before. I went with a good friend to one of his restaurants on a recent trip to London and had a wonderful evening. We laughed and caught up on our lives. We chatted to the barman. We ate delicious and unexpected things. I was captivated by that evening and how cool the surroundings were. I was wowed by the choreographed service, how everything lifted my spirits and opened my tastebuds. I think this could be just the type of fun, part-time job where I can learn tons of new things, specialised knowledge, and stretch myself in a number of ways. On top of that, it occurs to me that surely, some of the transferable skills of a radio show presenter are being able to read guests effectively and empathise with them, to entertain them. Add to that good communications, organisation and making things happen on time.

Once I get it into my head, the idea of working at that restaurant begins to take on outsized importance. Getting a job there would fill a need I've identified – making some money – but more than that, it's the beginnings of an answer to that other fundamental question, am I eventually capable of doing something other than broadcast journalism?

The whole thing begins to take on the form of an adventure. I am leaving Montreal for six months, leaving my routine for six months. It turns out, the only thing standing in my way was my failure of imagination, or just my fear.

Looking back, it was like that lemon-peppery sample of goat's cheese I talked the young goat's-cheese sceptic into trying. Like that Tomme de Chambrouze, this restaurant seemed the perfect bridge to somewhere, a gateway to a new world of discovery. Maybe something big was about to happen.

It is Saturday morning in London, month of May, and I am on my way to Fitzrovia, just north of Soho in the heart of London, to the Ottolenghi restaurant called ROVI. I have a trial shift.

If you have ever worked in the hospitality industry, a trial shift is no mystery to you. Unpaid, it is a way of separating the wheat from the chaff, to see what happens when you throw someone into the deep end. Some will sink, some will swim. I am hoping to at least tread water, but I am nervous. I have waited tables before, but it was cater-waitering, not the same thing.

When I visited the restaurant previously, I crushed so hard on the place that at the end of the evening I spoke to the bartender about the possibility of applying to work there. He seemed open enough to the idea and gave me the contact of the recruiting manager. Being a bit pushy is one of the hard-won skills from my BBC producer days, so when I arrive in town, I give James a call out of the blue and am invited to come by to say hello. I pass that initial test – we have a good chat and I present well enough. They are ready to give me a chance. I am told to bring black trousers and shoes and prepare to serve Saturday lunch.

When I arrive, I'm greeted by Recruiting Manager James again. He's a late-twenties English bloke in the way you might recognise them, say, from 1990s Working Title films; think Hugh Grant in *Notting Hill* but with no bumbling. He's tall and fit, square-jawed with blond hair and blue eyes. He has a definite coolness about him. In short, he is intimidating in an English way, the way that makes you feel that you are being constantly judged, which I am, so best to get on with it.

James introduces me to Gabor, the floor supervisor. He is Hungarian, a big, tall man with dark features and piercing eyes. He shakes my hand in a professional way and walks away without any lingering. They've seen their fair share of trial shifts. I'm also presented to Andrew, the head server today, Scottish, early thirties. He is neat, wiry, bald and a good deal shorter than me. I can see he is sizing me up warily as I gush a big, Canadian, 'Hi there! How are things going today?'

Andrew pauses a moment, looks at me, nods once, and says, 'Fine.' He then shakes his head from side to side, only very slightly but noticeably, and walks away. I find myself wondering how he can have taken an instant dislike to me.

James, on the other hand, seems enthusiastic enough. He takes me away from the introductions and stands me in the middle of the dining room to outline the table numbering system. I am trying to put everything else out of my mind and focus, but all this novelty at once is sensory overload. The seats at the bar are numbers 0–20, the section to the right is the 100s, the 200s are over there starting with 201 in the far end. The 300s are beside. There are 400s as well, but they are not seating people there for lunch.

Then it's off through a door, hidden in the panelling, to the changing room. I'm given a shirt and told to iron it and put it on. I have a dwelling, perfectionist side, the yin which often needs to face off against my slapdash yang. Sometimes the battle between the two can get me caught in a feedback loop. I am trying first to imprint the table numbering system into my brain and then I am trying to iron a shirt flawlessly. Any creasing I am sure will be marked down.

Something that is clear talking to James is that he has googled me. I would do the same, so it's not that surprising but still off-putting. He makes a comment about me having worked in radio and asks for more information about where. I tell him really only the basics of the CBC and change the subject. I'm not sure my credentials as a morning radio show presenter are going to give me an inside track at an 'in' restaurant in Central London.

Soon enough, I'm wearing an indigo-blue shirt like the rest of the staff and for all anyone would know seated in the dining room, I have a job waiting tables at an Ottolenghi restaurant. Things are getting busy. James takes me over to The Pass. The Pass is where plates come from the kitchen to the runners to make it to the tables. Just on the other side of The Pass, which is about five degrees hotter than anywhere else on the floor, is the head chef, Neil. I know this because I've googled him, read bios and interviews and watched videos featuring him. He's Scottish and a serious customer as you might expect.

'Hello there,' he says, fixing me right in the eye. 'So what brings you here?'

'I mean the short story is that I love your restaurant. I ate here a couple of months ago and couldn't get it out of my head. The menu was so unusual, to me anyway. Fresh, tasty. Surprising, even. I'm a big fan, to be honest. Sorry if I'm sounding a bit gushy.'

He lets out a genuine laugh. 'Don't be. Chefs have huge egos.' He has a twinkle in his eye. 'Where from?'

'Montreal.'

He responds, 'Great city.'

I ask him how much of the food is grilled to order. He's standing near a grill where vegetables sizzle and spit.

'Aye, a good number of the items are. Keeps us busy. And hot.'

I mention to him that I watched one of his on-line videos filmed in the kitchen here, and he smiles, 'Listen, best of luck to you.'

Yeesh. I had to go just that one, smarmy step too far, didn't I?

While at The Pass, I'm taught how to make up the welcoming nibble they serve to people as they arrive, a small dish of butter beans that is drawn from a heated well in the warm table. I have not paid enough attention to what I was shown – because I was going over in my head my exchange with the chef, obviously – and when asked to reproduce the butter bean small dish, mine do not have the right number of beans, are not positioned correctly, and aren't as neat as they need to be. I am told as much.

My next set of butter beans looks better, even though I can't help thinking they still don't look as good as the one I was shown initially. Slightly sloppy butter beans would be no big drama, just move on, pay attention and do it right the next time – but for my grade 5 teacher, Mrs Linklater. She told my parents I would not get anywhere in life because I had bad handwriting. I feel I have an innate tendency to revert to my mean level of sloppiness. Whatever I achieve, I'm convinced one day I will be outed for my secret messiness, lack of attention to detail and laziness, which somehow Mrs Linklater spotted so early on.

I am paired up for my trial shift with a Spanish waiter – kismet! I love Spain and feel a cultural kinship with the Spanish. Lucia is a young woman who embodies a lot of things that make me proud of being a Quebecer. She's not pretentious, she has a sparkle in her eye, and she gets on with things.

The Spanish and the Québécois share a heritage that ranges from the smaller things like language ticks, saying 'Hostie' or in Spanish 'Ostia', as an exclamation (a reference to the communion wafer or host), to the fact of having lived for generations repressed by the Church and deeply conservative politics. In Quebec, it's referred to as '*la Grande Noirceur*', the Great Darkness. In Spain, it was outright dictatorship under Franco around about the same time. The famous Québécois 'joie-de-vivre' really exploded on to the scene afterwards, similarly in Spain with the death of Franco.

'Nice to meet you,' Lucia says with a big smile. 'Come with me.'

Lucia gives me the crash course with efficiency and a good measure of patience – the computer system, which to my surprise I mostly get, the menu, which I've studied before getting here, and how to take the orders. It is a further avalanche of new information, and there is no way you can possibly feel you have registered it all. I have this feeling that if I just push on, in a sort of a 'fake it till you make it' way, I'll get by. It requires force of will and asking the right number of questions without being a pest.

Lucia uses a small notepad to take orders. 'Don't put pressure on yourself to memorise orders. It's not worth it.'

The tone of Lucia's service is crisp and friendly at the same time, so efficient that I'm not even sure the guests can see that she's making small notes. When asked about the menu, she comes up with exactly the answers the diners seem to want. Before anyone has to ask again for something, she has delivered it.

'I like to keep their water topped up whenever I have time.'

She coaches me as best she can. I know that my brain is straining with the effort and if I feel that, you can bet everyone else can see it, too. Diners can smell fear and uncertainty. The floor supervisor, Gabor, is watching for it. At one point, I detect what I am sure is the evil eye from across the room. Sure enough, a short while later, he comes over to me as I am surveilling the tables and in a drive-by critique, says: 'Your arms are crossed and you're making everybody nervous.'

It's a comment that stings all the more for being spot on.

Lunch hour is busy at ROVI on Saturday. Lucia finally says to me, 'Okay, I think you are ready to do some solo work.' She lets me take on the service of two of her tables. One is two women having lunch together, and the other is a slightly chaotic table consisting of a mother and father, French, and their three younger children.

I take a beat and summon that skill I rely on while live on-air with several moving parts and unexpected things happening. I force myself into a calm place. I focus on the moment and the conversation I'm having now. I shove all the busy, unattended-to thoughts and anxieties off to the side.

'Hello. Can I get you something to drink to begin?' I ask the two women. As soon as I start to speak back and forth with them, I feel reassured. They want good service, I want happy customers, we click.

For the French table, I speak French, which they acknowledge with satisfaction, though not what you'd call delight. They are all about the classic French reserve. Their order is much more complicated, as you'd imagine and especially with kids in tow, but I take careful notes and feel I've got it all.

I come back to the till, and Lucia watches me key in the order. I've recorded everything correctly, except for one thing. Much of the food is sharing plates, and there is a way to key in the order that splits up the service and allows time for guests to breathe and appreciate their meal. The second flight awaits your signal before being prepared. I've forgotten to ask which plates they want first. I should have broken it down clearly while taking the order.

'I'll go back and ask.'

'No, wait,' Lucia says. 'Let's figure this out. I don't think you need to go back.'

She teaches me a default system for which of the dishes are better to come first – the freshest ones, the colder ones, with grilled meats and more elaborate food towards the end. Children's food orders go in straight away always.

One of the clues about how tense I really am is that I notice I am clutching my pen and keep hearing Gabor's voice in my head. Still, I see food is making its way to the table of two, with big smiles from the guests.

I have enough basic knowledge of the menu to answer or blag my way through any questions, runners and bartenders deliver what I've punched in, water glasses are topped off, I am pleasant and conversational. Huh. It works. I am plausibly waiting tables in an Ottolenghi restaurant.

It is draining, however. My cheeks are burning from the effort. I am only just beating down my lingering anxiety about looking unsteady.

Then a moment I'm dreading arrives. It's time to clear some glasses. Mostly, it's the bus staff that take care of it, but Lucia has handed me a tray and asked me to go give them a hand. I'm being tested, I reckon.

As a cater-waiter in my university days, we cleared tables at banquets and weddings but with huge oval trays that we were allowed to keep nearby on a stand. Somehow, the fact that they were bigger made me feel they were easier to balance. Removing glasses with a smaller tray that I can't put down is making me anxious. I struggle with carrying anything on a tray at home and have had some spectacular accidents.

I'm at the table with the French family, dodging sudden movements from the kids.

'Here, let me get some of these glasses out of the way for you.'

'Oh, merci.'

I lean in to pick up two rosé glasses and some of the kids' glasses to boot. My hand is tense under the tray, but I have good grip from years of gym work, so I should be fine, right? I try to position everything on the tray so it's balanced. Everything looks good as I start to head away from the table but just as I pick up speed, a wine glass leans and looks like it may topple.

Time slows. I see the glass tip ever so slightly. My heart leaps into my mouth. My eyes are screaming, 'Please, don't let this happen.' I shift my angle of departure ever so slightly to compensate, accelerate, and focus on keeping my hand steady with sheer willpower.

The glass straightens.

'Hey, you're doing fine,' Lucia says to me as I get back to the station. She puts a hand on my shoulder. I am in a cold sweat. Thankfully, I have worn an undershirt.

In the back where you drop off the dirty dishes, a hefty West Country woman gives me a warm hello that is unlike anything from the floor staff. 'You've a nice smile, you have!' she says to me. She shows me a little shelf where staff keep glasses of water for themselves. I start to imagine how you could gradually settle into this place and make connections.

I walk back on to the floor feeling better than I have since I arrived, as though I am almost getting the hang of it, and then I'm tapped on the shoulder by Gabor.

'That's enough,' he says to me. 'Go get changed and we'll be in touch.'

Being taken out of the game hits me as a let-down. In the same moment, though, I seize on the relief of finishing and realise just how tired I am, sore feet to go with my sore brain from all the new information. I am wound up tight.

In the staff area behind the secret door, I change back into my civilian clothes. As I'm packing my bag to go, I see Andrew, the head server, and feeling that I did okay, I decide to press my luck a bit.

'Hi again, Andrew. I just want to say that I really appreciate having the opportunity today. What a great team you have. I loved working with Lucia. I hope you'll put in a good word for me.'

Andrew's eyes narrow. 'I will do that. Only if I get good feedback and if I judge you to have been exceptional.'

Nervous smile from me. 'Oh, well, fingers crossed! I thought it went pretty well, actually.'

He casts his eyes down and walks away out on to the floor.

I leave the restaurant thinking the place is as much of a gem as when I entered. I am in awe of them for what they do, all so well. The service purrs along with hard work that never appears like strain, even though it clearly is. As for my contribution today, you would not call it crisp and effortless.

Then there's Andrew. He was obviously suspicious of me, in fact, as much as I don't want to admit it to myself, I think he really didn't like me. I rubbed him the wrong way from minute one. What could it be? I was a chunky kid – I am a big adult. My go-to self-doubt is to think he was put off by my size. Did I look and act sloppy? Was it that, or maybe the way I tried to ingratiate myself to him? Maybe he thinks I'm far too old to be trying on a job like this? Honestly, at this moment, I can suddenly come up with a lot of reasons for him not liking me. I'm not feeling so good any more.

Shit.

Seriously, is this what I want to do with my break from broadcasting? Push myself this hard at a job that requires so many new skills, plus the pressure, the judgement and all the manual labour? As much as I need work and as thrilled as I would be to possess the kind of flair these people have, is this really a good move for me? Having arrived in London ground down by my routine, am I really in a place where this level of intensity can be therapeutic?

Five days later those questions are answered for me in an email from James:

> Thanks for your patience on this. We wanted to get the chance to sit as a management team and go through all the candidates.
>
> Unfortunately, on this occasion we have decided not to take your application further. We had one position open on the waiter team and a lot of high-quality candidates. It was a difficult decision and whilst we all appreciated your enthusiasm, we felt it right to give the position to someone with more experience.
>
> Having said that, I do believe you have a lot of the qualities we look for at Ottolenghi, if you would like me to forward on your application to a different site within the group, I would be happy to recommend you.

It is a rejection – I wasn't good enough. I am disappointed as I read it on the screen of my mobile phone, during a pause on a walk through Soho. I was about to get on the Tube to go home. Instead, I decide to walk through the back streets of London and all the way home.

Actually, I am feeling crushed. There was just something about this job and this restaurant that appealed to me. It's the only place I bothered to approach. It was a reflection of many things I aspired to, from the awesome staff from across Europe, Ottolenghi, of course, his fresh, inventive cuisine, the accent on vegetable dishes and flame-grilling, a wine list that read like a magical European holiday. I had spent days studying and decoding the menu and the obscure terms within, new types of food from places I hadn't heard of. It was young and vibrant and cutting-edge, it drew on transferable skills from my journalism and performance but also required plenty of things I knew little about but thought I could learn, things that would make me better and stronger. I would have grown. It was a place I could be proud to say I worked at. I imagined people saying, 'Wow. That's cool.'

After an hour of walking, I reach the South Bank and take a seat on a bench looking out over the River Thames. I take out my mobile phone and forward the email from James to a friend in Montreal, David, who's a chef at a popular, well-reviewed restaurant.

'Feeling a bit bummed out about this :/' I write.

I keep walking east along the Thames, weaving in between the tourists and the joggers, past Tate Modern and the Globe, seagulls swirling in the air. Within twenty minutes, a buzz from my phone, it's David writing back. Calm down, he says. That email from James was a big win. He says most people don't get a try-out, and most people don't get a kind email afterwards if they're not hired. He thinks I aimed high to try suddenly to become a waiter at one of the hottest restaurants in London having only had experience from cater-waitering in my twenties. He says that to be honest, restaurants hesitate to hire people over fifty in what are demanding jobs.

I know he is trying to lift my spirits and in some ways he does. It's true, I did just have a trial shift at an Ottolenghi restaurant in Fitzrovia and came close to being hired. Fair enough. Something else is bothering me, though. At first, I'm not sure I can quite put my finger on it but it's this: I have never really imagined myself as older. I weirdly have seen myself as ageless – boyish face, still all my hair, plenty of energy. If my youthfulness is imagined, what else am I deluding myself about?

On the spot, I force those thoughts down, thank David, and write back to James to say I'm interested in work elsewhere in the Ottolenghi fold. Weeks later, tellingly, he never writes back, and I never prompt him to. I don't bother to look for anything else. Maybe I can eke out the six months with my savings after all. Maybe Sheila was right and radio presenters don't have transferable skills.

Castillon Frais

'C'est un paysage qui sait, un paysage où se reflètent les lois profondes de la vie, où le dépouillement des cimes dénudées dessine le contour des grands rythmes élémentaires.'

– Henri Bosco, author, describing his beloved Luberon, a massif in Central Provence, 'where the profound laws of life are reflected, where the bare peaks outline the great elementary rhythms'.

Origin: A fresh, unpasteurised sheep cheese, these little beauties hail from the Luberon, from the farm of David and Fanette Ladu and their flock of Sarda sheep, originally brought to Provence from Sardinia. It's a fresh cheese, meaning it is light and bright, not funky at all, made only of raw milk, a few drops of rennet and a good dose of love and know-how.

Presentation: Each cheese is about 3cm in height and 6cm in diameter and has a vivid ivory hue from the rind through the

paste. It is an absolute stunner, with a velvety texture.
Un délice.

How to serve: You can make short work of these little sheep's
cheeses just on their own. Because of their freshness and total
absence of funk, I hesitate to put them on a cheeseboard
unless trying to make a point. Instead, try serving them as a
palate cleanser between courses, with a spring salad, or some
fresh fruit, berries or even citrus. They can have a beguiling,
almost sesame flavour which complements fresh, Asian-
inspired cooking, but don't heat them.

Fun fact: Few cheeses invoke the first, tender days of spring the
way these do. They arrive in London along with the buds, the
daffodils and the dawn chorus.

11
Picking Myself Up

FOLLOWING MY EXPERIENCE AT the Ottolenghi restaurant, it becomes a favourite pastime to throw on a pair of shorts, grab a towel, then head out the door and around the corner to one of London's hidden treasures, a little park in my neighbourhood south of the River Thames. You might walk from one end to the other of the busy street that runs along it and not even realise it is just on the other side of an old brick wall covered in vines and hidden behind bushes. I lie down with my shirt off for an hour or two, stretch out like a cat, bring a book and bring my phone but not use either of them. We are blessed with sunshine this spring. I have somehow forgotten about the restorative power of the sun after years of getting up in the middle of the night.

What I do in the park is an extension of what I have been doing in the weeks since I arrived. I am a broadcaster who has turned transmission functions off. I am a receiver now - the sun first, which moves in and out from behind the clouds of the English sky. I imagine a phone plugged in and recharging - that's how I experience the radiating warmth of sunshine these days. Then there are the birds and the bugs and the dogs and the smell of flowers - all of that - and a London game I love to play. My eyes are closed and I flip my ears on to bring what were indistinct conversations into focus, sometimes phone conversations, sometimes it's people talking to each other. With my eyes closed, it's akin to listening to the radio almost.

I try to imagine the physical appearance of the person who's speaking. London is home to people from so many places, one of the crossroads of the world. My borough, Southwark, contains a cross-section of the city. There are neighbours who live in social housing. There are people here from their office on lunch break. There are all kinds of sparkling new blocks of flats around that charge huge sums of money to rent or buy. There are students and teenagers from the many nearby schools and universities. There are young parents and seniors. There are people who sleep in a nearby shelter. It's London in all its mad diversity: so many native English-speakers with so many different soundtracks to their voices, so many people for whom English is a second or third language and has a whole other musicality. It's language rich beyond belief and I don't know if there's any other place quite like it, a feast for the ears.

I am listening to two blokes having a technical conversation. They're on their work break, young, I'm guessing. One of them has a broad Glaswegian accent and the other is talking like a character out of *EastEnders*. I'm sure I'm not the only Canadian my age to have their Glaswegian preconceptions formed by the film *Trainspotting*. So I am imagining young Ewan McGregor speaking to a Grant Mitchell type from *East-Enders*. I squint my eyes open after about ten minutes to find two sharply dressed South Asian men with neat beards, pressed shirts and dress shoes, one vaping and the other drinking a fruit smoothie. I love this game, not least for how it shines a light on my cultural references and updates them.

It is in ways like these that the initial weeks of my sabbatical pass. At home, I have far fewer things, including in the kitchen. There is an exciting feeling almost like camping. I ban my devices from the bedroom completely. There is no television. I go to the busy Columbia Road flower market every Sunday and buy fresh flowers 'for a fiver', as the traders shout, always something different.

I have a pint with friends, go to the theatre a couple of times, receive visitors from Canada, eat out and buy new things for the flat, not a lot of shopping but some beloved essentials like a new blanket for cosy evenings on the sofa. I gradually deep clean the flat from top to bottom.

Cantal

'Que vous avez d'appas ! que vostre odeur me plaist!
Et que de vostre goust, tout horrible qu'il est ...
Qu'au poids de celles d'or on devroit mettre en vente!'

– Marc-Antoine Girard, Sieur de Saint-Amant, French Poet, 1661

Part of a much longer poem entitled 'Le Cantal' in which Saint-Amant writes that Cantal 'puts Brie to shame':

'How attractive you are! How I love your smell!
And how horrible your taste is ...
That we should put on sale at the weight of gold!'

∾

Origin: Cantal is reputed to be one of the world's ancient cheeses, made reference to in Pliny the Elder's *Natural History* (AD 77) as a popular cheese in Rome. Then, it was referred to as '*Fourme*', from the Latin *forma* (the root of fromage). By the seventeenth century, it became known as Cantal. From cattle grazing the volcanic hills of the Auvergne in Central France, farmers made the giant wheels in their stone huts, using it later to barter for other necessities. It has both an AOC and an AOP and is a firm French favourite.

Presentation: Immense, barrel-shaped wheels weighing 40kg, it is a handsome cheese with a striking, natural rind that can get a bit wild. It's a pressed-curd cheese, similar to Cheddar, which some believe owes its existence to Cantal, brought by Romans to The British Isles. The paste is firm and golden. It can take on a rusty hue as it nears the rind.

How to serve: Wouldn't look out of place on a medieval feasting table. Wonderful to nibble on straight from the board, unaccompanied. It has a tangy acidity, bold and buttery with a moreish, golden spice flavour. Grapes, figs, apples and salad marry nicely with Cantal. Try it instead of Parmigiano with beef carpaccio; it's also a winner in baking: quiches, pies, savoury cakes. Wine pairings vary depending on how mature your Cantal is. Go bolder with a more mature wedge, Pauillac or Châteauneuf-du-Pape. With younger wedges, go with something medium to lighter, a Valençay or a Chardonnay.

Fun fact: A close relative of Cantal is Salers Tradition, a truly exceptional cheese worth seeking out. It is as natural as cheesemaking gets, using age-old methods. Farmers begin making it while the milk is still warm – on site, in the field, straight from the cow – using the same wooden vats they use for cheesemaking. These vats, called *gerles*, are rich in the historical bacteria necessary for fermentation. The Salers cow is a magnificent beast with a rich mahogany red or black coat. She milks with her calf present; the calf suckles briefly before the milk begins to flow, ensuring the presence of plenty of lactic acid bacteria, as well as cleaning the teats. All the bacteria necessary for fermentation come through these processes. It is quite literally a taste of history.

12
The Answer Lies in Borough Market

FOUR WEEKS AFTER MY failed attempt at winning a job in the Ottolenghi restaurant and getting a polite but firm knockback, reality starts to sink in. I thought I could manage the six months in London on savings, but I am burning through money. At first, I think this amounts to making the most of my sabbatical. As I go deeper into my savings reserve, I occasionally start to feel queasy, mostly early in the morning when I am forced to face the reality of my current account. I am heading for a wall.

One evening, I crack open some whisky, a gift from Alison, a wise former BBC colleague in Glasgow. When I first arrived, I sought her out, making the five-hour train journey and renting a hotel room for a few nights just to see her. A career in journalism means crossing paths with a lot of people whose stock in trade is to be able to size up situations unflinchingly and see things from different perspectives. Alison was a deputy of mine at the BBC World Service in the early 2000s and stood out like a good Camembert in a selection of French cheese. She is as straight-shooting as they come, a journalist with a capital J, takes no bullshit and tells it like it is. Her stock phrases are, 'I'll tell you the truth' and 'I'm not being funny', delivered forthrightly in a Dundonian accent. Alison lived for years in the Arab world and travelled extensively, seeing the inside of several news organisations including the BBC and Al Jazeera. When I met her in Glasgow, she was a consultant in media management to Scottish nationalist politicians.

She was incredibly generous, taking a couple of days out to walk me around town, through the Kelvingrove Art Gallery and Museum, even on a day trip to the Scottish parliament in Edinburgh. My God, we talked. Everything was on the table, and it went both ways because there was a lot going on in her life. Her mother had died recently, and she had spent some considerable time caring for her in Dundee. It was tough going, losing her in difficult circumstances, grieving, coming to terms with life without her, dealing with her estate. I listened, as she did to me.

'Morning show presenting? Aye. Tricky thing to work into your life, isn't it?'

'I've lost count of the number of people I've given advice to about managing the hours and the demands. "It's all about the routine," I told them. I'm feeling a bit of a fraud now.'

'Aye. It's probably a bit more complicated than discipline and routine,' she said, looking at me and then letting out a burst of laughter.

We put in thousands of steps that weekend and did a lot of emotional digging around. Returning home on the train with the bottle of whisky she gave me, I had to pinch myself that such people are part of my life.

Now, glass in hand, I pick up the phone with the other, reflexively, dialling her number looking to talk to her again. She answers on the first ring: 'Hello there, and what is it now?' That mad laugh of hers.

'You and I managed a team of forty journalists together. We were responsible for six hours of world news and current affairs every day. We fought through all the BBC management bunk. What did you really think about my outing waiting tables in London?'

This time there's no laugh, just a thoughtful pause. 'I love that you marched right up to that Ottolenghi place, told them to hire you and then worked a shift. Sounds like you did a bloody good job, too. Good on you. Just don't tell me you're going to fold and give up after the first hurdle.'

'No,' I say. Did she detect my hesitancy, though? Because actually, yes, that's exactly what I feel like doing.

'I bloody well hope not. There's so many things you can do coming out of journalism. Look at me, a political advisor.' She's chuckling again. 'I wouldn't recommend it. Bloody fascinating, though.'

I don't say anything for a moment. Then Alison continues:

'This hospitality sector interest of yours, I can see how some people would be surprised, maybe even see it as a step down for you. But you're intrigued and there's a reason for that. And why not? Makes a clean break from journalism.

'Perspective's a good thing, and there's lots more to that work than meets the eye, especially if you put a bit more thought into what exactly you might do and where. London and all, there's lots to choose from.

'In the end, look – it's a six-month sabbatical. Six months is not nothing, but it will pass more quickly than you think, and here you are, you've taken some good time off already but you're a do-er like me. What have you got to lose from going for it, giving it a go?'

After the call, I make an inventory of the gains I have already achieved. I am rested, no longer either working or recovering from work. Gone is the pressure of night-time alarms, fitting in naps and bedtimes, worrying about finding new subjects for the show, updating my social media. It feels great. My days belong to me. In the four weeks since I arrived, I have de-stressed so gradually it's been nearly imperceptible; nevertheless, partly because of friends like Alison, I am feeling it profoundly.

She's right. I decide to look for work, but no more than part-time, something that connects to me, shares my values and is not too far away. I come to realise that I get a lot of comfort from being in the neighbourhood where I've lived off and on for twenty years. It has a Tomme de Savoie effect, I guess you could say, a comforting cheese that always feels like an old friend, gentle and dependable. This is my London, the Borough, and now I want to work here, too.

The Borough is just across the River Thames from the City, the financial district, and its history is firmly rooted in it being the approach to London from the south. Borough High Street was and still is the road that leads to London Bridge, which crossed over to palaces, courts, administrators and the seat of government.

The difference is that in the past, there was just one bridge. On the South Bank, clustered near the approach to the bridge, were gathered all the things people couldn't do on the other side: theatres, bawdy-houses and bear-baiting, for example. It was also home to undesirables, hucksters and prisons. It was a sort of Mos Eisley spaceport, to use *Star Wars* terminology. Charles Dickens' father was jailed in a debtors' prison on Marshalsea Road in the Borough, right around the corner from my flat. The church that stands near Borough Tube station is nicknamed 'Little Dorrit Church' after Dickens' famous novel.

The Borough is filled with winding streets, great brick warehouses, many now turned into blocks of flats, railway arches and old-style public houses. It is a proper neighbourhood right in Zone 1, with plenty of well-established, long-time housing: council flats that date back decades, rows of identical houses, and beautiful, manicured squares that seem to pop out of nowhere. Centre to the neighbourhood's identity is Borough Market.

My little flat is ten minutes away by foot and, for years, I would wander up to Borough Market as the sun rose, buy a coffee, sit, and enjoy the breaking of the early-morning stillness as traders went about their morning routine, hauling their wares from storage and opening up their stalls under the giant green, wrought-iron canopy. The rhythm of the market, then as now, is punctuated by trains rattling by on their journey overhead.

Borough Market started life as a market selling corn and cattle centuries ago but is now a destination for London foodies, actually, for foodies from around the world. There are fruit and vegetable stalls, wine merchants, butchers, fishmongers, bakers, cake and confectionery makers, plus Italian, Croatian, Greek, Baltic, Spanish and Asian speciality stores. I remember fondly a woman who used to sell only ostrich meat, eggs and feather dusters every Saturday morning. She no longer trades there, alas.

Recently, the market was targeted in an attack. I would like to wish it away or pretend it didn't happen, but that wouldn't be right. It was 2017, two years before my sabbatical began, and it marked me, even though I was in Montreal at the time. I remember sitting in my kitchen listening to Radio 4 over cups of tea, rapt, unable to believe what I was hearing.

For several long minutes, three attackers hunted people down, going from business to business. They had pink ceramic knives tied to their wrists and were wearing what turned out to be fake bomb vests. It was brutal – the attackers slashed and stabbed people along their path, some a dozen times or more. They killed eight people, five men, three women. Forty-eight others were injured, twenty-one of them critically.

People were forced to hide and take shelter, hoping they wouldn't be discovered. They were under tables, in toilet cubicles, holding doors shut, trying to figure out what was going on. Terrified. It must have seemed like hours. Some ran for their lives. Some stood their ground and threw crates, trays or glasses at the three attackers, who were eventually killed about ten metres from the cheese stall where I now work.

It's a wound, a scar at the very least. I know it is still felt deeply by traders, even though it's seldom spoken of. Walking around the market today, you'd never know it had taken place. There are no memorials or markers. Traders and the people who work in the area, they know. When you work in a market, you're exposed. You're on display, for better and for worse, something I've come to understand.

One of the things that sets the market apart is the many cheese vendors. One of them was where I first got hooked on Comté. They do a good business selling a few select cheeses, bigger wheels, right in the middle of the market concourse under a bright orange umbrella. They've become familiar faces, some of them friends.

One morning as I'm walking around Borough Market, I see an ad posted with a call for a cheesemonger. I'm not sure I have ever really seen the word spelled out like that on a job advert. I have an immediate, physical reaction, an excited nervousness, so much so that I hang back for a while and watch the cheesemongers do their jobs. Damn, they're cool, so animated with the customers, so confident as they handle and prepare the cheeses, so deft as they package and wrap without even seeming to look at what they're doing. The display reminds me of France. All those memories from my exchange family in Saint-Étienne come pouring back, a time of possibilities, a year that opened a gateway in my life.

As I look at the job ad in Borough Market, I wonder if chee-semongering may just be a job I can learn to do. Fortunately, I have no idea of the realities of what it entails. On top of all it has going for it, it is a job that's different from anything you'll find in Canada. It is quintessentially European, a cheese shop, and a Franco-British one at that, selling mostly French and Swiss cheeses. It connects back over centuries of market history at this same spot in London. It is a great fit for a Montrealer who lives in English and French. My only slight concern is that in the job ad, they speak of warehouse duties. It isn't that clear to me what that is: moving boxes around with a forklift? I imagine being extremely poor at that. Possibly a danger.

In the end, I write an email entitled, 'I'm interested in work as a cheesemonger'. I don't hear back at first, but I don't stress about that. So much tension is exiting my body these days that time passes differently. I put in a couple of other job enquiries at the Market, but I do so almost to give some context to the cheesemongering application, not to have all eggs in one basket even though my heart has already decided. I apply to a specialist coffee roaster and to a wineseller, bar and restaurant.

One day, in the midst of a longer run around the perimeter of Battersea Park, the phone rings. It's the cheesemongers.

Brillat-Savarin

'Un dessert sans fromage est une belle
à qui il manque un œil.'

– Jean-Anthelme Brillat-Savarin, noted French epicurean and
gourmet. 'A dessert without cheese is like a beautiful woman
missing an eye.'

Origin: Born in Normandy around the turn of the twentieth century, it started out as *Excelsior* or *Délice des gourmets* until it was renamed in the 1930s by the cheesemaker Henri Androuët in honour of Jean-Anthelme Brillat-Savarin. It's now produced in Burgundy.

Presentation: A soft, bloomy rind cow's milk cheese, ours are about 13cm across and thick at 3.5cm high, but they also come in smaller formats. It is white or off-white and the paste looks cake- or fudge-like due to its enrichment with triple cream. Some first timers think it is cake! We sell it in quarters, which is plenty, but some customers are so in thrall, they'll purchase a whole wheel for the weekend.

How to serve: It really needs bread, brioche, croissant or a cracker or else the cream is too intense on its own. If you fancy truffle, try cutting it in half, coating the middle with truffle, then re-assembling it. This can be cheaper (and more fun) than buying a 'truffled cheese'. Consider the triple cream (it's a lot) before attempting a recipe, but if feeling adventurous try it baked over asparagus. The fine bubbles of a chilled Champagne will complement nicely. For wine, try a Sauterne and for beer, a Belgian blonde.

Fun fact: It is decadence pure and simple, sometimes referred to as the foie gras of cheese. One of the food tour leaders who regularly comes through the market stops at our stall and pronounces it the 'best cheese in the world' to much discreet eye-rolling on our side. It has its passionate fans, but best in the world is a stretch. Besides, I hesitate ever to name one cheese as best – how do you think the others feel after hearing that?

Part III
Apprenticeship

13
The Cheese Talk

I T TAKES ME A while to find Cheese HQ the first time because Bermondsey is a part of town filled with streets that wind along and under the railway tracks. It's also not easy to know where the front door is to some warehouse arches. I wander around for half an hour, eating up the margin allotted to ensure an on-time arrival. Nevertheless, here I am, three full minutes early, waiting outside the big, orange metal door beside the roll-up shutters of the delivery bay.

I wait until I am exactly on time according to my phone before ringing the doorbell. This is one of those doorbells where the button does not produce a chime, but instead is connected to what sounds like my old elementary school fire alarm. I give it a good press and jump back, startled. I feel as though I'm standing outside some walled fortress waiting for the drawbridge keeper. Minutes go by with no answer. I ring the fire bell again but this time with more of a tapping motion.

The door finally opens, and it is Cheesemonger Emma. She is smiling a big, welcoming ear-to-ear smile. She takes me in. Emma is the biggest cheese extrovert I have ever met. She loves cheese in boundless measure and in all its diversity. Recently, I listened in as she told a customer at our cheese shop in East Dulwich about travelling outside London to where she discovered someone selling a Red Leicester toastie.

My mind began picturing the buttery, brothy-tasting, orange-hued cheese, oozing from between thick slices of toasted country bread. When she finished serving her customer, I locked eyes with her. 'Emma.'

She squealed, 'I know! I can't get Red Leicester toasties out of my brain now! Why did I say that?'

That's what Emma is like. Oh, and petite and gorgeous. Anyone who knows about cheese in London knows her. She has since moved on to set up her own company, which is all about developing Londoners' taste for artisan cheese.

That same day, the Red Leicester Toastie day, two and a half years on from me being hired, I remind her that she's the one who first pulled my CV from the stack of submissions and called me up to talk about it while I was running in the park.

'Oh, I know. I remember reading it and saying, "We have to hire this bloke."' That feels good, but it surprises me to hear her say it. It did not feel like that on that first morning in Bermondsey.

The Arch is a spacious warehouse under the railway tracks. Above the delivery bay are offices. Just in from the delivery bay is the kitchen corner with the mandatory large box of tea. She offers me one, I decline. She takes me a bit further back and says she's going to give me a bit of a tour through the cheese-contact area. That means the clothes I have on need to be covered over, so trainers become big white rubber boots. I also put on a white smock over my clothes and a hat.

The room is bright, and the smell is a cocktail of odours that I will soon learn to associate with the job and, in a strange way, crave. There is the smell of cheese, of course, different varieties, some gentle and some potent, but mixed in is the smell of a powerful detergent called Topax which is used to clean cheese residue off things like knives, slates, counters and floors. It has a hard-to-describe slightly sweet smell to it, a step beyond bleach.

I wave to a couple of the all-white-clad workers, and she takes me into the different cheese fridges where I see row upon row of cheeses of all different shapes and sizes, trays of delicate goat's cheese, stacks of boxed Camembert, giant wheels of Alpine cheese.

We exit. Emma then takes me back to the part of The Arch where dry goods are stocked, similar to what it looks like in the open-air stockroom at Ikea, my only point of reference for a warehouse. A table is set out, two chairs, and at this point, Emma introduces me to Cheesemonger Cian.

'I have to go now,' she says, and she turns to leave suddenly. When Emma leaves a room, you can't help feeling slightly bereft for a moment. So there I am, in an echoing warehouse, neon lights buzzing above my head, alone with Cian, a total stranger, me dressed in a shirt and tie, while he is looking cool and casual. And sceptical.

'Sorry about the tie. I thought I should make an effort.'

'Right,' he says, looking at my tie. No smile.

It is the wrong effort, as it turns out, and it means not only am I wearing the wrong clothes for the situation, but I know I am wearing the wrong clothes for the situation. I feel I need to overcompensate in other areas in order to tamp down the effects of the tie faux pas because I don't want to come across as stiff or in any way effete. I resolve to smile a lot, look eager and listen intently. Forget the shirt and tie, please. What was I thinking?

Cian is in his late twenties and from Essex, north-east of London. I lived in London for ten years before I learned where it was. I had to look it up on the map. It was always less geographical and more a state of mind to me. If you're from Essex, you have a reputation for being cheeky, for having a good time, for not being afraid to size up and pursue someone you fancy, and for being a bit of a chancer. In other words, less outwardly restrained than most Southerners in England are reputed to be.

Cian is all the Essex clichés and more. He's whip smart, he's political, he's questioning and unwilling to go along with things he feels make no sense. He's also fiercely loyal, if you've earned it. He is half English/Irish and half Italian on his mum's side. He's popular and good looking. On this first meeting, he is being circumspect.

Cian has been assigned to give me something they call 'the talk'. The Cheese Talk, that is: a dissuasion technique. It is meant to turn me back and it's part of the reason Emma has left. Emma is not good at dissuading people from doing things. Cian is good at it, but as he sets forth to deliver the talk sternly, I am detecting something else from him, just under the surface. It's cheeky and Essex-y, for sure, but what does it mean? I can't quite read him. He has a page of notes in front of him. I sit across the table.

'So you know there's more to the job than just being nice to customers and selling them bits of cheese.'

My mind immediately goes to the part of the job spec I'm most suspicious of. 'I know the advert talks about warehouse duties.'

'All right, it's more than that, see. I mean there's a lot of hard graft to it, right? Like at the market and at the shop, not just here. What do you think of that?'

'I think that's good. I'm not afraid of hard work.'

Part of the confidence I'm showing stems from my afore-mentioned decision to compensate for my shirt and tie, but another part goes deeper. It's a sort of 'bring it on' attitude now that I decide I want this job. I could use a bit of hard work anyway.

Then again, 'What sort of hard work are you talking about?'
I ask.

'I don't know, all of it. Moving the cheeses around, for one
thing. They're big, right. Lots of cleaning, too. A lot of cleaning. Scrubbing, actually. And sweeping, washing floors.
Everything, really. Every day, too. What do you think of that?'

I keep my game face on. 'I think I'm up for it.'

'You are, yeah? The hours aren't great.'

'How's that?'

'Well, you work on Saturday. Every Saturday. That bother
you?'

'Not really.' Part of me is tired of having Saturdays off. It was
my only day off in the radio job. How great is it to be off on
weekdays? Like Mondays and Tuesdays, free to wander
around London when things are less busy. 'I'm cool with that.'

'Shifts have flexible end times and firm starts. Actually
right, we like you there a bit early if you want a coffee or something. But like what I'm saying is the close, right, that takes as
long as it takes.'

Okay, that's not so enticing, I have to admit.

He continues: 'An hour, definitely. But with me, right, it's
gonna be a lot faster. I'm ace at closing. It's tough going, though.'

Cian has shifted into an attitude where it feels almost like a
bout to probe my weaknesses, a poke here, a jab there. I find
that I am starting to draw on an energy from my on-air hostile
interviewing days. He's trying to put me off but I'm going to
push back. This is all developing its own dynamic. With
everything he says, the barrage of detail, I am feeling more
confident, not less.

In terms of the actual content of what he's saying, I realise
it all falls into the realm of something that might have intimidated the pre-epiphany me. The kind of bone tired I was
feeling daily, before the sabbatical, might have led me to feel

incapable of rising to most of the challenges he is setting out. What can a morning radio presenter actually do, after all? Instead, I am sitting here listening and I suddenly can't help smiling as I become aware of what he's trying to do. I am feeling rested. I am feeling strong from the gym. I am feeling confident from having spent so much time with people I enjoy, old friends and colleagues. I have proved to myself that I can face down outsized obstacles and overcome them.

'I can do that,' is what I say to him, repeatedly. And I know I can.

Cian closes his notepad, looks at me with a sort of smile and then opens his notepad again. He takes out a page, writes on it, and gives it to me.

'Here. Tomorrow, 11 a.m. Trial shift at our shop in East Dulwich. Good for you?'

'I'll see you there.'

'Not me. Maybe see you later, though.' Cian gives me a grin, and he walks me to the orange metal door and the interview is over.

Chabichou

'Et qui l'aime, l'aime en chauvin.
Bien fait, il passe le divin,
Mais combien rare ! Deux sur vingt!
Il n'est qu'un Martin à la foire,
Le chabichou!'

– Emile Bergerat, 'Rondeau du Chabichou',
Ballades et sonnets, 1910.

Bergerat here proving an eternal point about cheese, that it has a way of bewitching people.

> *'Whoever loves it, does so chauvinistically*
> *When it's well made, it's beyond divine*
> *But how rare is that! Two in twenty!*
> *Just a Martin at the fair/Le chabichou!'*

Origin: A cheese whose origins date back to the Arab Saracens who remained in the Loire Valley, along with their goats, in the eighth century after their defeat at the hands of the Frankish army. It has since become synonymous with the Poitou region, referred to in travel guides dating back to the eighteenth century.

Presentation: Chabichou is shaped like a squat cone, with a wider base than top, about 6cm diameter versus 5cm at the top. It weighs around 100g, is white, sometimes brilliantly so, or slightly golden-hued. When cut, there is normally a gooey creamline just under the rind. Yum – this is due to bacterial cultures slowly breaking down milk proteins. The paste runs from fudgy to creamy in texture, depending on the batch and how mature it is. It has a pleasantly pronounced goat's milk taste and some lovely sweetness. I've always thought Chabichou a cheese that comes closest to how most might imagine a classic French goat's cheese would taste. It's delicious.

How to serve: Pleasing to the eye, it's a great choice on a cheeseboard and can happily be consumed on its own or with a cracker, or with the traditional goat's cheese complements: honey, nuts, jam, dried fruit, fruit paste, or try it with grilled pumpkin or a colourful squash, where its white paste will make an eye-catching combo. Works well in recipes, an example being a spinach pie or parcel. As with most Loire Valley goat's cheeses, it pairs well with a dry Loire white or a light red, but goat's cheese and dry (sparkling) rosé in the summertime are magic.

Fun fact: The name is said to have evolved from *chebli*, an Arabic word for the goats the Saracens kept in the region where it's still made.

14
East Dulwich and the Cheesemonger Avengers

NEXT DAY, I'M OUTSIDE the front door of the cheese shop in East Dulwich, in a t-shirt this time, once again exactly on time. My talk with Cian and my experience at the Ottolenghi restaurant mean I am mentally prepared for a challenging day. It's a sweet cheese shop among a row of other shops on Lordship Lane in this prosperous, middle-class neighbourhood in South London. Next door is a fishmonger, on the other side is an organic fruit and veg shop with other general store type speciality products inside. Across the street is a high-end butcher. A ways down are a gelato shop, a wine shop and a neighbourhood cinema.

Behind a black slate counter overflowing with cheeses of all shapes, hues and sizes is Cheesemonger Molly, bespectacled, apron-clad and with a reserved smile. She has a friendly tone to her voice. Molly is a favourite, partly for her no-nonsense manner, but also for her knack for getting people to buy cheese, which I envy. I covet her wrapping skills as well, which are neat and pretty. Molly herself is the picture of the twenty-something South Londoner who's been to university: open-minded and accepting, curious, comes off as confident and clever, and has a posse of cool friends. She's fashionable for not chasing after fashion or labels and obviously a foodie. I also love her for naming her cat Gimli, inspired by J. R. R.

Tolkien. In time, I realise that every member of the cheese team is exceptional: likeable, creative, personable, fun. I remember initially puzzling why and thinking, 'Could it be the cheese?'

Molly says that Emma and Laurence are downstairs. Laurence, she explains, is the shop manager, and Cheesemonger Emma we have already met. They come up the stairs.

I love thinking back on this moment, because Laurence grows to become someone I have big affection for. If this were a superhero movie based on the Cheesemonger Avengers, this scene would be where a well-loved central cheesemonger makes his first appearance and a big cheer goes up in the auditorium, hearts expanding in unison.

Laurence will forever remind me of someone slightly out of his time – he looks like an English junior officer from First World War photographs. He's got brown, floppy hair pushed back off his face, an ample, old-time moustache, *très tendance*, and he looks far older than he is. He's in his twenties but looks as though he's thirty-something. He's big and tall and carries himself with an easy self-confidence. He exudes magnetism. He mostly wears what they call a beanie – a relative of a toque, for Canadians. He is the cheesemonger who's often featured in the company's publicity photos.

Off the bat, we go downstairs to the crowded basement and get changed into some cheese kit: rubber boots, jacket and apron, and clean our hands. Long before Covid-19, one of the first lessons as a prospective cheesemonger is how to wash your hands thoroughly, and that you need to wash your hands over and over again, notably after any time you touch anything that is not 'cheese-contact'. Tie your shoe? Wash your hands. Unlock the outside door? Wash your hands. Handle the phone? Wash your hands.

We go upstairs and there are a number of bits of cheese sitting on a worktable. The first exercise is to see whether I am capable of learning how to wrap them. Before we start, I am trying to fend off that sinking feeling that I won't be able to do this. Why? Because it requires dexterity, hand-eye coordination, attention to detail, and a bit of art. The ghost of Mrs Linklater descends.

To become good at wrapping cheese, you want to be careful but confident because without conviction, it's perilous. Once you are engaged in a wrap, there is no turning back. If you turn back, change your mind on a shape and a style, you will end up having to start again because the paper will already be creased. It is an unforgiving skill and just the kind that I am pretty sure I will do poorly at.

We kick off with rectangles. Rectangles rock. We have three types of paper to choose from, also rectangle-shaped, small, medium and large. The only challenge with the rectangles is to ensure you're centring the cheese on a piece of paper that is the right size, and making tight, clean folds. You can imagine squares are straightforward too, with just a bit more paper involved. Where you start to get into trouble is with circles, half-moons, and then the dreaded triangles.

Shapes are associated so closely to childhood. I remember having a rudimentary wooden puzzle where you inserted the right-shaped piece into the spaces: I loved it. Shapes connect with something within us. Months after my trial shift, I have a fascinating experience with a customer which illustrates that well. I talk her through a series of cheeses. There are about two dozen on the stand that day. For some reason, she looks concerned throughout, anxious. She is stuck on all the triangles, the wedges of cheese – it's all she sees. After having taken her through the soft cow's milk cheeses, the goat's, the sheep's, the Alpines and the Blues, she says to me: 'I am looking for a cheese that is not shaped like a triangle.' I don't ask why.

She found her round cheese that day – they were all right there in plain sight, it's just she was focused on the triangles to the point of complete distraction. I hope it tasted better to her because of it.

Being an awesome cheesemonger means wrapping tidily when called on and doing it reflexively in the same way you do up your shoelaces. If you don't do it skilfully, you will look like an imposter. The problem with the triangle-shaped cheeses is that they can be a very long triangle as with a piece of Brie, or they can be a very high triangle like a piece of Cheddar, or a small equilateral one, or a quarter out of a round-shaped cheese like a Reblochon. All of them are going to require a different approach, and even though there are a set number of approaches, just about everyone has slightly different styles.

Emma and Laurence are trying to show me how to wrap a triangle-shaped cheese that has some height, and they are each doing it a different way. It's reassuring to know there's more than one way, except that I am trying to learn and not exactly sure who to copy. The big surprise is that I am just about getting it. They leave me to practise on six different shapes, wrapping and unwrapping repeatedly. A cloud lifts. I realise this is the first time I have ever felt dextrous with my hands at something fiddly. Could it be that this whole time I had written off a skill because it wasn't 'who I am', and yet it was there all along, just in need of practice and a bit of faith?

Next job is to walk over to the cooling cupboard where the big wheels of Alpine cheese are kept on shelves overnight. The temperature is around 10–12°C, unlike the refrigerator which is kept around 2°C. Laurence is showing me how to slide a thirty-five kilogram wheel of cheese from a shelf that is about forty centimetres off the ground, lift it safely and move it over to the counter. Years of strength training to the rescue. Tick.

Next test on my trial shift? Laurence turns to me and says, 'I need you to help me do a job that I've been putting off. It's these stairs. They need a good clean.'

I mean, the job does not look easy at all, but in a move that I'll later learn helped me to cinch the position, I don't hesitate before saying, 'Sure, let's do it.' Months afterwards, it's a running gag that I was asked to clean the stairs, a job no one enjoys, on my trial shift. What surprises me in retrospect is how straightforward it is, albeit fussy. Actually, all the cleaning is straightforward because it's done over and over and that means that systems are in place to streamline the task at hand. It's when the systems fail that things fall down, like when a plug gets stuck at the bottom of a basin filled with piping hot cleaning solution.

The trick to the stairs is it's a tight space without a drain and you end up with a puddle of bleachy water that has nowhere to go. The stairs are pretty mucky. Laurence mixes up some Topax solution. Normally, he says, we could just splash the bucket full of detergent on to the stairs and scrub away. Without a drain, the less water the better. He hands me a long-handled blue brush and off I go. In a few minutes, the stairs are shiny and clean, and dry after I soak up the detergent solution with disposable blue towel.

Task accomplished, they take me into the basement office and we have a seat around the table. I notice off to the side a covered platter of what must be cheese. I'm slightly intimidated at the thought of being tested on it. However, something you forget in job interviews is that sometimes they want you to be the person they're looking for. I feel that energy from both Laurence and Emma in a way I did not from Cian.

As the interview starts, they ask me the question you should always expect and somehow, I didn't prepare. I did lots of homework, read through the website, swotted up on the history of the company and watched a series of videos on the cheeses they sell. Despite my preparation, when they ask me why I think the job is a good fit for me, why I want it, I have a moment that I can't control. Having not workshopped an answer, I blurt out spontaneously, 'Because I think it will ground me.' Thing is, though, as I say it my voice cracks. I'm having an uncontrolled and unexpected surge of emotion that has welled up organically from somewhere in my core. WTF.

I wonder whether they notice my voice quavering. How can they not? I wonder whether they've ever had anyone want the job 'because it will ground them'. Odd.

The interview part of our session over, they set the platter of cheeses on the table and take the cover off. They ask me to taste the cheeses in turn, name them, say where they are from and describe what I am tasting. I am slightly nervous because I don't know whether I'll find the words I need. I'm not sure, either, whether I can count on my tastebuds. I'm new to this. Also, I am acquainted with a fair few French cheeses, but I don't know much about other countries' cheeses and sure enough the first thing I'm given is an English cheese.

I don't know what it is, but I know it's English and I say so. I am right. I describe it as buttery, and crumbly in texture. It's Kirkham's Lancashire, rich and tasty, but they could expect pretty much anyone from here to know that cheese and I didn't name it. The next one is a goat's cheese – I know it's a Crottin. I am not particularly good at describing it. I end up saying simply that it's firm and has a balanced richness, which is obvious and unimpressive, but I know its name.

I'm given a hard cheese afterwards. I know it's an Alpine cow's milk cheese and I say so, but I don't know which one. I describe its creamy texture, its crunch from the crystals in the paste, and its salty, caramelly goodness. It's Gruyère. I'm doing just okay.

Next comes a piece of Roquefort, the premium French blue cheese that is salty but with a sweet fruitiness as well. It melts on your tongue. I get full marks here. Lastly, it's Munster, which I have down to rights. With its punishing aroma filling the room, there is a split second where I wonder whether I will be able to put it in my mouth without gagging. On the positive side, I watched a video about its production in Alsace from the company website and I'm able to describe it and tell its story in some detail. Thank you, Munster, for taking but also for giving.

At the end I feel elated, as though for an afternoon I crossed the threshold into a peculiar new world that I'd never imagined, peopled by beings known as cheesemongers with an array of traits and powers that – hang on a minute – maybe are lying dormant inside of me. Having spent more time with the cheeses, always a source of curiosity to me, they are starting to feel more like wonders of human endeavour, miracles of alchemy, or both. As I leave the interview and step out on to the pavement, back into the bustle of East Dulwich, I turn back and see Emma, Laurence and Molly chatting and laughing as they tend to the cheese and the shop. It's a moment of unexpected, involuntary melancholy because having only just stepped out, I wish I were back inside. Then the nerves: I wonder whether I did what I needed to get the invitation to join the fellowship of mongers. Can they see in me the potential to become like them?

I get the phone call, finally, later that week, and a request to come to The Arch for my induction. Barring a few formalities, I'm hired.

Soumaintrain

'When I was a boy, my grandmother sold it at markets. For me, it tastes of childhood and family dinners. I love its duality, at once rustic but also a fine French cheese. When customers are looking for a cheese to expand their horizons, I always point them to Soumaintrain.'

– Ludovic Bisot, cheesemaker, Meilleur Ouvrier de France

Origin: Hails from the village where it was first created, Soumaintrain in Burgundy, with a history dating back to the twelfth century. Cheeses were used as payment for rent on land.

Presentation: Soumaintrain is similar to Époisses in that it's a soft, washed-rind cow's milk cheese, often sold in a round box, with a wrinkled rind and a white, gooey paste. It's a much rarer find but seared into my memory because I have only ever experienced it with a pink rind, sometimes hot pink. It can also present as lighter pink, or bold ochre in colour. Key difference with Époisses: its rind is washed with a simple saline solution whereas Époisses is washed with a spirit – Marc de Bourgogne. Soumaintrain is a funky cheese as well, but gentler than its cousin. Intensely moreish, it's complex: a deep, earthy richness with a pleasing, farmy, lactic quality.

How to serve: A Soumaintrain can be so impressive as to make a cheese course centrepiece on its own. Serve with crusty bread or crackers and chilled Chablis. For reds, stay in Burgundy. A wedge with rocket salad is a sublime starter, or go all out and place a slice or two on top of a hamburger or steak fresh off the grill. It will melt there and then.

Fun fact: Soumaintrain production and expertise faded with the Second World War but saw a full renaissance beginning in the 1970s. Most of the production comes from three principal cheesemakers. Soumaintrain has a *fermier* version which is produced exclusively on farms.

15
First Shift

SINCE THE MONTH OF June when I first began training to become a cheesemonger, I've started associating summer with French goat's cheese. Combine it with a glass of rosé, a bit of sunshine, some friends and an English garden, and it's hard to go wrong.

Summer is a whole new world at our stall in Borough Market, where the goats take pride of place, front and centre in an open fridge, pushing the hearty raclettes, fondues and Vacherins out of the picture. Things look so different in the summer that customers will stop and comment: 'I almost thought you were another stall. You've changed everything!'

Here's another one we get often, pointing to one of our goat's cheeses: 'Is that a leaf? Or is it cheese?'

'Yes, it's a leaf, and it's cheese, our Mistralou. Gets its name from the wind that blows through Provence.'

'How do you eat it?'

'Just untie the bit of straw that holds it together, then unwrap it from the sweet chestnut leaf and inside is a square of goat's cheese.'

'What's it taste like?'

'Delicious. It's creamy, notes of Provençal herb, a bit floral, honey and egg yolk. Hard to go wrong, really.'

Mistralou flies out of the fridge, especially at the start of the season. We also stock a goat's cheese in the shape of a little log, with a sprinkling of herbs on top. Damn, the French are good. The *Buchettes* and the Mistralou sit alongside half a dozen other goat delights, some with ash rinds, each one a different shape: cones, pyramids, cylinders, none of them terribly big. If you step back from the display and look only at the seasonal goat's cheese, it looks like a box of chocolates, a cheesy box of chocolates.

My first day as a trainee cheesemonger falls on the first day of summer and Manager Tom won't let me go anywhere near the goat's cheese. I'll be honest, it's a relief. They just look too precious for my untrained fat fingers. They scare me.

Instead, we kick things off with a good sweep around the perimeter for mouse droppings. 'The pest control says we're the cleanest stall in the market and the mice just use us as a transit point,' he says. 'We want to keep it that way.'

'What, they poop as they scamper along the wall?'

'They do, actually. They're incontinent.'

Tom makes sure I sweep in every corner, nook and cranny, and that I run the brush along the little ridge above the floor. I see eight poops. I brush them into the bin.

'Did you say eight?' He's taking this sweep seriously.

'Yes. Eight poops,' I answer dutifully.

'That's about average – see, not much mouse action.'

As I begin my cheesemonger training in Borough Market, I work mostly with Tom and Daisy. As her name implies, Cheesemonger Daisy has something of the bright and wild nature of an English field flower, and, of course, enough heft to sling Alpine cheese with the rest of us. She has shoulder-length auburn hair. She's not long out of university and dating a roguish musician. They both more than hold their own down the pub. She's tremendous company, has a playful, mischievous streak, and she sells a lot of cheese.

She is wrapping the goat's cheese today. 'Is that very fiddly?' I ask.

'It is. Funny you should ask,' she continues with a strangled smile, struggling to wrap a cone-shaped goat's cheese. 'The trick is to stay calm and pull your edges tight like you're making a bed.' She pulls the cellophane to demonstrate. She seems close to crossing the border from calm.

Tom is the Borough cheese stall manager when I start my apprenticeship. He is tall and fit, with blue eyes, ginger hair and a neat beard. He's twenty-seven, half my age. He knows a lot about cheese. He has all the tasting notes down pat and is also familiar with the cheese producers by name, the animal breeds, the feed regimens, the seasonal variations. He's visited several farms and dairies. He's smart, confident and has good manners. His parents are doctors.

Tom is serious by nature. He doesn't like it when people touch the cheese. Even I get startled when he calls out, 'Watch yer hands, mate!' He's a superb teacher.

On my first day, I am struck to the core by the feeling that no matter what I do, I can never be as good a cheesemonger as he is. He is blindingly proficient. When he works, it all happens so fast, I can almost not detect all the different things he's doing. In the Cheesemongering Avengers, Tom is another founding member.

Tom has decided to start me on the big Alpine wheels of cheese. He gets me to pull them one by one from the cupboard – squat down on my haunches, balance the wheel firmly in my hip and pelvis area, lift cleanly with my legs without any sudden twists or turns – and carry them across the stall to be stacked on to the display in towers.

Every day they come out of the cupboard, they need to be flipped. At night before they go to bed, they are given a saline wash with a brush like the ones you use on horses. Their topside was brushed last night and tonight it'll be the other side. You can see why it's so tempting to anthropomorphise them – I do from the minute I meet them.

It reminds me of something a cheesemonger from another stall at the market once said to me: 'I love how all the cheeses have personalities. It's just a shame they all think they're Mariah Carey.'

Did I mention Tom is patient? He spends hours walking me through the many-step process of cutting the Alpine wheels of cheese into wedges. You need to cut them into stackable halves and quarters, and also into working pieces, eighths or sixteenths. When people want to buy a couple of hundred grams of Comté or Gruyère, you can only make reasonable cuts from the smaller pieces. The wheels, halves and quarters are heavy. They're hard to manipulate. To cut through them, you need to use a cheese wire with a handle at either end.

'Okay, you forgot the knife again.'

You can't just pull the wire through the wheel without propping it up on to a knife, otherwise the wire has no clearance underneath and you end up with warped and wonky bits that are near impossible to work with and look like objects from a funhouse. If you accidentally cut a wonky wedge, it becomes a scarlet letter that you need to live with until it is, mercifully, sold. Even the next day if you're not working, other cheesemongers will ask, 'Whoa. Who cut that?'

'I'm sorry!'

I apologise a lot in those first weeks. Working with the big cheeses is stressful. They cost a fortune, and I do not want to screw up. He takes the time to watch over me, though, and stop me before I do anything badly wrong. I'm grateful for the way he's not letting me follow through on mistakes.

Where I get frustrated is wrapping the faces of the cut wedges with cellophane.

'See these wrinkles? And these dusty bits on the face of the cheese? That's the rind dust that you need to clean off the face of the cheese with a knife edge. Do it again.'

I do it again. And again, and again, and again. I spend most of the first week cutting wheels of Alpine cheese and wrapping the resulting wedges.

At closing time, since I don't know yet how to do anything and we all want to go home, I'm assigned the washing up.

There aren't many actual dishes to be done at a cheese shop, so doing the washing up means cleaning all the knives, wires and lyres used to cut cheese. All the black slates that the cheeses sit on need to be washed, as do the cutting boards. There is a lot of everything. You have two sinks: one is for the rinse, one is filled with the detergent solution for the wash, which is highly toxic, designed to be sudsy and break down animal proteins without intense scrubbing.

The guidelines are to wear goggles, black rubber gloves, and a wipeable smock in order not to get Topax anywhere on you. It has an uncanny knack for splashing. When you don't put the goggles on, it immediately splashes into your eye. If you ever don't wear a smock, it splashes instantly on to your trousers. I have a drawer full of trousers with discoloured spots all over them. Don't wear rubber boots? Guaranteed your shoes will be soaked in it. Black shoes turn a strange orange colour. You should see mine. It is unforgiving.

After that first shift, when I get home, I break out in a tight, angry red rash along the insides of my forearms. It is ugly, itchy and painful. I begin to have this sinking feeling that I may be allergic to Topax. That would surely disqualify me from doing the job. The rash looks awful.

I am on probation for three months – they can let me go for any reason whatsoever with a tap on the shoulder. Even if they allowed me to work and serve cheese looking like this, I don't think I could bear having such a bad rash for any length of time. For the rest of that evening, my first as a trainee cheesemonger, I feel an awful dread. I don't want to stop now.

Mistralou

'Le ciel était lisse comme une pierre de lavoir; le mistral y écrasait du bleu à pleine main; le soleil giclait de tous les côtés; les choses n'avaient plus d'ombre, le mystère était là, contre la peau; ce vent de perdition arrachait les mots aux lèvres et les emportait dans les autres mondes.'

– Jean Giono, *Le Serpent d'étoiles*, well-known Provençal author writing of the storied Provençal wind, the Mistral: 'this wind of perdition tore words from lips and carried them away to other worlds'.

Origin: The cheese was conceived by Vanessa and François Masto, who took over a farm that was all but abandoned in Provence. The milk comes from the Mastos' herd of seventy rove goats, a breed that was hard to find not that long ago, but is now in healthy numbers, prized for its sweet, protein-rich milk.

Presentation: Wrapped in chestnut leaves that the Mastos collect themselves at the farm, the paste varies depending on the batch and how mature it is. Most often, it will ooze slightly as you cut into it, but Mistralou can also be so runny that you're best advised to have some baguette ready to mop up whatever remains on the leaf. The pastes can also present firm. Mistralou is a low-salt cheese with a lighter taste – herb, lavender, egg yolk, honey. I've been surprised to taste even the more mature batches and find them pleasantly rich without tipping into bitterness. As they're hand-ladled, no two cheeses are ever the same.

How to serve: This is a cheese to be admired, handsomely wrapped in its chestnut-leaf parcel. It can play a starring role on a spring or summer goat's cheeseboard served with a chilled, dry Provençal rosé and some fruit, such as raisins or figs. Also, a wonderful picnic treat with a crusty baguette. It's not a goat's cheese to cook with.

Fun fact: The seventy rove goats who produce the milk that goes into Mistralou graze freely, munching away on local herbs and flowers, giving each batch of the cheese slight variations based on the seasons. Take a moment to look up a photo of a rove goat – their horns are unique, majestic.

16

Did You Just Lick Your Fingers?

O N MY SECOND DAY as a trainee, I arrive early and am leaning against the side of the stall when Tom arrives. I am wearing a long-sleeved fleece to cover up my rash. It hasn't gone away. I've had a difficult night's sleep, tossing and turning, wondering what to say about it. Say nothing, is where I've landed.

'Morning, Michael!' Tom seems in a good mood.

'Morning, Tom. How's things?'

'Yeah, all right. I need a coffee, though. Pub last night. What about you?'

'God, no. I was knackered, went to bed early. When you go to the pub, do you ever go with people from the market?' I'm curious to know more about it.

'Sure,' Tom answers, 'but not so much. Susan, who did the job before me, she did. She had a market boyfriend.'

Okay, that sounds exciting. 'Her boyfriend worked at the market?' I ask, at which point Daisy arrives. 'Oh hiya, Daisy.'

'Morning, Michael. No, he doesn't mean actual boyfriend. She had one of those. She means, you know, they flirted a lot.'

Right, now we're getting somewhere. 'Who was he?'

'Lanky Ukrainian with a moustache, works at the raw milk stall around the corner. He was here all the time chatting to her,' says Tom.

'Gruyère was exchanged frequently for pints of raw milk. Full fat, delicious in tea. So creamy,' says Daisy, playfully.

'Do you two have market boyfriends and girlfriends?' This is the journalist inside me, always with the questions. I am making mental notes.

'I wish!' says Daisy.

'You have someone in mind?' And now I'm probing.

'Oh, I think we all fancy Pietro. Right, Tom?'

'I like girls, thanks,' says Tom. 'But yeah, he's hot. Here, Michael,' Tom is now through with this conversation and hands me the broom. 'Perimeter sweep. Mouse poop. Let me know what you find.'

I manage to keep my inner arms hidden from view most of the day. The aforementioned Pietro, on the other hand, arrives wearing a sleeveless t-shirt, guns blazing, down at the end of the alley at the cheese toastie and raclette stand. He's a big, curly-haired Italian.

As we go about opening the stall, I notice Tom takes time out to speak to the owner of the Italian cheese and cured meat stall just next to us. I later learn his name is Phil. He's very tall with a shaved head and seems to know everyone. At this point, I'm too shy to say hi and I'm not sure anyone cares to be introduced to me anyway.

Across the way and up a bit, there's a stand that sells bread, lots of sourdough and other loaves, baguettes and other baked goods such as decadent cinnamon rolls that are immensely popular with early-morning market goers. Every day, the same married couple work there, Allan and Barbara. I don't know much about them, except that they work hard, never seem to have a day off, and are from East London.

There are a few traders who do the traditional calling. It's a thing you'd be sad to lose because of the history behind it, but it can be grating. 'Get yer strawberries! Fresh-picked straw-berries!' Fine, once in a while, but five hours straight is a lot.

Down from Allan and Barbara's stand is a stall with products from the south of Italy. It is a magnet for colourful Italians and, apologies for the cliché, it gets loud. It's run by another curly-haired Italian, Francesco, who looks like a character from an Italian comic book, tall and lean with an impish grin.

Once everything is in order in our stall, tables in place, cheeses out and proud, Tom has me working on cutting down and wrapping more Alpine cheese as a refresher from yesterday. I'm getting there but it's so slow. More apologies.

'Michael, I'd rather you be slow and do it well. Just keep at it, worry about technique and the end result, not how long it takes.'

I'm still not allowed near the goat's cheese. That's fine by me.

Today's new skill is wrapping blue cheese pieces for display. We package up a lot of them in preparation for Saturdays. Daisy shoots me a look that reads 'better you than me', but I'm oddly enjoying the blue cheese. It's sticky and messy but reminds me of helping my mother out in the kitchen with cookie dough.

'Did you just lick your fingers?' asks Tom.

'Why do you ask?' I answer his question with a question, because I am that busted.

'Don't be funny. Yes, you did. Go wash your hands, please, Michael. Seriously, there's a difference between putting a piece of cheese in your mouth and licking your fingers.'

'Sorry.'

'Just work with this bucket of alco-wipes nearby. You need to keep wiping your fingers as you go. Wiping them and not licking them.'

'Sorry.' I am embarrassed. It was just second nature is all. I am learning that in cheesemonger training, you need to unlearn a lot of habits. Like blowing on surfaces to clear them off. Doh.

Tom and I spend time tasting through many of the cheeses — we stock a lot of them and it's overwhelming my brain. Tom says that to begin with, the best strategy is to choose a few cheeses that you enjoy, learn about them and focus on selling them. From there, you can expand bit by bit. It's good advice.

'You could do worse than just sell Gruyère. Actually, what a great idea. Let's do that.'

Tom sets me up with a piece of Gruyère and tells me to cut it into cubes, not too small. Next we take a long, flat tomme knife, blunted, and lay some of the pieces on top of it. 'Perfect, off you go.'

I have beginner's nerves, and I need to get them out in the open: 'I don't know a lot about it.'

'What does it taste like?'

'Creamy, caramelly, crunchy.'

'Beautiful. And where's it from?'

'Switzerland.'

'Right, from the Alps or the Jura or the mountains, however you want to say it. And it's cow's milk. Now go sell some. See what happens.'

'Go Michael!' Daisy says.

Finally a transferable skill. As a journalist, I have spent hours humiliating myself talking to strangers, sticking a microphone in their face and asking all variety of questions, sometimes in a language that they didn't even speak. I am the man for this job, and this time I have cheese to offer.

'Try some cheese? Anyone for some Gruyère? Sir, fancy some cheese?'

When offered free cheese, some people seem to be irritated. This surprises me only slightly because the same was true with the microphone. Others appear shy and move quickly along. In fact, so many people react this way that I wonder if putting me out here with Gruyère cubes is really such a good strategy. Am I chasing them away?

Then there are others who will take a piece drive-by style and move swiftly along, 'Thanks!' That's okay. Come back if you like it!

And then there are the 20 per cent or so who are up for free cheese, hungry or just sociable and like a sample.

'Goodness, what kind of cheese did you say this was?'

'Honey, come try this.'

'Bruh, that's good cheese.'

'Oh. My. God. This is delicious. I'd like to buy a piece, please.' I have sold my first piece of cheese. Tom is right, the cheese does the talking. I am fantastically excited, elated even.

'Great. Now sell some more.' Tom pats me on the back.

At the end of what was a good day, a great day, Tom pulls me aside.

'I like how you interact with the customers. The rest will come. How do you think it's going?'

'I think I had a good day, and I think you're patient with me.'

'It's a pleasure and it's my job. So let's talk about your arms.'

So he's seen the rash on my forearms, now my face is red as well. I roll up my sleeves to show him properly.

He winces. 'God, that looks awful. We need to do something about that. It must be bothering you.'

'Yeah, I think it's the Topax.'

'Makes sense. I've seen other people have a reaction to it, but not that bad. Have you got anything for it?'

'I'll stop by the pharmacy.'

My concern about the rash has made all the unexpected wins of the day fade into the background. The joy I was feeling is gone. This is an existential threat to my nascent mongering career. It can't carry on.

Straight after close, I walk down Southwark Street from the market towards the pharmacy, hoping by some miracle they'll have a bright idea. In my experience, creams don't work well on me. As I'm walking, I pass by a decorating and DIY shop and struck with an idea, I go in.

After a while wandering around, I find the protective equipment section, and a pair of gloves that go all the way to the upper arm with resistant rubber on the outside. They're called gauntlet gloves and are much longer than the rubber gloves we have at the stall. They're not cheap, but I rush to the till and buy them. I feel like I have solved the problem.

I text Tom and send a photo. Good idea, he writes, but he'll have to clear them with Jon. Owner Jon has final say on everything having to do with hygiene and protective equipment.

I am not used to being the person who causes problems at work. I'm used to being the one who solves them. I hate this rash – it's throwing everything up in the air.

Gruyère suisse

'*Un gruyère, pareil à une roue tombée de quelque char barbare.*'

– Émile Zola, *Le Ventre de Paris*, 1873, describing 'A Gruyère like a wheel fallen from some Barbarian chariot'.

Origin: Cheesemaking in the Gruyère region of Switzerland dates back to Roman times, perhaps even well before, as some archaeological digs suggest. In 1762, Gruyère was added to the Académie française dictionary. It has a long history, but only received its AOC designation in 2001.

Presentation: About 60cm in diameter and 10 to 12cm high, a wheel of Gruyère is hefty and takes pride of place in any cheese display. Its rind is a rich brown, often flaky; the paste will vary with the seasons, but is most often ivory. Cut into big wedges and stacked, it's a thing of beauty.

How to serve: Maybe it's just me, but I prefer my Gruyère to be chillier than room temperature, giving it a slightly firmer, substantial texture that then begins to melt while in the mouth: heavenly. Gruyère doesn't need to be served with anything, and in some ways doing so takes away from the rich feast it offers on its own. It is packed with complex, evolving flavour, so good on its own you could imagine a Gruyère course during a meal, or a board where it is the only cheese served with bread, crackers, walnuts and grapes. It's great as fondue or shredded then melted as a gratin. There are so many recipes that call for Gruyère: puffs, pasta, pastry, French onion soup; it's a natural with kale or ham or potatoes. In France, people will sometimes refer to generic, all-purpose Alpine cheese as Gruyère, so if you're looking at recipes in France, keep that in mind, and make sure to choose a recipe that does your Gruyère justice. A proper Gruyère suisse AOP is, after all, pricey and deserves to have a place of honour in your cooking. For wine pairings, if you can get your hands on a Swiss wine, now's the time.

Fun fact: Of all the cheeses I have tasted out to all the customers over the years, Gruyère is reliably the one that brings the most people back to make a purchase. There is something irresistible in its creamy, crunchy, caramel goodness. The crunch comes from tyrosine crystals. Tyrosine is a non-essential amino acid which triggers dopamine release, so there is actual science that suggests what we cheese lovers already know to be true: eating Gruyère reduces stress and makes you happy.

17

A Brief Introduction to the Art of the Squeegee

I T IS ONE OF those glorious, warm summer days in London, or stinking hot, depending on your point of view. As part of my training and probation, even though I will be assigned to work primarily at Borough Market, I am sent away for a week to the company cheese shop in South East London.

It's back to Lordship Lane, in the thick of the East Dulwich hustle and bustle. This is proper London middle-class; young parents and retirees are king and queen. Prams are Range Rover sized and everywhere being driven with purpose. A friend dubs these young parents 'The Praminators'.

Walking into the cheese shop is a bit like that moment when you step out of an aeroplane after a long flight and are greeted by an entirely different climate. Suddenly it's not mid-July, more like mid-November. The air is heavy with the promise of bursts of showers and it is the type of cold that penetrates down to the bone, just the way the cheeses like it. This is something I didn't realise when I showed up dressed in hot-weather attire, shorts and a vest, trainers with invisible socks.

Unlike at Borough Market, there is a uniform of sorts at the shop, not just an apron. In the basement, there are a series of bins containing work clothes, several for grey t-shirts, laundered but stained, sizes M to 3-XL. I choose an L when really I should be going for more fabric and an XL. I also choose a jean jacket, a faded, bruised blue colour, laundered but not ironed with collars that don't lie flat no matter how much you try to press and reshape them. I remove my trainers and pick a pair of wellington boots: bright blue with red accents. There's nothing to be done about my shorts. Finally, an apron completes the look.

It is a lot of clothing and when all kitted out you don't feel nimble or fleet of foot. I feel as though I'm wearing robes and clomp up the stairs to the shop floor. The spaces at the shop are tighter so I am exceedingly careful. I do not want to knock something over or in any way draw attention to my natural lack of coordination. If I felt slightly dashing with a sun-kissed glow on arrival, I am now comprehensively humbled and feeling like a costumed cheesemonger at a fancy-dress party.

Today, I report to Cheesemonger Molly at a time before we've established any rapport. She is second-in-command at Lordship Lane and I already have a one-way crush on her from my trial shift. There is also some awe and intimidation. She gets on with things, knowing exactly the sequence of tasks necessary to transform the shop floor. Soon it will be fairly bursting with cheeses of all shapes and sizes, luring passers-by to stare through the window.

I know almost nothing and have little idea where to begin. If she is assuredness and purpose personified, I am halting and slightly befuddled with an ample serving of self-doubt. 'Can I really do this?' That insecurity hangs over my every action all day.

'Michael? Would you mind squeegeeing the floor?'

Ah, no problem there, right? To keep the humidity up in the cheese shop, a bucket or two of water is spread on the floor before closing the night before. That means that the cheeses which are left on external shelves, the big cloth-wrapped

Cheddars, the Parmigiano and the butter-slathered Lanca-shire, don't get dry and cracked. Over on the wall are a series of blue-coloured implements. Blue signifies it can be used on the floor and must not come into contact with the cheeses.

The squeegee is like a big blue broom, but instead of a brush, a long rubber edge fastened to the end connects with the floor. How hard can this be? I grab a squeegee and head up to the front of the shop and begin to try to corral the water down the shop floor towards the drain. Oddly, it is making a loud scraping noise against the floor that I am not expecting. The water is not corralling at all.

Solution? I put a bit more muscle into it. Now it's really scraping the concrete floor. Molly looks up. 'Try flipping it over?' she says, deadpan. Ah, so the squeegee has a swivel head. This is a fairly minor task, I keep telling myself. I've got this.

Now flipped, the squeegee is something akin to a miracle. I never progressed beyond Grade 9 science, having been put off by a beginner worm dissection, so to see the way that rubber bonds to the concrete floor – totally other properties to the earlier plastic – is a revelation. This time, it's like I am just willing the water to move with my sweeping strokes, and it does. I am a squeegee pro. Except after a while, the water moves back.

I discover that in the time that I am working the length of the shop, pulling water from underneath the counter, the water I'd earlier moved is running back to the front of the shop. Time passes, the pattern repeats and I am transformed into Squeegee Sisyphus.

I am beginning to think that there is a plot to make me look incompetent at even the most rudimentary tasks. Maybe doing it a bit faster will be the trick, at which point I begin to do everything much more quickly and some water has flowed along with me, hurrah. Still, I turn around and the floor resembles an aerial map of the Great Lakes and I look slightly breathless and red-faced, having moved at Benny Hill speed. I now bow to the inevitable. Without intervention, I am defeated. I had hoped this was one newbie query I wasn't going to have to make:

'Erm, Molly. Sorry. Is there a trick to this?' As in, beyond making sure the squeegee is right way up.

'You need to make sure each long stroke is directionally towards the drain, even when at an angle. Don't try to do it section by section. It doesn't work.'

Molly walks over to the wall of blue, non-cheese contact implements and takes hold of one of the other squeegees. She walks up to the front of the shop on the other side of the counter. In long, steady, fluid movements, she reaches forward and pulls the water towards her. Ten seconds pass, maybe fifteen, and the floor is dry.

Much as I feared, the tasks are increasing in complexity. Molly has asked me to bring the boxes containing cheese out of the fridge and to set them on waxed paper along the counter. It's a walk-in fridge like at the market and on either side there are about six shelves. Each shelf holds a stack of boxes. There are wooden boxes, cardboard boxes, plastic crates and a styrofoam box containing Mozzarella in water. Some boxes are open, some closed with wooden slats stapled across them. Where even to begin?

'Molly? Sorry to bother again. How many of the boxes should I bring out?'

'Bring out all the opened boxes, and if there isn't much cheese in any of them, bring an unopened one of the same cheese.'

I begin to stack box after box on top of each other and move them out to the counter on to the waxed paper. Even months later as I think back, one thing I am proud of: I don't drop a single box. Ever. Oh, not that I am not constantly thinking that's about to happen. The bar is low.

'If you could start with the goat's cheeses?'

Gulp. Despite all my wrapping practice, it is still tough for me. Add to that the fact that at the cheese shop, the standard is higher and the mountain even harder to climb. This is a proper shop, not a market stall, and it can't look in the slightest rough and ready. They are looking for crisp, clean and wow.

I swear, I am doing my best. It is painstakingly slow, and my fingers seem so uncoordinated and oversized. The wrap needs to be tight to the point where the finished product glistens on the counter, corners neatly tucked. Think of a bed made so tight by a head nurse or a drill sergeant that a coin can bounce off it. A cheesemonger burn I hear long after I've started is, 'This wrapping looks like your Granny's stockings.'

Molly's wraps are precision perfect. She is watching, she is patient, and she helps: try it like this, use a bit less cellophane, hold that tight, make sure your fingers are clean. It all takes so much focus and I am so very slow and discouraged. My display begins to take shape and it's okay, but it's not great and is miles away from awesome. Finally, I decide I just need to say it out loud.

'I'm feeling like I'll never get this down right. I'll never be a patch on you and your wrapping, and I just want to apologise.' I am actually hanging my head, but it feels good to have said it.

Molly walks over from her station where faultlessly wrapped soft cow's cheeses have miraculously appeared in quarters, halves and wholes, the product of her swift, deft fingers. Her slates already have the air of a cornucopia of cheese.

'You're actually doing really well. I've seen a lot worse. Just keep at it. It'll come.'

I wish I could hear what her secret voice is saying but I'm thankful for the words of encouragement. I don't really believe her that she's seen worse, or maybe I do, but that 'worse' she's seen was someone who was hopeless.

Then a thing happens in this job that is exactly like live broadcasting. The clock has been relentlessly advancing and suddenly it's the appointed hour. There is absolutely nothing you can do about it; the show must go on. It's ten o'clock, the door is unlocked and people begin to come in to buy cheese, just like in the radio studio when the clock hits the top of the hour and the mic goes live.

'Morning!' What a relief. God knows I struggle in these first days but if there's one thing being a radio presenter trains you to do, it's to be there, present in the moment with your guest. I have a near boundless curiosity about people, love to chat, ask questions (sometimes impertinent ones), listen, have a laugh, smile and interact. It's my thing and in that moment, the world is a brighter place.

'Can I help you find anything?' I ask the first customer of the day.

'Just having a browse, thanks,' she answers, politely.

'Warm day, isn't it?' I persist.

'It's an absolute scorcher, twenty-four degrees already! Not in here, mind you.' She laughs.

'Nope. Always cool in the cheese shop. Stay as long as you like.' I decide to leave her to it, but she's now keen to chat a bit.

'I might just. What is that you're wrapping?'

'This? It's a goat's cheese called Petit Blaja, from the Pyrenees. I just tried it for the first time. I'm a total newbie, trainee cheesemonger.'

'Congratulations.' She has a warm, genuine smile. Conspiratorially, she adds, 'This is my dream job, you know. I'm afraid I'd eat the profits, though.'

'The Petit Blaja is really good. Do you want to try along with me?' I cut her a small piece. She agrees to taste it.

'Oh, that is nice. It's much moister than I expected.'

'Right? I find the texture almost like peanut butter. It sticks to your palate.'

'Yes, it does!'

'Even though the taste is warm and lemony, not peanutty, or maybe just a little?'

'Oh, I'll have one of those. It's nice to try something new.'

'I can also recommend the Gruyère.'

'You know, I haven't had a piece in some time but I love it. Thank you.'

After she leaves, Molly smiles a big broad smile, the first I've seen from her today.

'Gosh, you handled that really well.' Maybe I can win Molly over, after all. And sell cheese!

As the clock ticks closer to midday, we serve customers and I manage to finish my display of goat's cheese. In the same time, Molly has finished the hard cheeses, the blue cheeses, the soft cow's milk cheese, literally every other display.

As for all the manual labour, I am viewing it as a positive challenge. I'm not talking about the cheese wrapping, which to me is not manual labour, more an art form. No, I'm talking about the cleaning, the scrubbing, the sweeping, the loading and unloading, the lifting, and the bleaching. I call it 'the Drudgery' in my inner voice. There is also a phenomenon in this job that I call the Surprise Drudgery, where the goalposts seem to keep shifting. Someone has written proforma 'job sheets', one for every week of the month. Later on, I will become more familiar with them but at the time, I don't know they exist and their contents manifest themselves suddenly and cruelly.

Supervisor walks over to you around two in the afternoon: 'So, it's the second Wednesday of the month.'

I'm thinking: 'Yeah, that feels about right.'

'That means the cubby-holes need to be alco-wiped and the drawers emptied and alco-wiped in all the cupboards under the counters.'

Right – didn't see that one coming. I begin systematically to pull all the articles out from under the cupboards and wipe and clean. This is a logistical operation of some importance even if things are relatively well organised. I feel it's going to take a long time, although in the event, it only takes fifteen minutes.

On another afternoon on another day, supervisor walks up: 'So it's the fourth Thursday of the month.' I flinch, thinking I know what direction this is going, just not the destination.

'Can you take out all the tape dispensers and clean them carefully with alco-wipes?'

Yes, I can. Did you ever think about a tape dispenser and how many nooks and crannies they have, sharp edges, and how surprisingly unclean they can be after a while? In time, this will turn out to be one of my preferred surprise bits of drudgery. Like cleaning the slate crate. It says something about you which ones you develop a strange attachment to.

Another day at the cheese shop and this time it's 11.30 a.m. 'It's the third Tuesday of the month, we need to clean the chemical crate and the black bucket.'

What is she even talking about? 'Sure!'

Or: 'Last Thursday of the month, we wash the fridge doors.' And so on, and so on. There are a lot of things to clean.

On this sunny July afternoon where I have been struggling, albeit with a lot of heart, to wrap goat's cheese, to charm strangers, to clean surfaces and knives as they get dirty, to use the till, even to squeegee, this moment will live forever as the most surprising of all Surprise Drudgery moments.

Molly: 'So it's Thursday, and that means we need to clean the basement floor and the toilet. You feel up to that?'

There is a pause of several beats as I compute this information. It is definitely Thursday. Did she really just ask me to go clean up the basement and the staff toilet? 'Sure!'

I am standing downstairs in the basement in oversized rubber boots, stained grey t-shirt and rumply purple jean-jacket, collar sticking half up. I am looking at the basement, which looks not unlike most basements you can imagine – cluttered. I have surveyed the toilet room. I've looked over the different-sized cleaning implements, some in a new colour, yellow, and I have the feeling that I am hitting a low point that feels something like humiliation. Is it? It might be. This is a task where I know there will be a middle and an end but here at the beginning of it, it seems like it is going to take hours. I don't even really know where to start.

I am beginning to wonder about my judgement in taking on this job. I even feel a thought trying to enter my brain: maybe this was all an error. Weirdly, that's exactly the point at which my phone buzzes with a message from Tom. 'Good news. Jon says we can try the gauntlet gloves. We'll get past this rash thing.'

Persillé du Beaujolais

Origin: One of the more cheesily romantic origin stories belongs to Persillé du Beaujolais. It was first conceived fifty years ago through a friendly rivalry between the French cheesemakers, the Lapierre family from the Beaujolais region of France, and the Italian Gorgonzola producers who travelled to their farm to buy their young calves for veal. The Italians would go on about the merits of Gorgonzola during their visits, the 'best blue in the world', until finally, the Lapierres decided to rise to the challenge. They took the exact same bacterial starter culture and blue moulds as for Gorgonzola, and created their own cheese, setting it instead in the shape of local *fourmes*. (*Fourme* cheeses are set in cylinders. The word *fourme* comes from the Latin meaning 'shape' and is the root of the word *fromage*.) This is how Persillé du Beaujolais came into the world.

Presentation: There is a sometimes vigorous debate over how to cut Persillé du Beaujolais, or for that matter Fourme d'Ambert or any cheese that comes in the same drum-like shape. Some, more often in France, say thick slices should be cut right through the middle so that they're round. It allows them to present distinctively. Others cut the wheel once in half and then proceed to make half-moons or triangular wedges to get the desired portion. In any case, as the name suggests,

Persillé is parsleyed with greeny-blue moulds. The paste is fudge-like in texture with a golden hue. The rind tends towards a slightly darker, caramel shade. It's a handsome cheese.

How to serve: A gentle, crowd-pleasing blue that has a warm tang to it, it's supple in the mouth with a good balance – no unpleasant edges or acidity. On a cheeseboard, it will surprise fans of blue cheese as it's not your usual and might even win over blue sceptics with its sweetness and balance. Serve simply with crackers; you can add grapes, pears, walnuts, or a bit of fruit paste. For pairings, try a sweeter wine like a Muscat or a porter beer, a cider or a perry, not too dry.

Fun fact: Many rap lyrics reference blue cheese. I'll let you explore those on your own – they're varied – but one common meaning of blue cheese in rap lyrics is a $100 US bill, because just to the right of Benjamin Franklin's likeness, there's a blue security ribbon.

18
No Maure Like This, Please

O VER TIME, YOU DEVELOP relationships with all the cheeses. Some of them get complicated. All of them feel personal because they are central to everything. You need to sell cheese to make the company money and pay your wage. However, it's not easy to forge a good relationship with a cheese when it's acting out. They can get especially irritating when you know their potential but are having to put up with their sass.

Some cheeses are the teacher's pet. I like to work having the Tomme de Savoie nearby because it's so solid and dependable by nature, and a crowd pleaser. Other cheeses are difficult but that is just fundamentally who they are – Époisses, for example, even Camembert. I can't hold it against them when they get wild.

Then there's a cheese like Sainte-Maure which is constantly throwing curveballs at you for no obvious reason. It feels random or worse, spiteful. Sainte-Maure is one of my cheese frenemies. Cheese history tells that the Arab Saracens in the eighth century instructed their captors in how to make it. It is steeped in warfare and deceit.

Sainte-Maure is an absolute classic French goat's cheese. You'll recognise it from its ash rind and its form in the shape of a log, but a log that is thicker at one end. It has a straw running through it that is often marked with a number denoting its producer.

Sainte-Maure is a pleasing, medium grey colour due to the ash on the outside. Inside, the paste is ivory. The contrast is stunning. It's firm but not without give, with an inviting breakdown along the rind. It is normally creamy and feels luxurious in the mouth.

When you get a good Sainte-Maure, all is right with the world. It has just enough goat's milk taste to make for a pronounced flavour that is not over the top: nicely balanced, earthy-tasting, not too acidic. It's a joy to cut into, to eat straight off a cheeseboard slice after slice on its own, with a cracker, or any of the traditional goat's cheese accompaniments like honey, dried fruit and nuts.

I once built an entire evening around a jar of jalapeño chilli jam and a popping Sainte-Maure, just the three of us. So much pleasure. For wine pairings, it's versatile: pink bubbles, Sauvignon Blanc, even a slightly chilled, light red.

So imagine the betrayal when a new tray comes in and goes wrong before you can intervene in any way or put your finger on why. This happens just often enough that you can't write it off as a phase or a one-off.

You will get Sainte-Maure where the paste is so tight it doesn't give up anything in the mouth and might as well be on a supermarket shelf. It can also go aggressively the other way and develop an unpleasant, strong goat taste. The rind gets tacky and distressing to the touch. Sometimes it just collapses all over the place as if it's lost its skeleton entirely. When too far along, its harsh, bitter or acidic notes seem to come roaring to the fore.

Finally, let's address the elephant in the room, its shape. Honestly, it is penis-shaped. I have overheard Owner Jon employ the word 'dong' in reference to it, something I can't unhear. When it's particularly weathered, it invites further, related comparisons that do it no favours either.

So, to reiterate, taste it before you buy it where at all possible. I know I love them, until I don't. And then I love them again.

Sainte-Maure

'C'est le Saint' Maure de Touraine
Le fromag' de chèvr' qu'on aime
Quand on l'arrose d'un petit verre de vin blanc
Ah mes amis rien n'est plus succulent
Il vous met le coeur en fête,
La joie vous monte à la tête;
Il vous suffit d'y goûter une fois
Pour vous en lécher les doigts!'

– Song composed in its honour, this is the second chorus,
proposing a good feed of Sainte-Maure with a glass of
white wine which will put you in a great mood and have you
licking your fingers (NB if mongering, no. You'll need an
alco-wipe to hand).

Origin: The story passed down through the ages: Arab women
remained in the Loire Valley, along with their goats, after the
defeat of the Saracens at the hands of the Frankish army in
732 AD. They taught the locals their knowledge of the making
of goat's cheese. Sainte-Maure-de-Touraine obtained its AOC
status in 1990.

Presentation: Shaped like a log which is fatter at one end, it measures 16–17cm and weighs about 300g. It has a blue-grey ash rind and a straw runs through the middle of the paste. The straw is decorative (sometimes it is plastic and stamped with an identifier), but in the past, it served to help stiffen the paste.

How to serve: A beautiful-looking cheese, it makes a solid addition to any cheeseboard. Eat it with nuts or fruit if you fancy, fresh figs especially. I love it with jalapeño chilli jam. I have had it served melted on little croûtons in a *salade de chèvre chaud* in Paris (a fine way to eat it, especially the Paris part, but I usually prefer to use Crottin de Chavignol), and while it melts a bit runnier than some other goat's, it was supremely tasty. For pairings, try a Loire Valley red, Chinon or Bourgueil, a Touraine white, or cider. For me, at the risk of repeating myself, nothing beats a crisp rosé with goat's cheese, bubbles if you want to add a sense of occasion.

Fun fact: Superstition has it that you must begin cutting a Sainte-Maure from its thicker end or else the goat whose milk was used in its production will stop giving milk.

19
Knackered

As I approach the three-month mark in my chee-semongering and the end of my probation, Tom goes through my trainee file with me every couple of days. It is on a clipboard and we check off the competencies learned after discussing them together. The list of checkmarks is growing. I am now au fait with some of the finer points of running the stall, dealing with the cheeses and selling them.

I can now take and fill a wholesale order. I have memorised most of the price codes for the cheeses and my hands fly across the old-school French till. I have the cheese contact rules down. I know how to take the temperatures and fill out our logs for inspection. Oddly, none of this makes the job any easier, because expectations rise for the skills I've been trained on, but I am still an apprentice and less than proficient at most of them.

Most of the time, I work with Tom. Once a week, normally on Friday, it's Cheesemonger Cian who's there, back in my life.

'Is that how you wrap the Crottins?' he says, looking over my shoulder.

'Yeah. In twos, you mean?'

'In twos with the sellotape. That's how you do it with Tom?'

'Yes.' What am I doing wrong, I wonder.

'All right.'

'Why?'

'Well, what's that like at closing time?'

'It's a faff. Takes forever to get them out of their wraps and back in their trays.'

'Yeah, it does. Also, they'll go flying as you try to cut through the tape. Take six of them altogether, see.' He cuts a piece of cellophane and puts six Crottins in the middle and then, in a flash, has wrapped them tightly and set them on the slate, no sellotape. 'Unless you like working late?'

'Not really.'

'Me neither. I'm a fast closer, see? That's what I like. I like to see how much time we can shave off every close.'

'Got it.'

After we set up, Cian tells me about a business idea he has. He wants to start a pizza oven operation in a pub he knows and sell pizzas while people drink. He thinks this could be a real money-spinner.

'What do you think?'

'I think you can make a lot of money selling pizza. I mean how expensive are they to make, really? Plus people love them and drunk people get hungry.'

'Exactly. I know a guy who's looking for someone to take over a pizza operation in his pub.'

'What kind of outlay would it take?'

'That's the thing, see. He wants me to pay him for renting the equipment and the space, plus access to his punters. Not just that – I can't do it alone or I'd be working all the time. I'm thinking about it.'

Gradually over the weeks, he starts to share anecdotes from his London adventures, his mates, his girlfriend, his football matches, his business ideas, his music podcast, his band. He's got a lot going on.

Cian is competitive when selling cheese. Whereas I like to be at the front, trying to entice people in with samples and chatting at length to customers, Cian will swoop in for a sale, sometimes from elsewhere in the stall entirely. He'll be in the back where there's a lunch corner for the staff, checking some messages, then spot a good potential customer approaching the stall. He has an eye for people who will buy cheese – and like a flash, he's beside you with his smiley eyes, turning on his rogue's charm, burning up the till with fresh sales.

One day a customer in his forties with thin, straight blonde hair and wire-rim glasses comes to the stall holding a book to his chest, hugging it so it's impossible to see the jacket. He asks for some Beaufort. Beaufort is a big Alpine cheese.

'You know the French call this "The King of the Alps",' I say to him.

'I've heard that. Is it that much better?'

'Depends on the wheel, is what I'd say. It's bigger, though. Higher fat content.'

Now obviously, journalist needs to know what the book is, since he's hiding the title.

'What are you reading?' I ask.

To his credit, he answers straight away, 'It's a book about microdosing LSD.' He shows me the cover.

'Ah. This is a big new Silicon Valley thing, right? Greater focus? Have you tried it?'

'Not micro-dosed.'

We have a good laugh at that comment and taste through some cheese. He leaves with just the Beaufort he originally asked for.

After he leaves, things slow down a bit and Cian walks over to me and says, 'Not everyone wants to chat, you know. Some people just want to buy cheese.'

I get the message, not so subtle. Maybe I am boring people, talking their ear off, or going too far.

The next day I ask Tom, 'Do you think I'm too chatty with the customers? Like am I slow?'

'I think you're finding your style, and your thing is to make a connection with the customers.'

'I love chatting with people but maybe I get carried away.'

'Did Cian say that to you?'

'Maybe.'

'Okay, don't listen to him. Please. He has his style. You have yours. We can't all have the same selling style. People really like talking to you, Michael. Some of them stay chatting for ten minutes. That is going to pay off. You'll see. It builds trust and loyalty.'

'Or it really annoys them and they don't come back.'

'I really don't think so, Michael. I'm the manager. Listen to me, not him. You be you.'

That night, I am knackered. Lying on my bed, I don't want to have a shower. I don't want to take off my work clothes. In fact, I don't want to move any part of my body. Every once in a while, I shift imperceptibly just to feel the duvet underneath me – so soft! – and to smooth out the aches in every last one of my muscles.

I smell like cheese and bleach.

To climb the stairs of my flat up to the bedroom, I was slightly hunched over. It's hard to describe the soreness I feel deep in the soles of my feet – it feels almost as though someone has been taking a hammer to them. My hands tingle slightly and I have only half-feeling in my right thumb and forefinger.

I have three bright blue plasters on my hand. One is from where a cheese wire snapped as I was pulling it through a slab of Comté. It broke, suddenly swung up and embedded itself a millimetre or so beneath the skin of my right index finger. I should have looked more closely at it before acting, but I am squeamish and I wanted to get the wire out of my finger as quickly as possible. I grabbed it and yanked it out. Mistake. Not only was it a couple of millimetres deep, but it had a crook in the end from where it snapped so it took out some flesh. There was blood – not great customer service, we can agree. I stepped back and let Tom carry on and went to bleed on my own in the corner.

Another of the injuries is from the teeth of the tape dispenser. They are sharp like the teeth of baby crocodiles. Blood again, though not too much, and lingering irritation. The other wound is from a paper cut right at the folds of a knuckle. Surprisingly few injuries are from knife cuts.

The most common injuries at the cheese shop are from crushing an appendage. The wheels of cheese come in around thirty-five kilograms and as you try to set them down on a surface and remove your hands, you can easily get the timing wrong and the cheese comes down on your finger. I have slammed the fridge door on my finger often enough that I should know better. Then there are your feet and the panels that cover the contents of the cupboards. They are off the floor and held in place by knobs at the side. If you don't keep holding the panel as you turn the knobs, they fall exactly at the point where your toes meet your feet. I have damaged a big toe nail before due to this and it's not attractive, takes forever to heal. There's a rumour of a cheesemonger once breaking a toe.

But let's get back to my bed.

I am feeling the cumulative effects of cheesemongering, where every day starts with sweeping, hauling out wheels of cheese, moving large tables, climbing ladders, moving boxes, wrapping with focus and precision, manipulating slates, cutting down through the thick pastes of Cheddars and Alpine cheeses with both hands on a knife, scrubbing surfaces to free them of cheese residue, bleaching and squeegeeing floors and rearranging the furniture. Once more every day, all of the above. Saturday, 7 a.m. start and 6.30 p.m. finish.

I am not hungry. I am not thirsty. I just want to gradually allow my body to be fully horizontal again. I am unfolding. In my mind, I try to re-establish contact with myself.

I was a soft youth. I never attended a secondary school gym class. I didn't make my bed or my breakfast – my mum did that for me. My chores were lame, taking out the bins, and even that I complained about and thought was a burden. Some of this is payback.

One of the differences between this and a gym workout, where likewise afterwards you lie on your bed and don't feel at all like getting up, is that I realise I have no choice but to get up and soon, because my toes are burning. We are all kitted out with rubber boots, but at Borough it is just not practical to wear them throughout the day. Sometimes when I should wear them, while washing up and washing the floors, I am so focused on getting on with things and not finishing late that I end up still wearing my black canvas shoes, which are now orange canvas shoes because of all the Topax that's been spilt on them. My toes by now are so familiar with Topax that they react immediately when my socks get wet with it. They need attention.

In the shower on days like this, I actually lean against the tiled wall. I am brought again to wonder why I've chosen this job. I do not need a job that requires this much physical labour, or really any physical labour. Radio presenter? Zero physical exertion. That's when I remember that it's part of why I wanted to do the cheesemonger job in the first place. This tiredness is so far superior to that radio presenter tired. What I feel is muscle fatigue, not sleep deprivation and the constant mental burden. I feel weary but it feels good.

As I let the hot water soothe my muscles, I look down at my arms. My rash is definitively gone.

Beaufort

'Le beaufort est sans doute un exemple de l'efficacité des rapports humains, établis dans la confiance et la dignité, sur un plan d'égalité réciproque et de respect des hommes.'

– Maxime Viallet, noted alpagiste, effectively saying 'it takes a village' to make a cheese like Beaufort, which is 'established on the basis of trust and dignity, on a level of mutual equality and respect for people', an apt reference to the communal nature of Alpine cheesemaking.

Origin: An AOP since 1968, Beaufort has one of the stricter sets of specs *(cahier des charges)* for producers to follow. It must come from only a few valleys in the Savoie, including the Beaufortain Valley, of course. Milk from only two types of cows is permitted: Abondance and Tarine. The first cheese called Beaufort dates back to 1865, but Beaufort has origins which pre-date the French Revolution (its predecessor was named Grovire). It's a French Alpine cheese, but the cheesemaking knowledge behind it migrated originally from the Swiss.

Presentation: A wheel of Beaufort is massive, often weighing a bit more than 40kg and 36–75cm across. It's typically high, as high as 16cm, and one of its distinctive characteristics is the concave heel to the rind. This is due to the wooden hoop cinched around its middle as it's set. Two theories as to why they've gone for the concave, other than to set it apart: first, that it makes the cheese easier to carry, and second that it helps to ensure the cheese doesn't cave in on itself during maturation. Beaufort tends to have a white/ivory paste. Summer Beaufort has a rich yellow hue, and Alpage Beaufort is even brighter yellow. This is due to the cows feeding on a variety of wild grasses and flowers as they graze in the Alpine Valleys of the Savoie. Beaufort without the prefix Summer or Alpage comes from cows fed local hay (no fermented silage) during the months when they are mostly in barns. Beaufort is not crazy about heat, or even room temperature. It's a supple Alpine cheese, hard, yes, but instantly yielding en bouche due to the higher fat content. In fact, it doesn't grate well for this and other reasons. Instead, if melting, cut it into strips or cubes. Because it's expensive, you will typically not get a large piece, but if you can splurge for a special occasion, a piece that runs the entire height of the cheese showing off the full concave of the rind is a showstopper.

How to serve: Nothing beats a Beaufort that is on point. In my experience, it's one of the more finicky Alpines, though, and can vary wildly. Ask for a taste before purchasing so you know what you're getting. Different batches each have their own qualities. Beaufort can have a big, beefy flavour to it, but it can also be intensely fruity: stone fruit – apricots and peaches. My favourite wheels have a line of sweetness that's almost like marzipan. It is the smoothest of the Alpines, regularly served on posh ski trips in France, a perfect way to replenish your energy. At home, as a cheese course or apéro on its own with some pre-cubed pieces? You'll be a star. One of the more surprising complements to Beaufort is raspberry. It will make a succulent fondue with a bit of kirsch. Soufflés, cheese tarts, gratins, all will be pimped to the max with Beaufort, but check out the official website for inspiration such as an 'Iced velouté of Beaufort, beetroot and raspberry'! For pairings, I would opt for bright, more acidic reds that can set off the roundness of this luxuriously higher-fat cheese. For whites, try a Savoyard white.

Fun fact: Beaufort inspires royal qualifiers. I've often seen it referred to as the King of the Alps, or more often, the Prince of Gruyères (Jean-Anthelme Brillat-Savarin, 1825, *Physiologie du goût*). When there's a good wheel of Beaufort at the stall, Cheesemonger Nuala will bounce off the walls all day with infectious delight, selling through whatever stock we have. It can be difficult to source in Britain, and when in stock, customers can get as excited as Nuala.

20
Like French Kissing a Sheep

WITH JUST DAYS TO go before the end of my probation and growing in confidence, I begin butting heads with a cheese called Pérail. It's pronounced pair-eye, a sheep's milk cheese. Summer now over, Cheesemonger Fionnuala has come back from Ireland and rejoined the team as we head towards colder, busier days and the end of the year. Despite knowing her for only a few weeks, we immediately establish a rapport.

'God, Fionnuala, this Pérail. Remind me why we stock it.'

'What do you mean now?'

'It's so acidic, it almost burns your tongue. The minute you cut into it, it runs all over the barquette. It has a bitter finish and en bouche, it's like you're French kissing a sheep.'

'You've done that, have you?' She lets out a big laugh.

'Fine, then. Tell me you like it.'

'It's not a cheese I run to.'

'It's a cheese I run away from. And I can't sell it. Seriously. I don't know what to tell people.'

'Some people like strong, gooey sheep's cheese.'

'I suppose some people like being slapped in the face, too.'

'Some people definitely enjoy a good brawl. What's brought this on, anyway? What did that poor Pérail do to you?'

'I just can't bear to see them looking up at me like this first thing in the morning. What are they, blue, green and grey now? Except where the paste erupts from the crust on to the surface. I've wrapped the same five cheeses every morning for the past three days. I haven't sold one of them. And neither have you.'

'Right, give it here.'

'What?'

'Pass one of them to me, we'll crack it open and give it a go. Otherwise, they'll just sit there for another three days.'

I hand Nuala a Pérail, one that's a bit weathered and crusty. She sinks the knife in. As soon as the top is broken, the runny paste starts to ooze in all directions. There's no such thing as cutting a piece of this cheese, not this batch, that's for sure.

'God, look at your face,' she's laughing now and nearly keeled over. 'Come on, it's part of the job.'

I run my finger along her knife, put it into my mouth and close my eyes. She does the same.

I wince. 'You first,' I say to her, wanting an unvarnished opinion.

'I mean I haven't ever got past Ben describing it as "calamine" to be honest, but you're not wrong. This is a lot. Let's mark it down and present it as a strong sheep's cheese for anyone who's in the market for one.'

'Well, I don't know what else to do, so yeah. I just need to see the back of them.'

'There's a new tray in the fridge.'

'Please, make it stop.'

'If you feel that way about it, talk to Jon, maybe.'

'You don't?'

'God, what a downer. Michael, I don't have strong feelings about it but you seem to be in a bit of a rut on the matter. He'll be here on Saturday.'

I have begun to see Pérail as irredeemable.

Tom is nervous that Owner Jon is coming to open the stall with us on Saturday morning. He is well known in Borough Market and although he has his hands full overseeing the business, he loves to retail and likes to see how things are going with his cheesemongers.

Tom thus spends the whole week ensuring things are ship-shape for his arrival. Trays are topped up, tape dispensers are shining, the fridges get their monthly clean a week early. Due to our work rota, Tom's not in on Friday, the day before Jon's appearance. Friday is the day I work the stall with Cian, so I get a call late on Thursday evening after I get home. It's Tom.

'Sorry to call you late. One last thing I forgot to mention when I saw you today,' he says.

'Sure.'

'I know you do this all the time anyway.'

'Go ahead.'

'But Jon is coming in on Saturday first thing to open and set up at 6 a.m.'

'So I hear.'

'Don't be funny, please. That means make sure everything is 100 per cent clean – no missed spots on the tables. Make sure all the cheeses are wrapped well for bed, I mean with the right protocols. Ask Cian if you're unsure of anything. Oh, and can you take a photo of how the stand looks on Friday and send it to Jon?'

Each different cheese has a separate protocol on how it likes to spend the night. In showbiz, these special requests are known as 'riders'. For instance, the Castillon Frais needs to sit in its box unwrapped, underneath some waxed paper but its box needs to be kept in a plastic sheath. Also, it can't be on an upper shelf too close to the refrigeration fan. Brie de Meaux and Munster stay wrapped in cellophane, but the Brie is under a layer of straw on a top shelf, Munster is in a cardboard box on a lower shelf. Comté sits unwrapped in a cool cupboard, about 10 to 12°C, and has a quick saline bath before bed. Reblochon needs wrapping in paper, middle shelf, cardboard box. I could go on. Oh, and sometimes they need to have a change of routine depending on how they are feeling, for instance, the Tomme de Chambrouze is mostly kept wrapped in paper but if it's too moist, wet even, it will want a night unwrapped but lightly covered over. They make Mariah Carey's rider calling for tall, leafy plants in her dressing room look amateur.

Saturday lives up to the hype. It is like no other to date since I began working as a cheesemonger. When I arrive, Cheesemonger Nuala is pulling the soft cow's milk cheeses one by one out of their boxes and wrapping them for display. The tables are set out already. The big wheels of cheese are in place. Jon is working on the hard and semi-soft cheeses. Tom, having just arrived, is going through his early-morning checklist, making sure everything's in order. This is way ahead of where we'd normally be on a Saturday.

Tom hands me the broom. 'Morning, Michael. Perimeter sweep, if you don't mind. Let me know how you get on.' Only two mouse poops this morning. Maybe they also got the memo about Jon coming.

To see him now, here at Borough Market in the predawn with us, working with his cheeses, almost bouncing on the balls of his feet as he does, I have nothing but admiration for him. I get this rush of feeling: he is the captain of my ship and I would sail away with him anywhere. Jon is going through all the bigger cheeses, doing a careful triage, wrapping and re-wrapping wherever necessary. It's a cheese care and beautification process which is a wonder to behold.

Where he takes time is in their initial assessment. He is peering into their eyes, he is reaching out to them, trying to understand where they are in their lives, how they are feeling, what kind of night they've spent in the fridge, how they've been treated by others all week, what their genealogy is, all of it. All the answers to those questions inform how he is about to proceed: what needs to be cut away, scraped or re-shaped, how they need to be wrapped, whether they need to be sold as a priority or 'focus' or discounted.

He'll pick up a piece of, say, the Cantal au lait de Salers from the Auvergne, a rare find in London, and where it was looking a bit dull, cracked and weathered, after a careful trim and a scrape from Jon and a pristine wrap with cellophane, it looks smarter than the day it arrived. Oh, and he's doing all of it while chirping away to all of us about cheese, about the news and about the music of the 1980s – we are listening to an 80s radio station.

On this Saturday morning, the big news is an interview Prince Andrew has given to the BBC where he says he has 'let down the side' by frequenting Jeffrey Epstein, and by standing accused of sexual assault himself, despite always having denied it.

'Let down the side!' Jon's voice rings out in mock disbelief. 'He's let down the fucking side!' He laughs a big laugh that carries out the stall and down the alleyway.

'Can you believe how creepy this Sting song is?' says Nuala. The esprit de corps of these early hours is powerful. We are united in purpose and enjoying each other's company.

The hard cheeses Jon is working on, the Gruyère, the Comté, the Maréchal, the Ossau Iraty, L'Étivaz, the Beaufort, they've all changed in the twelve hours since we last left them. Oxidation means that a half-wheel of Gruyère is not a bright off-white in the same way it was. Holding the blade of a knife with your thumb and three forefingers and scraping it along the face pulls ribbons of cheese away with each stroke. Underneath, it's a purer hue and a brighter taste that's revealed. When I do this job, it takes a long time. It's awkward. The cheeses are heavy and I stop to check my work often. When Jon does it, it's second nature like an extension of his arm – it happens fast.

Occasionally, he'll decide to throw open the process to the room. 'Michael, what do you think of this Gruyère?'

Okay, stay calm.

'Um. I mean, I think our Gruyère is pretty dependable. I guess this is tasting a little meatier than usual, but nothing exaggerated.'

'I'm liking this wheel, Jon.' Nuala jumps in.

'Yeah, it's lovely. Bright,' says Tom.

Nothing further is said on the matter. I should probably have kept my comments more general. Do I seem like I'm trying too hard?

As customers begin to arrive, Jon proves he is an all-around marquee presence, a draw. A crowd forms around midday to listen to him talk about cheese and to buy. With him, it feels like they are all building a cheeseboard or hoping to learn something.

I hear him talk at length about the Cantal and why he stocks it. At one point, someone asks him to describe the Selles-sur-Couffy and he says succinctly, 'Vegetal, cooked asparagus.' It strikes me instantly as he says it that it is exactly that, only I had never made the association. I know he's also taking the measure of us as the day goes by, and Tom slips a word in my ear to say, 'You're doing a good job. Jon likes what he sees.'

There is a bit of a lull towards the end of the day, and before he leaves – he's on a high from spending a day with the customers – I decide to try my luck and ask Jon about the Pérail, get it off my chest.

'Jon, could you tell me about the Pérail?' I ask.

'What about it?' he asks, enthusiastically.

'I'm struggling to sell them. I just don't think they're tasting great. I get a lot of bitter acidity from them. I'm trying to find a way in.'

'Is it this latest batch you're worried about?'

'It is, but the last one was no better. Worse, actually. They end up hanging around, then they get so weathered.'

'The idea is to shift them before that point,' he says. Then he takes a long pause before saying anything else.

Did I mention I can come across as brash? No surprise for a radio presenter but for a cheesemonger? That's what's worrying me at this exact point. My confidence is suddenly deflated. It's good to have a strong presence but I've been cheesemongering as a trainee for all of twelve weeks. I start to get worried. Jon is never at a loss for words, but he is obviously considering his response.

Finally, instead of an answer, he tells me a story about when he first worked for a well-known London cheesemongers. He begins with his trademark, pensive-sounding, Yeah ...

'I remember one day when I was working at the Dairy and had a real down on the cheeses. Things just weren't tasting good and I said so. Another monger answered me, "I'm not sure which cheese you're talking about." "Most of them, actually," I answered. And he said, "Well, what should we do with that information?"

'I mean the thing is, we work with these cheesemakers day in and day out, across the seasons. It's a tough bloody profession. You know, they have rough patches and yeah, sometimes the cheeses don't taste their best. We stick with them. We make that choice and they get better, dependably, in most cases.

'Michael, the cheese varies, is what I'm saying. We know that and we work with that. But the mongers also vary. Pérail's a good cheese. You might ask yourself, "Is the problem the Pérail, or is the problem me?"'

I don't say anything, just nod my head. I'm a little stunned.

He goes to the back to pack up and go.

Before Jon leaves, he huddles with Tom and checks the day's sales figures. They were strong. We all sold a lot of cheese and I had the second best sales. It was a great day, a fun day, until the Pérail closer.

Walking home that night, my head is spinning. I stop by the Co-Op to buy the only wine I can afford these days, a store-brand bottle from Chile, £5. I feel awful. It feels like the appropriate pairing.

Jon's comments to me are sinking in. You need confidence to survive in a new job, but I have gotten too confident too fast. My writing off Pérail is bordering on petulant and it says so much about my limitations as an apprentice cheesemonger. There are considered reasons why Pérail is a part of our offer. Somehow, I am unwilling to stretch far enough to see them. I think part of the problem was not fully embracing how different people's tastes can be. I can't imagine fancying Pérail and was not open to doing the work necessary to imagine how others could. I found more release, more satisfaction in writing it off because it didn't appeal to me after what, three months as a trainee cheesemonger? Something that should be so basic dawns on me, that people can desire something I reject.

I haven't bothered to look into its history, either – it's a cheese that is originally made from milk left over from the production of Roquefort. Our Pérail is made by a family of cheesemakers, the Dombre family, who bought some land abandoned after the Great War in the Midi-Pyrénées region and started a farm they named 'Les Cabasses'. Imagine the undertaking, not just the farming and raising the sheep, but taking on ancestral cheese recipes and starting up a raw-milk cheese production. Now their cheeses are sold in London and Paris.

Then there's the actual cheese. I take a moment to do some research and discover Pérail has a history that reaches back across generations. Peasant farmers hundreds of years ago made them for their own family's consumption. The name originates from Provençal, one of France's regional languages: it was called *Peral*. It was only in the nineteenth century that they began to be sold in markets throughout l'Aveyron and Les Causses. Our little Pérails, it turns out, have so much to tell you if you'll only stop and listen. Later in my cheesemongering career, I develop a soft spot for one of our regular customers, a tall, quiet young man from Eastern Europe who orders three Pérails without fail every weekend. 'I just love the taste.'

Pérail is teaching me a life lesson I thought I'd learned before, though apparently I haven't internalised. When you reject a thing that's been around a while instinctively or emotionally, even go so far as to hold it in contempt, it is often out of ignorance, or what the French call *inconscience*, a reckless disregard that's more a reflection of your own shortcomings. It's so boring, so shallow, the antithesis of what I'm supposed to be working towards with cheese, and for that matter in life.

As if the whole Pérail episode isn't bad enough, it is also time to reckon with the guilt I am carrying. In fact, I am racked with it, feeling it physically in my body, not just my head. All day long, this amazing bunch of people, these cool cheesemongers, make me part of the team, 100 per cent. Tom trusts me to prepare for Jon's arrival. Nuala hardly knows me but is so friendly already, respects me and my opinions even though I'm on probation. I've even started to have my own small group of regulars who like being served by me.

And yet, what exactly are my intentions here? I have never told them I am on a sabbatical. Never told Tom, never told Molly, never told Emma or Laurence, never told Daisy or Cian, never told Owner Jon. I have another job as a radio presenter. The clock is ticking, and I have to go back in the next few weeks. It dawns on me at that moment how selfish and unfair I'm being to them, making them think I want to be a legit cheesemonger. Is this all a game to me?

Right. Calm down. Of course this isn't a game. I know it means much more to me. So much more! Although, what precisely?

Thing is, this isn't just about me. This is their life, their job, their business. While I'm trying on life as a cheesemonger for a few months, they are living it. If they knew the truth, would they respect me? Honestly, in their shoes, I wouldn't.

It brings me right back to my brash question to Jon about the Pérail. It was a radio presenter's question. And his answer: 'Pérail's a good cheese. You might ask yourself, "Is the problem the Pérail, or is the problem me?"'

After an hour alone and half a bottle of Chilean plonk, I have the answer now. It's me.

Pérail

'On essaie de faire perdurer ce que nos parents ont créé ... on est fier de ce qu'ils ont fait ... On se doit de maintenir ces traditions-là, ces valeurs de travail et de qualité.'

– Élise Dombre, Pérail cheesemaker, speaking about the duty she feels to maintain the traditions of her parents, and pay homage to the values of quality and hard work.

Origin: For centuries, sheep grazed in the part of France where they make Pérail, L'Aveyron, and a version of Pérail will have been made throughout that time. However, it's only since the 1980s that Pérail has been successfully commercialised.

Presentation: Round and flat like a small, thick pancake, it is white or off-white and is mostly sold in a barquette in fitted paper. It has a natural rind, covered by the beautiful, intricate patterns of *Geotrichum candidum*, a yeast-like mould.

How to serve: Some bread or crackers are essential, especially to mop up the juices if you have a runny one. Some people love the barny, sheepy flavour, but if you, like me, can sometimes find it a bit much, look for a complement such as a spinach salad or figs, or something a bit sweet. For wine pairing, try a Saint-Chinian or a crisp, slightly bitter cider.

Fun fact: Pérail is made in the same region as Roquefort, and often uses sheep's milk left over from Roquefort production.

21

'I think we should move into the fridge'

I T'S SUCH A SPECTACULARLY beautiful November morning that I snap a pic on the way into Borough Market and post it on one of my social media accounts.

```
Friday morning in The Borough #SE1, #sunshine
Wherever you are, have an awesome Friday.
```

Walking to work in the first, indirect light of morning, I'm in a great mood and looking forward to my Friday selling cheese.

I have given myself the gift of a reprieve and it's helped with some of the guilt that I've been feeling. My six-month sabbatical drawing to a close, I wrote to my boss in Montreal and asked her if I could extend until after the holidays. She said yes almost immediately. It makes sense anyway, she said, to take up the mic the first week of the new year, 2020. That's three more months and crucially, it means I will be cheesemongering for the period they really need me here.

To have packed up and left at the end of September just as I am finishing my training would have been a slap in the face and a blow to the company, a small business that works the whole year getting ready for the explosion of sales at Christmas. It's no exaggeration to say that without the holidays, this kind of artisan cheesemongering wouldn't be profitable. They've invested in me, long hours of training. I owe them that much at least.

The reprieve I am feeling is exactly that, however. It's temporary. My notice period is four weeks. With the extension of my sabbatical, I no longer have to rush the difficult conversation about quitting. I can push that to the side on a day like this one and walk into Borough Market with purpose.

Londoners approach Friday with a type of hedonistic enthusiasm I have not witnessed elsewhere. I love them for that. The weekend is about to be unleashed and there is a palpable sense of it in this town, strong party energy. After five days of hard work, they hit the pubs for an after-work drink or make the rounds at the market to prepare for a fun night in with friends or loved ones. That means we get some good customers coming to the cheese stall at Borough Market.

During the week, many will pop by for a quick purchase, something they need. On Friday, they tend to be up for the full cheese-buying experience. The dynamic is exhilarating for the mongers, heightened by our incredible cast of cheeses. I get a real blast out of connecting them to the people who want them.

Flush with these good vibes and high expectations, I am also looking forward to seeing Cian today, my Friday workmate. This morning, I am fully here for his faux-laconic outlook on life. His body language, the way he speaks – 'Cool, yeah' – they all broadcast remove but the reality of Cian is that you know he loves to bite into the apple. It's the unspoken joy of him. Cian has required a lot of work from me. I feel the effort is paying off.

Just finishing the perimeter sweep for mouse poops (a scant haul), I am bombarding him with questions as we open the shop. 'How's the planning going for your girlfriend's birthday?' He's dating a beautiful girl who he clearly adores and is planning on re-upholstering a set of chairs for her, an exotic animal-style pattern. It's a creative, ambitious gift. Also, if you don't 'know a guy' in London, you know that's going to take up some money, time and effort.

'Mate. They look amazing. I'll be a fucking hero, just wait.'

Friday openings are busy. It's not Saturday, but you get early birds. Also on Fridays, we do a fair amount of prep for the weekend, cutting down big Alpine wheels, wrapping smaller pieces of blue cheese, restocking shelves. The time goes by quickly as customers start to arrive.

Cian's in a good mood, good company, but his leg is bothering him since an incident earlier this week. To hear him tell it, it's downright painful.

'Could be a hernia, maybe,' I say, in front of the customers we're serving.

'Oh, a hernia. That's painful – where is it exactly?' asks a thirty-something woman who ordered 150 grams of Gruyère and is choosing from among the goat's cheeses.

'Yeah, it's like, up here.' He points. 'At the top of my leg.'

A Kiwi cyclist with a yellow backpack is our other customer – he's a regular. Unsurprisingly, we refer to him as 'the Kiwi cyclist'. Lovely fella, sporty. 'Nah, that's not a hernia, not there.'

'HE said it was a hernia,' Cian points at me.

'Could be,' I say. 'I said it could be – but yeah that's not looking like the right spot for it.'

'How's it feeling exactly?' The first customer, the woman, asks.

'Like a sharp twinge.'

'Is there a bump or a bulge?' asks the Kiwi.

'Nah.' He rubs the area again to check. 'Definitely no bump.'

'Not a hernia, then.'

We all feel a bit relieved for him.

'I made the mistake of playing on it,' says Cian. 'I said I'd play goal, but it's so boring in goal I moved to mid-field and now it's started hurting again.'

'Sometimes,' I decide to weigh in again with my sporting expertise, 'what an injury really wants is a bit of action to heal. Motion is lotion. I had a back thing last night and almost skipped my workout but I went this morning – like a warrior – and guess what? Pain gone.'

'You're not wrong there, mate,' says the cyclist. 'I say that all the time. Motion is lotion. Careful, though, there are a lot of injuries that can be aggravated if you don't give them time to heal.'

The woman, meanwhile, has taken a scrap of paper out of her bag and is writing on it. 'Sports physiotherapist,' she says. 'Come see me. First one's on me. We'll figure it out.'

Cian flashes a big smile, takes the paper and says, 'Thanks!' I feel this is how things generally go for him.

As we get to lunchtime, Tom arrives from Cheese HQ, bounding in to cover our breaks. Cian's off to eat.

'All right then. What should I do?' Tom asks me. There's a thing he's trying out now, to get me to take charge sometimes and to tell him what to do. I see the point but it feels awkward. I'm not crazy about it.

'If you could perform the Tom magic on the stall, that would be cool,' I tell him. The place is looking messy after a busy morning. Tom hates it when things are like this. It's rubbed off on me. I'm surprised he hasn't said anything.

Tom's innate orderliness is in equal measure impressive and exasperating. More than once, he has put things away which I have placed nearby seconds earlier, to have within reach. To Tom's angel, Cian, meanwhile, is the devil on my other shoulder. Where Tom would have every working piece of cheese in its place and preferably wrapped, Cian's presence has led to a decadent spread of cheeses of all sorts, covering almost every workspace.

Within minutes, the Tom tornado does its work, and the place is shipshape. And here's the thing about him, you can read annoyance when we transgress – the manager whose stall is being improperly tended – but it is never deeply felt and it passes like a cloud in front of the sun on an English summer's day. He is fundamentally a lovely bloke.

When I return from my break, Cian is back, Tom is gone, and we get back to the business of selling cheese and putting things in place for our busy day tomorrow. I have the piece of Coulommiers we use as a taster in my hand – Coulommiers is a soft cow's milk cheese, and despite the cooler weather, it is running. I am tasting it out to a customer whose order I am filling. It's just after 2 p.m. when suddenly: commotion.

Something is very wrong.

People are running past the stall out of Borough Market, left to right from our vantage point, towards the nearest exit on to the street. The sound of it is uncanny; you can hear running footfall like a percussive chorus.

At first, I think it looks bizarrely staged, like a scene from a comedy horror film when everyone is over-dramatically running in the same direction, or a stampede from a wildlife documentary.

Instinctively, I turn to Cian and he to me. We duck slightly, reflexively, and move to the back of the stall, back away from the commotion. Some of the customers who were waiting at the stall decide to take off running in the same direction as the crowd. Others, some of those we are serving, decide instead to move away from the crowds like we're doing, further into the stall. They are a couple in their late sixties and a young man in his twenties.

At the back of the stall there is a small alcove out of sight, a space where we can sit on a stool and eat lunch or make a tea or coffee. There isn't room for any more than one person back there. We both look towards it, look back at each other and shake our heads.

It feels longer but all this is happening in a matter of seconds. The flow of people has grown, the pace has increased and the look on their faces is now distress, alarm, fear. Honestly, at this point, I am just a little bit stunned. I don't know what is going on but it's seriously not good.

Cian, on the other hand, has seen all he needs to: 'I think we should move into the fridge.'

There's no debate. He is right.

'The fridge?' asks one of the customers, the older man.

Cian: 'Yeah, it's a fridge where we keep things overnight.'

'Let's go,' I say, and we are all off. The younger man turns out to be an American; he is walking just behind me. Cian is behind him and then the couple.

I open the fridge, usher the customers in, then Cian and I enter.

I can feel that I'm scared, genuinely afraid – nothing like this has ever happened while I've worked here. I can't stop myself imagining the attack on Borough Market two years earlier: angry guys with sharpened knives, roided up and believing God wants them to maim and kill people. It was a grisly attack – so many people died or were hurt while trying desperately to defend themselves. It all suddenly feels so real that my head is buzzing.

With the fear comes a moment where I think to myself that if there's not enough room in the fridge, Cian and I will go in, not the customers. We work here, not them. It's primal and instinctive. The thought only lasts an instant but it's enough to disturb me then and now. 'God, that's just wrong,' I tell myself. I suddenly feel ashamed, and I push the thought away. I remember having a moment of clarity, thinking this is not how I want to act in a moment like this. I won't be that person.

Having got a better hold of myself, I wonder whether maybe we should secure the customers in the fridge and then stay outside and stand in the little alcove. I could do it. I'd be able to hear more clearly and have line of sight to the market. We'd have a bit more control than inside a fridge with a thick door not allowing us to see or hear.

Alongside that thought, I have a flash of myself peeking around the corner just when an attacker is out front. I imagine him looking right in my eyes and then rounding on me, coming in for the attack. I can almost see the long blade of the knife and me raising my hands up to protect my face. My heart is beating so fast.

We all fit in the fridge. These are split-second decisions – it turns out I'm too fearful to hide outside and stand watch. It's a bit of a squeeze but it's amazing how you can do something when you need to. Once the door closes, we feel immediately safer and the heightened fear subsides a little.

'Breathe, breathe,' I repeat to myself.

Now that we're here, it's crystal clear that we are doing the right thing, that we should be sheltering our customers, responsible for them. In fact, they become the priority. They are in our care. I am still kicking myself for having thought differently moments ago.

The young American is pressed at the back against the boxes of Mont d'Or, a seasonal cheese for the holidays that comes in wooden round containers. I am up against the soft cow's milk cheeses on the right-hand side of the fridge, Cian is across from me against the goat's cheeses and the couple is in between. He is wearing a Canada pin, and we learn later they are from Vancouver Island.

Cian closes the door firmly behind us.

'Do you think it's an attack?' the woman asks.

'Oh yes,' says her husband.

I think it is, too. I have more flashes in my head of news reports from the attack two years ago, trying to remember exactly how it played out, but I say nothing.

Hearing a clamour loud enough to carry inside, we all fall silent, listening. It's impossible to discern what's happening. The only thing certain is that there is a lot of noise, a lot of movement. I think I hear men shouting, possibly a fight. It sounds to me like shouting in anger.

Finally, I break the silence, 'Is everyone okay? Are you all right?' I ask the customers.

They all respond more or less calmly, looking me in the eye.

'Yes.'

'Yeah, I'm okay.'

'I'm good.'

I suggest we call the police to find out what's going on. Cian gestures that he hasn't got his phone. He's left it in the stall. I remember seeing it now on the counter towards the back. I have mine in my pocket but before I think to draw it out, the Canadian man hands me his.

'Here, use mine.'

'Can you dial 999?' I ask.

He does and I take it. It answers on the second ring: '9-9-9 Police, Fire or Ambulance?'

'Police.'

The police operator comes on. It's a woman's voice.

'Hello,' I say. 'We're calling from Borough Market. We've shut ourselves in the fridge. There's some sort of commotion going on outside, people running out to the exits looking upset and we don't know what's going on. We were hoping you'd have some information.'

'You're at Borough Market?'

'Yes.'

'In a fridge?'

'Yes, in a fridge. And we can hear voices outside shouting but it's hard to tell what they're saying.'

'Okay, bear with me one moment. Won't be long.'

Several moments go by with everyone in the fridge looking at me expectantly before she returns on the line to say exactly what I was expecting her to say.

'Okay, listen closely. It's an attack. So you need to stay where you are. You've done the right thing. Stay hidden. Is that clear?'

I look at everyone and repeat what she's said: 'It's an attack.' Their eyes are so big.

The police operator answers as though I was speaking to her: 'Yes – that's all I can tell you for now. Stay where you are and when we have more information, we'll let you know.'

'Okay, thanks.'

The line disconnects.

The shouting is now louder. Much closer, but still impossible to make out through the door. No one says anything for a while. All we can hear are the fans from the fridge and the noises intensifying.

The young American at the back looks at me. 'What should we do?'

'Okay, if someone tries to open that door, we pull to hold it shut, right?'

'Right,' says the Canadian man. I learn later his name is Terry. I return his phone to him.

Reading everyone's fear, Cian looks at me and says in a steady voice, 'It's a cheese shop. We have a lot of knives.'

I have one in my hand. It's a small, black-handled, blunted knife that we use for cheese tasting. It won't even cut through cellophane. Nevertheless, Cian's moment of bravado gives me a welcome burst of empowerment.

In my other hand, I'm still holding the tasting wedge of Coulommiers and it's doing what Coulommiers does best. It's running everywhere it can, all over my hand, almost as though it's bleeding.

The box I'm standing next to is not the box it would normally go into and this cheese really should be wrapped – such is the absurdity of how the mind can work during a crisis – but I set it down anyway, wipe my hand on my apron and reach into my pocket for my phone.

'That sounds like dogs barking,' says Cian.

That could mean the police are on the case. Listening, we can also now hear a helicopter overhead. There's some relief in that but police presence doesn't mean they have things under control.

'Can we try to see what's happening through the Internet,' says the Canadian woman, Margaret.

Cian uses Terry's phone and starts searching for information.

I decide to get a message out to our people. I go to our company group chat and type in the first thing that comes to mind, without any context, in exactly these words:

```
Me: We are locked in the fridge. [We
weren't locked in, just shut in. You
can't lock the fridge from the inside,
but that's what came out.] There is
shouting outside. We have three customers
with us. They say there has been an
attack. We are staying put for the
moment. Please report if you have any
info.
```

Seconds later, Tom appears in the chat.

```
Tom: Holy fuck.
Cheesemonger Emma: I've seen there has
been a knife attack on London Bridge. What
can we do?
Me: Keep us informed. We don't know when
it is ok to leave the fridge.
Cheesemonger Daisy: Omg. Please keep us
updated how you are. Hope u are ok
Emma: The Metro says they have been shot
down. Please be safe.
Me: This is helpful. We will call the
police again. If you have copy of a story
to send us. We are struggling with the
internet. But WhatsApp is working just
about.
```

There are so many people using the local mobile networks, data has slowed to a crawl. I write some more:

```
Me: We are nervous and a bit chilly.
There's been a lot of shouting. We have
no idea what exactly it is. Cian is on to
the cops again.
```

Cian is trying to get through on the emergency number as I message.

```
Warehouse Cheesemonger Llewi: Stay safe
guys.
Cheesemonger Manager Laurence: Shots have
been fired by the police at someone on the
```

```
bridge itself. There was apparently a
stabbing and likely more than one person
injured. We will try and find out more.
Stay put for now.
```

I read Laurence's message out loud to everyone.

'How's everybody doing?' I look at each of the customers one by one. 'Not too cold?'

'No, we're okay.'

We are still hearing shouts and loud noises. I am listening for the crack or pop of shots fired as Laurence mentioned but haven't heard any. Finally, a message comes through that signals things are going to be okay. It's Tom.

```
Tom: Hi guys. I've phoned security. They
know you're in the fridge. They will come
let you out when safe. But the market has
been cleared.
Laurence: Nice one Tom.
Tom: They are in action. The whole market
has been shut down and roads have been
closed. Please let me know you receive
this message.
Me: Message Received.
```

In the final moments inside the fridge, once I've read out the latest messages, the tension breaks. The Canadian couple takes a group selfie. In it, I look stressed. Cian gives a half smile, he looks assured.

Cian has got through to the police again and is in the middle of what sounds like a slightly confusing conversation when the police call back on the other phone, the one I originally used. Cool trick. Not sure how they did that.

'We're calling to tell you that the situation is under control. It's safe to go outside now. Report to the police who will show you to safety.'

I am still wary and suggest we could maybe open the door slowly, but Terry has thrown caution to the wind, opens the door wide, walks straight out and begins to explore the stall.

It's a slight blur what happens next because I'm stunned and still on my guard. Then suddenly, hands are shaken among our group, thanks conveyed. The young American dashes off.

Terry and Margaret grab me by the arm and say, 'But we haven't paid for our cheese.'

Honestly, who knows where we were with their cheese order? 'Don't worry about it.'

'Yes, but we didn't get our cheese.'

Pragmatic Canadians.

I give them what's wrapped on the counter. It's probably theirs? Cheese in hand, they finally head off. They ask my name, and I tell them, 'It's Michael. Safe travels.'

I go to my bag which is hanging on a peg at the back to put my house keys in my pocket, but for some reason I leave my bag in the stall. I am not acting too rationally.

I come out of the stall to look around. I have never seen such a mess at the market. Half-consumed food, drink and packages are littered everywhere, the alley outside our stall is thick with them. Police stationed at the exit to the market spot Cian and me and gesture us over. I motion towards the shutters indicating I should bring them down, but they call to us to say no. They point us down Tooley Street and around the corner.

We have left the stall completely open. All the cheeses are out, though wrapped. My money belt is under the counter in a cubbyhole unprotected. Nothing is locked. My bag is hanging on a hook. Dazed and zombie-like, I walk past the police, as told, and to the other side of the cordon.

As we emerge on to Southwark Street, south of the market, we meet traders one after another. I see Allan and Barbara who work in the same row of stalls as we do.

'Are you all right, Michael?' Allan asks, concern in his eyes.

'Yeah,' I answer reflexively. 'We were hiding in the fridge.'

'Good for you,' Barbara says. 'The fridge? How many?'

I tell her our story, then Barbara tells us hers: 'When it all started kicking off, we should probably have run, but we didn't. We were just ducking down behind the stall. I was, anyway. Allan kept popping up his head. I told him, "Get down, you fool." Eventually we just lay flat on the floor behind the cabinet. Michael, I was scared. I swear I could hear people shouting in Arabic. We heard the police calling for people to run as well, but it was too late for us to leave – we didn't feel like it was safe to come out. Then we spotted three police walking down our lane, the armed ones with the big rifles. That's when I stood up and called out, "Please help us!" and one of them says to me, "Right, you're not supposed to be here." They moved us out of there fast, but Allan insisted on taking two bread crates!'

'Bread crates? I don't understand.'

'Neither did I! You know the stack of crates the bread arrives in? He said he wanted something to throw if we were attacked.' We ended up round the corner downstairs with a group of others in a restaurant. We were there for a good while. They even gave us something to eat.'

'What a story!' I grip their shoulders. Cian's moved on down the street, so I tell them I have to catch up with him. 'I'm so glad you two are okay. You did well.'

When I'm close enough to Cian, who's telling our story to a market trader I don't know, I take a moment to update the group chat.

```
Me: We are out and safe now.
Emma: Great.
Daisy: Thank goodness. Xxxx
Me: The stall is open with shutters up.
Police wanted us to go. I asked to close
the shutters they said no. Sorry. My
money belt is in the stall.
Emma: Michael it is most important that you
guys stay safe. Do not worry about the stall.
Me: I asked when we could go back and an
officer said "Watch the news."
Cheesemonger Yasha: This is all that's on
the BBC news website at the moment (in
case you can't open the link).
```

A number of people are believed to be injured in an incident at London Bridge, police have said. The Met said they were called to a stabbing at a premises near the bridge just before 14:00. The force said they had detained a man. London Ambulance Service has declared a 'major incident'. The BBC's John McManus, at the scene, said he had seen a group of men in a fight on the bridge. Police then arrived and shots were fired, he said. London Bridge station was currently closed and no trains would be stopping there. Police have advised people near the scene to follow directions from officers on the ground.

I put my phone in my pocket. Cian's now talking to a younger guy with a thick South London accent. He says he works in the kitchen in a restaurant near to where the attack took place.

'We came out of the restaurant to see what's going on and this cop is just screaming, like: "Run! People with knives! Run! Run! Run!"'

He tells us he did run, but then saw a bus to shelter in, and was on the upper deck when he saw the attacker on the bridge.

'He was wearing a suicide belt. There was cops around him. Then they just started firing at him. I don't know how many times. They hit him in the head.'

Because of the alarming details, I remember him telling the story clearly, but that's not exactly what happened according to the inquest held much later. The inquest jury heard that six firearms officers confronted the man who'd told them he had a suicide belt.

It turned out to be a fake. With no way to know that, the police were cleared to take him down, to carry out 'a critical shot'. The police testified they opened fire as soon as it was safe to do so. The jury heard twenty shots were fired and twelve hit the man in the chest and abdomen. Jurors concluded he was lawfully killed.

The incident is known now as the Fishmongers' Hall attack. Fishmongers' Hall is where the attack began, on the north side of London Bridge. Borough Market is on the south side.

The attacker was one of the participants in an event marking the five-year anniversary of a prisoner education scheme. In the midst of the event, he went to the toilet and prepared his attack. He emerged with a pair of knives and the fake suicide belt.

He stabbed to death two much-loved young people who had worked with prisoners involved in the scheme, Saskia Jones and Jack Merritt.

What happened afterwards led to the awarding of the final Queen's Gallantry Medals from Queen Elizabeth II. The medals were awarded to four men who put their lives at risk to stop the attacker. They used what they could: a ceremonial pike, a narwhal tusk and a fire extinguisher, all items they found at Fishmongers' Hall, where the meeting had taken place.

They fought the man and wouldn't back down, both inside, then following him outside as he fled. On London Bridge, they corralled him with their weapons until the police arrived. One of them told the BBC that the attacker had told him he was going to kill them all, to blow them all up with his explosives belt. The man held his ground anyway and answered back, 'Blow it then and get on with it.' Instead of running to save himself, he aimed the fire extinguisher at the attacker and doused him, making it hard for him to see.

I read a lot about Saskia and Jack in the days and weeks following. To lose such vibrant young people implicated in work in the community was absolutely gutting, and felt so cruel. Their families were devastated. Imagine how many more lives might have ended if it weren't for the bravery of the men who stood up against the attacker.

It all set people running, terrified, south across the bridge and into Borough Market. So many people were calling police to report a commotion there that police shut down Borough Market out of an abundance of caution. No doubt, they were also thinking of what had happened two years earlier and weren't sure how many attackers there were and whether other places would be hit. Borough Market was a likely target.

That's what happened, but it's a story that only became clear months after the fact. For us, the people who work at

Borough Market, we had no idea at the time what had really happened, except that people had been killed, and the police shot the attacker dead. We gathered in groups, telling our stories.

We end up down Ayres Street and converge on the Rose and Crown pub, a classic English response to a crisis. Traders walk in and out of the pub and gradually, we all end up with a pint of beer in our hands. I have no idea who paid. I notice a lot more smokers than I thought there were.

Outside the pub, I give Cian a big hug.

'I can't think of anyone I'd rather be holed up in a cheese fridge with while under attack,' I say to Cian.

'I feel the same, mate,' he says.

We snap a pic of us still in our aprons, pints in hand, and I post it on to the group chat. 'We are happy to see you!' comes an immediate response. Cheesemonger Emma sends through two hearts. Cheesemonger Molly kicks it up a level and sends two sparkling hearts. Cheesemonger Anne writes, 'Takes more than a terrorist attack to stop a cheesemonger!'

Then, Cheesemonger Manager Laurence adds: 'Aprons on. Even in emergencies. That's the spirit.'

Cian taps out a response: 'Aprons so we look legit.'

Cheesemonger Nuala: 'Glad you're ok guys.'

Phil from the Italian cheese and ham stall is with us. His people are all safe, he says, but it was a hairy few minutes. They have a place to hide above their stall but to get to it you have to pull a set of stairs down from the ceiling.

Traders are now wondering when they can return, now that the danger is over. When we last left the area, the police were extending the cordon, pushing us back. I got so many different signals from them, from 'watch the news' to check back every fifteen minutes. It seems clear nothing is going to move fast.

My phone is running low on battery and I am beginning to feel a penetrating cold. I say to Cian that I'm going to go home and warm up and I ask whether he wants to join me.

'Nah, I reckon this is as close we'll get to this year's Borough Market Traders Christmas Social.' I laugh. I leave him headed back inside the Rose and Crown to order another pint.

'Phil, what are we going to do about the stalls?'

'Tell you what,' he says, 'go home and warm up. I'll add you to the Borough Market Traders' group chat and as soon as we get the green light, I'll post something and you can come back.'

'Cheers, Phil.' Then I give big Phil a bear hug – I have to stand on my tiptoes because he's so tall. It seems only slightly to have taken him aback.

'Ah, thanks,' he says.

'Thank you,' I answer, and I head down the street to the flat, take off my boots and make a cup of tea.

Tom sends me through a message:

```
Jon says to stay warm but close by. The
concern is vermin (mice and rats), so if
they let us in before the shift is due to
end at 7, you are close by to close the
stall as quickly and efficiently as possi-
ble.
```

I sit down to wait it out. My journalist's side kicks in then and I tweet about what happened along with a photo of the traders outside the pub. BBC Radio 5 Live gets in touch as a result and I agree to an interview. In it, the presenter asks me this question:

'Does this make you feel different about working at Borough Market?'

I answer without hesitation:

'Yes, it does. I was proud of working at Borough Market before, I am now one hundred times more proud. I always knew my fellow traders were awesome but watching them in action in uncontrolled circumstances, how calm they were and how compassionate, I am blown away. And I can't wait to put my apron on and be there tomorrow. And I say, if people are trying to scare us, fuck them! Sorry. Excuse my language.'

Cian's dad hears the interview and sends him a message: 'Not sure whether Mike Finnerty should get a theatre award for his dramatic retelling of your story on 5 Live or a marketing award for promoting your company and Borough Market!'

Cian listens once 5 Live posts it online. He texts me.

```
Cian: Legend - just listened to it.
Me: Notice you come off the hero in my
interview.
```

I had told the presenter about Cian suggesting we hide in the fridge, making sure the customers were safe and about his comment, 'It's a cheese shop. We have a lot of knives.'

```
Cian: Dude u r my hero. But actually I
come across as a bit stab ya.
Me: Thanks for your awesomeness today.
Cian: Shit man. Thanks so much.
```

After the sun goes down, traders are still cordoned off from the market. There's a lot of frustration on the group chat. They want to get back to their stalls, but the police keep saying no. Then the mood changes and there's a sense the police are about to open things up again in a controlled way.

I get myself dressed to go back and I send a message on our chat with an update to say I'm on it. I'll take care of the close because I am close by.

A short time later, I am back on Park Street. It's just south of the market and around the corner, an Old London streetscape that has appeared in a lot of period films and television. The traders are bunched up next to the police cordon. We are told to get into three separate queues and to stand near people who work in the same or an adjacent stall.

I see Barbara and Allan at the top of the queue, so I gesture to them and they wave me over.

'Michael,' says Barbara. 'How are you? It's about time they let us back in. Can you believe this?'

The police are allowing the traders in, but in groups of six only, under escort and constant supervision. Just then, I hear my name being shouted out from across the road.

'Michael!' I see someone waving. It's Owner Jon.

It surprises me so much to see him. I am only now getting to know and understand him. He wasn't in the chat all day, relaying messages only through Tom. I honestly didn't think he was overly concerned, but he was there all along just at a remove and here he is, in person.

Seeing him, I get emotional again. I'm a grown man and I've held a lot of responsibility in a lot of tough situations, not least during live radio shows when things went wrong. Hell, I was in New York City for the BBC in the days following the September 11th attacks. I saw firefighters and police coming back covered in soot and dirt from Ground Zero. A sense of pride in Jon and all of us overwhelms me. In the end, we all want to be led well, with courage, competence and compassion. For me, in that moment, he embodies all those things.

He makes his way over to us through the crowd.

'Jon! You're here! That's so cool.'

'It's good to see you,' he says. 'Are you okay? What a fucking day, mate.'

'I'm okay. I mean, I reckon I'm running on adrenaline now. I'm so relieved everyone at the market's okay.'

'Thank you for coming back.' As Jon says thanks, the police wave us through. Jon takes the lead, explains who we are, and we are led over to the stall.

Jon asks the cop, 'All officers okay?'

'Yes, thanks.'

Right thing to ask, I think. He continues with the police officer, 'Thank you for doing this.' And with a smile: 'Do we get our own officer as a guard while we close?'

'A sergeant!' he says.

Jon explains it's going to take a while and the sergeant signals that it will take the time it takes.

There have been a few times when witnesses have been present to see what takes place at closing and I've felt proud of pulling off the transformation that we do, but no time more so than now. I swing into action and start moving the big wheels of cheese into the cupboards. Jon is assessing the softs and putting them away carefully. We move, fast but methodical.

It is so much work. After about half an hour, the police sergeant looks at us, sticks out his lower lip and nods his head. 'You do this every day?'

Jon: 'Yep.'

At that point, the first bucket of Topax hasn't even been prepped. When we get into the home stretch, things going well, Jon turns to me and says, 'Michael, thanks again for doing this.'

I look up from the sink and meet his eyes. 'It's my job.'

Days later, he'll joke in a self-deprecating way about stepping forward out of nowhere near the end of the drama to be present for the close. He says, 'Couldn't miss getting in on the hero shift.'

At the end of that surreal day in November, I feel truly part of our cheesemonger family in a way I haven't up until then. Since I started as a trainee, what I've wanted above all is to do the job well and to be a valued member of our team, but I hadn't arrived there.

That night, I feel a bond to every one of them and especially to Cian and Jon. What Laurence texted about our aprons, what Cian answered – 'Aprons on / Aprons so we look legit' – really touched me. Something changed that day, deep inside. Since then, I look at my cheesemonger's apron like it belongs on me.

Coulommiers

'Tel fromage que vous nommiez / Jurant sur les saintes Images / Que sur tous les meilleurs fromages / Prévaut celui de Coulommiers.'

– Raoul Ponchon, French poet, chronicler, food writer, 1848–1937. A poet's way of saying 'Coulommiers is the best', direct translation: 'Whichever cheese you name, swearing on the Holy Images, Coulommiers prevails over all the best cheeses.'

Origin: Beloved by workers and nobles alike, Coulommiers originated from the same region as Brie. In fact, it's a close relative to Brie, smaller in diameter, meaning easier to transport and less breakable. It rose to prominence at the Exposition Universelle in Paris, 1878.

Presentation: 13cm across, about 350g, Coulommiers lovers will buy a whole wheel, but it's most often sold in quarters and halves. It's a bloomy rind cheese, the same family as Brie and Camembert. They start out life firm, with a bit of chalk at the heart of the paste, but as they ripen from the outside in, they get oozier and become one of the absolute classic runny, French raw cow's milk cheeses. When ripe, they're strong. You should be able to tell how ripe they are just by looking.

How to serve: A delight on a cheeseboard, but make room for the rivers of cheese that will flow from it, especially in warmer temperatures. You'll want plenty of crusty bread to mop it up. I find it can have a slightly garlicky taste, incredibly moreish. In fact, I've made a whole meal of it. Try it with toasted raisin or fig bread. Blanc de Blancs Champagne or a crisp Chablis make fine pairings, as does a pint of bitter or a brown beer.

Fun fact: Some folks thought it helped cure the plague, so it was regularly given to those who came down with it.

22
The Morning After

ON SATURDAYS, OUR BIGGEST day for sales, we come in to work early, around 7 a.m. Before the real rush begins around 9.30 a.m. we get a short break. I pop out, apron on, and do a quick tour of stalls I like around the market.

On the day after the Fishmongers' Hall attack, I head over to the café at the heart of Borough Market. It's located in a container. The proprietor has a grill fired up with rashers of bacon and a fry-pan full of bubble and squeak. I didn't eat much last night and I am starving.

Maria's a large presence in the market, physically and spiritually, as famously irascible as she is adored. 'Hello, young man! What can I get you?' She has just recently started calling me 'young man', which I've chosen to take as a compliment.

'Egg and bacon roll, please, Maria. Cuppa tea, as well, please.'

'Egg and bacon roll!' Maria shouts, as she moves over to the grill, takes an egg with one hand, cracks it open on to the heat and shifts a couple of rashers into place. 'Coming right up, young man.'

Bernie, short for Bernadette, is making my cuppa and taking money today. 'Michael, how did youse over at the cheese stall handle all the excitement yesterday?'

'Shaking in our boots in the cheese fridge. Were you on?'

'Nah, I wasn't here. Everyone's okay though. Shaken up a bit, mind you. Cheese fridge! That's a good one.' She lets out a big, hacking laugh, then coughs.

Then she lowers her voice and leans into me. 'These attacks are such bollocks, can you believe it? I don't expect it'll be busy today.'

'I was listening to the radio this morning. People saying folks should make a point of coming by to support us. I guess we'll see.' I give her four pound coins, grab the roll and take my leave.

'You take care, now, and will you say hi to Fionnuala?'

'She's not on today, Bernie, but I will when I see her. Thanks.'

Next stop is towards the back of the other side of Borough Market, across Bedale Street, a stall that does Baltic foods, notably poppy buns. Poppy baking reminds me of my Czech granny who used to make deep-fried buns filled with poppy, like a doughnut. There's not a taste in the world that connects me more to home and family. Eating one provides me with a shot of happiness, even a sense of security. It's like I'm eight years old again in Granny's warm kitchen on the farm in Saskatchewan. Poppy pastries are hard to find.

The stall is being run by two young women I don't recognise today and just as I come up and start to order, Hector darts in and says, very loudly, 'Good Morning, Lesbians! How are we today?'

'Can I have a poppy rose, please?' I ask. That's what they call it. It's a poppy bun but baked to resemble a rose from which you pull poppy-coated pieces, not the same as what Granny used to make but it's similar.

'Sure can,' one of the young women looks at me and then rolls her eyes with mock exasperation at Hector. 'This is how he is.'

Hector says, 'What! Don't be shy. Oh hi, Michael!' Hector works at the market as well and is dating a dashing young Italian bloke who works next door to us. Hector hangs around as they close sometimes. He's something of a doting boyfriend. This is the first time he has ever said hello to me. 'I heard you and Cian hid in the fridge yesterday?'

'Yeah, with some customers. All's well that ends well, I guess. For us, anyway,' I realise immediately it's a stupid thing to say.

'Fucking panic, though, wasn't it? Pandemonium.'

'How much do I owe you for the poppy?'

'It's on the house today, my love.'

'I have to run back, short break – stay warm, everyone. See ya, Hector.'

As I get near our cheese stall, I make a brief stop to chat with Barbara and Allan. We've already said the quickest of hellos as we were raising the shutters.

'Now what have you got there, Michael?' asks Barbara, pointing to my two packages.

'Poppy pastry left hand – reminds me of my granny. Bacon and egg roll right hand.'

'Comfort food, is it?' asks Allan, teasing slightly. 'After yesterday.'

'You're not wrong there. How are you two feeling this morning?'

'Oh, we'll be all right,' says Allan. 'It'll scare away the crowds today, you'll see.'

'How are the nerves, Barbara?'

'We'll be fine, Michael. But what a day!' She turns very serious now. 'Did you read about those two young people killed on the other side of the bridge? Such lovely souls. Breaks my heart, it does.' She looks right in my eyes, 'This has got to stop, you know.'

'I know. I feel like I've lived a lot of emotions in the past eighteen hours. There's some anger. Best not to dwell too much on it.'

'Mmm-hmmm,' she nods her head. 'Now, I won't keep you from your breakfast. Go eat.'

It's Tom and Daisy for today's shift. I arrived before Daisy. Tom took me aside first thing, 'Listen, thanks again for yesterday and great job. Really.'

'I feel like we were lucky all the violence stayed on the other side of the bridge.' He nodded but didn't comment, looking serious. I went on: 'I was reading about the victims this morning, two young lives ended like that,' I snapped my fingers. 'People who were making a difference, and for what?'

There was a pause then, like he was searching for his words. Tom looked to be clearly moved. 'I feel so bad I wasn't here with you guys. I wanted to apologise to you. I'm sorry, Michael.'

'You what? No way, Tom. Don't be crazy. Things happen as they happen, and you weren't here. It's nothing you did or didn't do. In fact, you were a huge help calling security for us and letting us know what was going on. We should have thought to do that, but we didn't. Total lifesaver. I should be thanking you.'

'I felt useless sitting at The Arch. I wished I hadn't left you guys. I was kicking myself. Then I wanted to come over but everyone said that was a bad idea.'

'Definitely a bad idea but I appreciate the sentiment. Very much.'

'Listen, are you gonna be okay, today?'

'I think so. Honestly, there's no way I wouldn't have come. I wouldn't miss this shift for the world. They are not going to scare us from living and working.'

'I hear you, but just tell me if you need a break at any time today, okay? We'll sort it out.'

'Okay, I will.' I didn't sleep well. I am running on a full tank of determination instead.

There is a German lady who comes regularly to the stall. She's in her sixties, stern but scrupulously pleasant, white hair with wire-rim specs. She usually buys a slice of one of the Alpine cheeses, Comté normally, and one of the bloomy rind cheeses like Brie or Coulommiers. Occasionally, she'll take a goat's cheese depending on the selection.

I was discussing bread with her the other day. Cheesemonger Fionnuala was working with me.

'Where can you get good bread around here these days?' she asked.

'Do you want my honest view on that?' I responded to her question with another question.

'I wouldn't ask otherwise.'

'I don't rate any of the places around here. No one makes a decent baguette. Lots of sourdough, mind you. And obviously nothing as good as German bread.'

'Ach!' she said. 'There's only one place in London to get good German bread.'

'Oh? Where's that?'

'In my kitchen. I bake it.'

'Do you? That's so cool. It can't be easy, either.'

'It's like anything, once you get the hang of it.'

'Well, if you ever want to bring any by the cheese stall, I'd love to try it.'

As soon as it came out of my mouth, I thought that I'd possibly overstepped. Not a first for me! Radio presenter's privilege at play – I don't know her well at all.

She'd looked confused when I'd said it, then asked: 'Say again?'

Sheepishly this time, I repeated, 'I said if you're ever bringing around samples, I'm keen.'

'Oh, I see.'

Cheesemonger Nuala arched an eyebrow and then after she left said, 'That was a Teutonic response to your invitation to share some bread if ever I heard one.'

After my breakfast, stationed at the front to serve again, I notice the same German woman across the market, walking towards the stall. She is with a man this time.

'Good morning!' I give her a big smile. 'Nice to see you.'

'Nice to see you! We heard about what happened yesterday. How's everyone doing?'

'Oh, we're doing okay today. It was tense yesterday. We hid in the fridge until things calmed down.'

'Brilliant idea. Good for you. We weren't planning on coming to Borough this morning, but after yesterday, we made a point of it and here we are. What's good this morning?'

'Well, we appreciate the custom. I know you like the Coulommiers and it's lovely and gooey this morning, not terribly strong.'

'I'll have a half, please, and tell me about the goats.'

'I might go for the Sainte-Maure today. They're behaving.'

'Excellent, a whole Sainte-Maure. And this is for you.'

She hands a bag to me across the counter. It's a loaf of her bread.

'What? This is so kind of you! Thank you very much.'

'It's Vollkornbrot. Lovely with the butter you sell. In fact, I'll take some of your salted butter as well, please.'

I prepare her order and thank her once again.

Cheesemonger Daisy looks over, 'That was nice of her. I think you've won her over.'

'I don't know what to say about that, Daisy. It's so sweet and so unexpected.' Her gesture of solidarity is so moving it is choking me up a bit.

'Are you okay, Michael?'

'Better than okay, thanks. It's just ... people can surprise you.'

'Pleasant surprises are more than welcome today,' declares Daisy.

That Saturday, we get a number of customers coming by to express their support. Our numbers are down considerably, though.

In the afternoon, Phil comes over to talk to Tom about it. 'Expected as much,' he says. 'It'll take a couple of weeks before things get back to normal.'

'Do you reckon?' asks Tom.

'It's not as bad as two years ago, not by a mile, but this is the last thing we needed.'

The good news for traders is that with time and as more and more people begin to learn the details of the Fishmongers' Hall attack, the association with Borough Market fades. After all, the drama unfolded on the north bank of River Thames. Borough Market had not been targeted. Even though the fear we lived that day was real, some of it was an echo of what had happened two years earlier. Footfall and sales rebound in time for the holidays, to the relief of everyone.

There's a moment on Saturdays when things sour a bit at the market. You can pinpoint it to within about fifteen minutes, around 3.15 p.m. Those who come for provisions arrive earlier in the day. Cheesemonger Fionnuala has labelled this moment with the single word 'aquarium', because the customers just swim on by. They're passing through the market after lunch or on their way to the pub.

'Feels like things have just gone aquarium,' she'll say.

People begin to drink and that's a big part of it. A thing that never fails to impress me is how loud people can be in Britain once they've a few pints down them. There's a joke about Canadians that goes like this: How do you get twenty drunken, rowdy Canadians out of the swimming pool? Answer: 'Excuse me, could you please get out of the swimming pool?'

That's not the vibe in Central London and over the next few weeks after the attack, it becomes a problem for me. Lads coming out of the pub shouting, arguing, making sudden noises. I flinch uncontrollably. In an instant, it takes me back to that Friday afternoon. I wonder if maybe something's wrong, or worse, whether we need to hide again.

One late Saturday afternoon, there is a lot of shouting going on as I am preparing an order for a customer. At first, I am just startled. Then I start to zone out as I am cutting down some Gruyère. Time slows. I am thinking to myself, 'What the hell is wrong with these guys?' I maybe even say it out loud. I don't know how much time passes.

'Michael, are you all right?' Cheesemonger Nuala asks.

I turn to her and she looks at my face and says, 'Yeah, okay. I'm going to take this order over for you. You go to the back and put the kettle on.'

I put my knife down and walk to the back.

Nuala comes back later and has a few sips of tea. I made two cups, as you do.

'It's perfectly normal to be jumpy, you know. I don't know what the hell's wrong with people. Such arses. You know, if it'd been me on that day, I don't like to think.'

Two weeks later, on another Friday, a number of people who were at the stall during the Fishmongers' Hall attack return to say hello, including Terry and Margaret who hid in the fridge with us. I'm frustrated, though, because Cian's not there when they drop by and I want him to see them, too. Margaret says that after the drama they went off to do some travelling in Britain and have just arrived back in London. It was a relief to get out into the countryside. They fill me in on some of their travelling stories and, as luck would have it, himself shows up just in time. Cian's as thrilled as I am to renew our acquaintance. There are big hugs, we take a photo in front of the fridge, exchange contact details, and they buy a lot of cheese, including a Mont d'Or, a piece of Gruyère and some Ossau Iraty. I still hear from them regularly.

A young couple returns to us on the same day as well, but they have to remind me that they were the ones I was serving when everything kicked off. As they recall it, it suddenly makes sense – yes, that's what happened! – but I could never have picked them out of a crowd. They were the ones to whom I was tasting out that runny piece of Coulommiers. They explain that the crowds of people running by made them decide in an instant to leave the market. It was the right thing to do. They tell me they are keen to finish their cheese purchase. Coming back helps them to put it all behind them, they say. Me, too. I thank them and give them the royal treatment along with a small discount.

Things get better, gradually. My jumpiness subsides. Even today, though, sudden shouting takes me back to that surreal Friday afternoon.

Vacherin Mont d'Or

Origin: Served at the dinner table of King Louis XV, Mont d'Or dates back to the eighteenth century in official ledgers, but it's probably much older than that. Nowadays it is protected by an AOC and an AOP in both Switzerland and France, with guidelines that differ slightly but significantly. When cows which had returned from Alpine pastures started giving less milk than required for Comté and Gruyère production, farmers used it to make Vacherin instead. To this date, it's still made only seasonally, from mid-August to mid- or end March.

Presentation: Vacherin Mont d'Or is produced in wheels that are then packaged in wooden boxes. Around the rind of each cheese, a strap of spruce bark is attached. The cheese is also matured at least 21 days on spruce boards, so it has both the taste and aroma of the forest and the farm. In those first weeks, the rind is given a saline wash daily, which gives it a deep beige hue bordering on pink or ochre. If you've only ever eaten it straight out of the box, take one out to admire.

How to serve: For many, Vacherin Mont d'Or is synonymous
with Christmas, but there's no reason to wait until then. They
begin to arrive in October. The key to enjoying one is to figure
out how you like them: milder, stronger, or somewhere in
between. This is a cheese that can have a big, forward taste
and aroma if you get one that's more mature (some might say
stinky!) or be positively gentle for a less mature wheel. If you
flat out say you don't like it, then I would wonder if you'd had
the wrong batch for your tastes. The next decision is whether
to eat it with a spoon right out of the box, slice it in half and
put it on a cheeseboard, or put the whole box in the oven and
warm it through (don't cook it – it just needs warming for
about 20 minutes, no hotter than 150°C). If it's going in the
oven, you may choose to score the top and add a splash of
white wine and garlic. You could also go for honey and thyme
or be creative. Then dip chunks of bread into the oozing
paste, or French cornichons, or pickled onions, or a slice of
saucisson. They are wonderful for sharing and so festive, an
absolute treat. For wine pairings, think mountain reds or
whites, or go with an artisanal beer of your choice.

Fun fact: Each box is stamped with its date of production,
allowing mongers to advise customers on how far along they
are. As the season continues, you end up having a few batches
on hand at any given time, which can become tricky. In
constructing a Vacherin tower, it's important not to have all of
one batch at the base of a tower in case that's the one a
customer has his or her heart set on, otherwise you get into a
Jenga game scenario.

23
A Clean Slate

EVERY EVENING AT THE market, we take the black slates upon which we displayed the day's wares and we scrub them. They are gooey and sticky from an entire day's contact with the cheeses. Our super-strong detergent loosens fats and proteins from surfaces. Then the slates get a rinse in hot water. When they come out again in the morning, they are gleaming.

The slates can be arranged as you like on the day. Some are sat atop wooden props, giving the display height and depth. It's a blank canvas, though of course, the medium you paint with are the day's cheeses. There are big and small ones, softs and hards, cut wedges and individual packages, all in a variety of hues: blue, white, golden and ash grey, even moleskin and ochre.

The finished product should appear like a cornucopia, overflowing with abundance, a thing of beauty. Unveiling it is one of the most exciting moments of any day. I will admit to once giving a customer the evil eye for wanting to purchase the cheeses we had so lovingly just assembled – it was too soon. Okay, more than once. In fact, it is a running gag at the market that I don't like it when people disturb the display when it is looking just so. They ruin it.

You'd probably recognise the type of customer that bothers me most in this regard – handsy.

'Can I help you find something?' I ask, trying to keep the edge out of my voice as an early bird set of young parents reaches in to pick up a cheese.

'Just having a look, thanks,' they say.

'More like a touch and fondle,' says my inner voice. Out loud, I say: 'How about I give you a wee taste of something?'

I find the diversionary method works best. Now that they've got something to snack on, they're distracted from touching anything else. While they're otherwise occupied, I put anything they've disturbed back into its rightful place. I am doing this as nonchalantly as I can.

'Oh! That's delicious. We'll take one of those.' They move back towards the display to pick out a cheese, but I see them coming.

'That's okay. Here, I'll get you a nice fresh one, straight from the fridge in the back.'

They pay and they're gone.

In the trickle hour, early Saturday morning when there are just a few market early birds, I can usually manage to fend off most customers.

'Nice work, Mr Prickly,' comes the voice of Cheesemonger Fionnuala behind me.

'What do you mean? Oh, them. They didn't notice.'

'That you wanted to social distance them away from the display? No, not at all. Subtle.' She lets out a cackle.

When we're on our game, our cheese displays are the subject of posts on social media and people will comment out of the blue while passing by: 'I just want you to know that your display is gorgeous.' Or less formally, 'Look at all these beautiful cheeses! I'm gonna die!'

You can imagine how good this feels. Maybe for someone who has always had artistic flair, doing the display at the beginning of every shift could be dismissed as a routine artistic act like so many before it. For me, who suffered through years of ugly creation at school, or no creation at all – really a total absence of flair or talent – the displays matter deeply.

I remember during my training how Manager Tom would critique them and how inspired, and sometimes hurt, I would be.

To get some variety, some artistry into a soft cow's milk display, you need to cut the round, bloomy rind cheeses into quarters and halves; I'm talking here about the cheeses covered with blooming white mould such as Brie, Coulommiers and triple-cream Brillat-Savarin. Each piece needs to be wrapped tightly in cellophane – no granny's stockings.

'Do your best,' Manager Tom used to say, 'and let me know when you're done so I can review it.'

Tom has a few spectacular design tricks, like making a five-petalled flower out of Gour Noir, a medium-sized, ash rind goat cheese that looks like a leaf.

I just wasn't a person who could manage pretty. I got so discouraged. I tried to imitate Tom's simpler designs but they always seemed to come out looking like little building sites, or just mounds.

One day after three weeks of training, Tom walked over: 'Yeah, okay. Here's what you're doing wrong.'

My heart sank then because actually, I thought that what I did that morning was okay – I'd worked on the display for the better part of an hour.

'You need to think of little islands, each separate from the other, even if only by a little.' My ugly mounds had no borders, it seemed.

He started to rearrange my work. Each time I thought he might leave one set of cheeses the way I'd arranged them, he moved in and switched it around. Not even the boxes of Camembert made the cut.

'Here, these quarters can be placed almost like a cascade or a mini avalanche.'

Cascading avalanches. See? I never would have imagined that. 'Basically, I'm a clod.'

'Hang on a minute, it's good what you've done! The wrapping's getting better. We're into the finer points, now. I like these Munster pieces.' Looking at my crestfallen face, he left my Munster pieces exactly as I'd positioned them.

I took a breath and re-focused. Come on, man up. It'd only been a month. Anyway, Tom was right. I was getting faster, a bit cleaner in my folds. Plus, if he thought I was not a lost cause, then there had to be hope.

In time, I learned by stealing his tricks. I'm not proud. Then when he was away or someone new was starting, they'd be well impressed as I tried my hand, say, at a goat's-cheese Aztec pyramid.

Fast forward to late autumn, training near over, and I develop a reputation for the most outrageous Vacherin displays in the Market.

'Beautiful, Michael! Gorgeous!' Allan calls out in his East London vowels from his stall across the alley.

I have built an undulating block of Vacherin boxes modelled on the famous apartment building complex, la Grande Motte, in Montpelier in the South of France. Then one day we have a special on Camembert and the first of the new-season's Vacherin, so I compose a peaking, S-shape of each cheese which meets in the middle and crosses over.

Under an orange umbrella, at another cheese stall in the centre of the market, Jonny is looking over, staring at my display from his station, his eyes squinting. Then he comes out from behind the umbrella and saunters over in his apron with his blue eyes and twenty-four-hour stubble. Everyone swoons over Jonny. He is a part-time cheesemonger, part-time actor. Cheesemonger Simon, a colleague of his, says he played the back half of War Horse one season in the West End.

Jonny slows to a halt in front of our stall.

'What's this?' he asks, jutting out his chin in the direction of my Vacherin design.

Surprised, I take a beat before answering. 'Special on Camembert,' my voice quavers nervously, just enough to be noticeable. 'And the first of the Vacherin.'

'Well, well,' Jonny shakes his head and looks it up and down carefully. There's a long pause before he finally says, 'It looks fucking amazing.' Then he looks at me and flashes his big, West End smile.

Being an apprentice cheesemonger is full of rewards in the end. I am taking direction from a twenty-seven-year-old manager and the other cheesemongers, most of whom could be my children. It is pretty much a one-way street. I do not feel I have much to impart to them except my hard work, my gratitude and my sympathy for the patience they are showing waiting for me to skill up.

The way I see it now, the whole process is like a washing clean of sorts, like the slates at the end of the day. It requires buckets-full of humility. Funny thing, the more humility I display, the better I feel. I work hard and I am hard on myself, impatient to become a valued colleague. I always show up inspired and enthused. I latch on to any simple task I can perform well, like bleaching the slate crate, or even the morning perimeter sweep for mouse droppings. I am willing to do and do-over as necessary. I pull out all the stops to be the best cheesemonger I can.

How liberating it is to don the apron, free of all baggage, except those that appearances and accent confer. I feel like I am getting an opportunity fully to be the person that I want to be at work, someone who is keen to do things well, eager to learn, irritable never, interested, charming, funny, committed, never shirks duties even when I'd rather not do a thing. I am also rested and no longer deprived of sleep.

The first six months are such slightly unreal, precious months, months where I am never asked to take a leadership role except with myself. I do not want to have my decisions govern the way things are run.

It is only by working in these conditions that I fully come to understand the weight of leadership, especially outsized leadership. In other words, I am able to size up the true burdens I've been working under for years only once I am working at a job where I am shorn entirely of them.

One of my happiest and most fulfilling days, even more so in retrospect, is at my performance review where I sit down with Owner Jon and Manager Tom and they tell me how they think things are going. They have solicited 360-degree feedback, having asked all the different people I work with to make comments.

What a joy to hear in words written on a page by others, yourself being described exactly as you would wish. It feels like an out-of-body experience. One of the comments comes from Cheesemonger Laurence who hired me, 'What can I say about Lovely Michael?' 'Me?' I think to myself. He goes on to say pretty much everything I would ever hope he'd say about me. I am in disbelief. The power of that affirmation isn't just that other people have noticed what I am trying to do, what I have accomplished, and verbalised it, it is that I have created it entirely by myself, through my efforts, and without input from 'CBC's Mike Finnerty'.

'There you have it, Michael,' says Jon. 'Probation over. Well done. And with it, we'll give you a pay rise retroactive to the beginning of the month. Oh, and thank you. Really great job.'

I am a cheesemonger.

To get hired by Cheese HQ, I have made no reference to my media reputation. It is satisfying and empowering that they hired only what they saw and what I demonstrated. They hired someone called 'Michael', not affiliated with the BBC, the CBC, or the *Guardian*, and at age fifty-four to boot.

In many ways, that review is the culmination of my sabbatical. It is one of the most fulfilling days of my life. Thinking back to it still suffuses me with happiness.

I have found my own answer to the dilemma my CBC colleague Sheila raised all those years ago. Yes, radio show presenters can do other things.

Maréchal

'C'était un peu hérétique.'

– Jean-Michel Rapin, cheesemaker, inventor of Le Maréchal,
speaking about the risk he took when he first developed the
cheese: rubbing the rind with hay and flax. The rind represents
the pride of the cheesemaker, he says, and covering it over was
considered a heresy. Then, as now, he felt he needed to be
daring to set his cheese apart from other regional offerings.

Origin: In 1994, the Rapin family of cheesemakers in the Vaud
region of Switzerland decided to shift from Gruyère
production to a new cheese, their own creation. They settled
on a cooked-curd cheese (like Gruyère) but in a smaller
wheel. The other bold move was the use of herbs, notably flax,

which are included in the feed of the cattle and rubbed into the rind, giving the paste a distinctive flavour, almost sage-like.

Presentation: A wheel of Maréchal is about 30cm in diameter and can vary in height, though they are at least 8cm high. The rind is a deep chestnut to dark brown colour, herbaceous, flecked with the different herbs and grasses that are rubbed into it. The paste is typical of a cooked curd, Alpine cheese, off-white to golden, though the wheels don't tend to be as aged, usually 12 months or less.

How to serve: If you can't be eating it in the Swiss mountains on a picnic blanket, Maréchal is a handsome focal point to a cheeseboard. It is intensely moreish just on its own, and reminds me of the delights of a roast chicken dinner with its notes of sage and flax. Try it with fresh-baked bread, some butter and a slice of cooked or cured ham. Serving it with olives or dried fruits works well. It's wonderful in fondue, though pricey. For recipes, think soufflés, croquettes, polenta, melted over cooked endives with ham, or a decadent Alpine mac and cheese.

Fun fact: The name of the cheese is a reference not to a military man, but to a *maréchal ferrant*, a blacksmith, Émile Rapin, the great-grandfather of Jean-Michel who first conceived of the cheese. Jean-Michel says he wanted his cheese to embody the values of Émile, a hard-working, generous man who cared deeply about his trade.

24
Michael, What Have You Done?

ONE THING THAT CHANGES at our Borough Market stall – we add a sign that reads, 'Cheesemonger's Choice'. On it, we give some daily suggestions for cheeses people might like based on what we have in stock and where the cheeses are in their lives. The calculus involved in coming up with that list is tricky.

There is always a cheese that is Best in Show on the day compared to the others. When a cheese is really popping, it packs an experiential wallop that will leave you looking for something to hold on to. These are cheeses that will redefine what you think you know.

One day, a batch of Saint-Félicien comes in that is beyond my imagination. This is a double-cream French cow's milk cheese which we sell in a round barquette, and on this particular day they are plump and cloud-like in texture, rich with a hint of enticing funk, oozing cream but just slightly, like an elixir. When you put some in your mouth it feels as though you are lifting off the ground. This is a cheese you cannot eat with your eyes open.

We have plenty, or so it seems at the time, and I am so overcome by it, I have an urge to share it with others so that I can see them have a similar reaction. I'll never forget two young servicemen from somewhere in the centre of the US who had never had artisan cheese before. I say to them, 'I'll give you some cheese to try but I warn you, it's going to be intense.'

They take it and put it in their mouths, then their eyes roll heavenward before they close their eyelids altogether. Their world stops turning. After a few hushed moments, one of them says slowly and simply: 'I ain't never tasted anything like that before.'

Cheesemonger Daisy looks at me after they leave, 'Oh my God, that was sexy!'

When I had my episode with the narcotic-grade batch of 1924, previously discussed, it was not just a personal challenge, it presented the company with a problem. People had been coming to put together their Christmas cheeseboards with a set idea of what they wanted, until I would say to them, usually with my mouth full, 'You have to try this cheese.' At the end of the day, Manager Tom came to collect some of our 1924 to send to another location. He had promised ten boxes of it, but there were only three left.

'Michael,' Tom said. 'What have you done?'

Owner Jon has had to explain the problem with this method of selling cheese several times to me until it has sunk in. It may be the hardest lesson in all the cheese universe. It helps for me to imagine a cheese shop in Paris. I have had several people recount their frustration and joy with certain *fromage-ries* where you can't get the really good stuff unless you have a relationship with the owner or the cheesemongers.

Let me explain the problem as clearly as I can: if you get carried away with one cheese that is top of its game and firing intense flavours to the point where it is felling cheesemongers and customers alike, what about all the other cheeses? What is happening to them? They are getting pushed to the side, sitting unsold, often becoming less than in every way, and crucially, less attractive to the buying public as time goes by. That is no way to get through your stock.

Back to this outstanding cheese, the precious commodity which is now worth more than the price you are selling it at, except you can't raise the price. So how do you decide who gets it? Who deserves to have it? Do you give it to a passing tourist from Kansas who will never set foot in the cheese stall again? No, it is not enough to derive pleasure from knocking a stranger's socks off. You have to be strategic.

These ultimate cheeses, the supreme batches, must go to people who are top-tier customers, who are regulars, who will carry your business in leaner times, people to whom you owe a debt, close family members (not your estranged cousin), spouses and/or lovers, food reviewers, Nigella Lawson. You get the picture. These are not foodstuffs to be trifled with.

As the boss went on to explain, you simply don't have the luxury of selling only the most excellent of cheeses, only the Number Ones. There just aren't enough – this is artisan cheese. If you did that, their finite supply would quickly be depleted and you would be the cheese shop that tends only to have lesser cheeses to offer.

At the other end of the spectrum, there is a whole category of cheeses that have certain flaws, that are not at their best but that someone will enjoy either because they don't see the flaw in the same way you do or they're happy to enjoy a lesser cheese if the price comes down.

For instance, a wind-burnt or slightly dried Cheddar might be something you think best to toss out. Okay maybe, but you could give a particularly delicious Cheddar that is somewhat dry as an extra to a client and explain the situation. A slightly dry Cheddar to someone you know loves to melt cheese on a jacket potato or a toasted slice of bread? That's a fine gift and will make someone happy. I will often stop colleagues throwing Raclette trimmings away, 'Hang on a minute! I'll take that.' It can be the basis of a meal, melted on morning toast or in a cheese sauce. I love trimmings partly because they allow you to step outside of convention.

Around Christmas time, we get bushels of Vacherin and we sell through most of them. However, we are often left with some that become very mature. At a certain point, a Vacherin will become so ripe as to make you wince slightly just from the smell. Some newer cheesemongers will say, 'No one will eat this. It's too ripe – we need to throw it out.'

I remember once throwing out what I thought was a rancid banana at my brother-in-law's house only to be upbraided for having thrown out a precious foodstuff that was apparently maturing to just the right state. With ripe Vacherin, cut them up into oozing slices, wrap them as best you can, put them on display and watch people flock to them and snap them up. This was Cheesemonger Nuala's strategy one Saturday, and it worked. I couldn't believe my eyes.

There is a whole breed of cheese aficionado who is looking for ripe, powerfully strong cheeses. Many times I have said about a cheese that others want to write off, 'Leave that cheese with me,' and within the hour I have made someone's day.

So the hard truth to buying cheese is that you might not get the truly great cheeses unless you have earned them and you definitely will not get them if you don't ask, 'What's exceptionally good right now?' If you make a point of asking that, it's hard for an honest cheesemonger not to give up the goods. Being a knowledgeable and trusted customer has benefits.

Fourme d'Ambert

'Dieu est avec les gros bataillons, surtout quand ses soldats ont un morceau de Fourme d'Ambert dans leur gibecière!'

– Henri de la Tour d'Auvergne, maréchal de France (1611–75), declaring that 'God is with the big battalions, especially when his soldiers have a piece of Fourme d'Ambert in their satchel!'

Origin: The agreed-upon history of La Fourme d'Ambert dates to the eighth century, but *fourmes* were said to be used by Druids in the age of the Gauls, long before. A *fourme* is essentially the mould that gives a cheese its shape, in this case a cylinder. This is a cheese that is emblematic of the Auvergne, in the centre of France. The mould for this blue cheese, *la fourme*, comes from the village of Ambert, thus the name Fourme d'Ambert. It was produced by farmers in the area around the Haut-Forez and used as a currency to rent farmhouses. Already in 1900, 200 tonnes were being produced. Now that it has both an AOP and an AOC, production is standardised and it's become a favourite French blue.

Presentation: The form of a Fourme d'Ambert is 11cm in diameter and about 22cm high (they can compress somewhat). They usually weigh about 1.5kg. The cheeses come wrapped in foil. Once opened, the rind ranges from tacky to gooey, with a mottled blue-grey-pink hue. Cutting it in half or on an angle reveals the creamy white paste, blue moulds and often enough, splashes of pink.

How to serve: Insanely moreish, Fourme d'Ambert on a piece of
crusty bread is all you need. Skip the bread, even. It will work
well in sauces (it's a great melter – try it as a raclette option).
In sandwiches and baking, it's a natural. A quick internet
search will yield tantalising recipes for breads and pastries.
For salads, the challenge is that it's less a crumbly blue, and
instead is known as one of the creamiest of all French blue
cheeses. It's a cow's milk blue, and pairs nicely with honey
and nuts. For wines, try round, fruity or floral whites. Go
sweeter with Sauternes, a cider, or an iced cider.

Fun fact: It's hard for a monger not to love Fourme d'Ambert
because when you taste it out to blue cheese lovers who've
never had it before, you get such a wave of love in return.
However, cutting up and wrapping a cold and gooey wheel at
-3°C on a January morning at Borough Market is an exercise
in mind over matter.

25

Christmas Eve

O N CHRISTMAS EVE IN the year I become a cheesemonger, I arrive along with the full second wave of mongers at 7.30 in the morning. There is a sense of us giving one last heave-ho. It's been a long, long week and we sold A LOT of cheese.

Owner Jon and Cheesemonger Fionnuala have the tables in place and much of the cheese is out. Even at 8 a.m., people are approaching, looking to get their Christmas cheeses. There are some hearty customers who have been several times since things got busy. 'I was here yesterday but it was so delicious that I've decided to come back and buy some more.' That feels good.

Christmas Eve is a tough day for me and I need to focus on the business at hand to keep it together. This is it, my last day selling cheese. My leave of absence at the CBC has come to an end. Time's up. I need to be back in the presenter's chair straight after New Year's. I have considered packing in my broadcasting, because I am so bonded to mongering and to these people who have done me so much good. However, I have made a commitment to the station managers in Montreal to return, and to the listeners. Finances are an important part of the equation. I cannot afford at my age to forego the next year's presenting wages in favour of part-time chee-semongering.

Five weeks earlier, I sent Tom a message. 'Can we meet for coffee this week?'

'Sure. Come to Peckham?' I did. He picked a quiet coffeeshop with a backroom. Just as I arrived with our coffees and set them on the table, I started to speak.

'Sorry, I can't start with small talk. I need to get this out. I'm sending in my notice. I'm leaving. I have to go back to Montreal.'

Tom didn't appear surprised. I was worried, perhaps fool-ishly, about him feeling betrayed after all the work he put into training me. He did look unsettled. It was an awkward conver-sation and there was no way around that fact.

'I thought this was going to happen,' he said.

'What do you mean?'

'I mean you're good and you've got other things in your life.'

'Um ...' I was casting about for how to explain it and I hadn't really expected him to give me what sounded like praise in response to my announcement.

I ended up just saying what was in my heart: 'I love it, Tom. I love this job. I love you, man. I am so, so fond of you, I'm sorry to embarrass you. Or is it me I'm embarrassing?'

'Ah, Michael. I love working with you, too.'

'Thanks for saying that,' I laughed.

'It's true!' He let out a laugh but then was serious. 'It's true.'

'There's just a bunch of things I have to take care of in Montreal.' That's what I said to him. It wasn't the whole truth but it wasn't a lie. I had never gone into the details of my broadcasting with him because I was keeping that part of me scrupulously separate, something I'd set out to do as part of the sabbatical. 'Things to take care of in Montreal' was the same thing I'd said to the management team, along with this: 'I want to come back.'

I felt bad about leaving the company. Having said that, they've heard it all before. There's a lot of turnover in the service sector. Cheesemongers come and cheesemongers go. Any impact of me giving my notice was blunted at that point anyway because we all had a lot of other things on our minds: the busiest four weeks of our lives were approaching like an oncoming train. At this point in the year, for cheesemongers, anything on the other side of Christmas feels like a concept and not reality. Instead, we are all focused on shifting insane amounts of cheese in record time.

At the height of the rush, we sell as much cheese in one day at our Borough Market stall as we would over a normal week or more. The logistics are overwhelming.

Christmas Eve is when things finally start to loosen up. There is a steady flow of customers all morning, sure, but most people have already bought what they need. Then at noon, Cheesemonger Nuala is on her way. Her good-bye, over to Ireland for Christmas, starts to feel like my good-bye. I can feel a tug at my heart as we embrace, a big hug. She is a gem, an absolute star, and the best company imaginable.

When I arrived at 7.30 a.m., I hadn't even taken off my coat and the first thing Owner Jon said to me was, 'Michael, can you go look after Fionnuala?' Something was wrong. She was in the back, fumbling with bandages.

There was a fair amount of blood on one of Nuala's hands and she was a bit rattled. Often with cuts you get a stupid amount of blood, out of proportion to the cut. That seemed to be the case here, thank goodness.

'I think I just reopened that cut from the other day.'

We got new black knives the other day, un-blunted, and I was fooled, too. We're so used to them being dull that when they aren't, we end up with sliced hands and fingers.

'Okay, don't worry,' I said to Nuala. 'Just let me have a look.' I was calm. She gave me her hand and I could see the cut, see from where the blood was coming. Most of it wasn't fresh.

'You're fine – it's just that same stubborn cut. Here,' I helped her with the bandage.

She relaxed immediately and it was never a big deal but afterwards she came up to me and said, 'God, you're good at that, Michael. Made me feel immediately better. Thank you.'

We had that moment and dozens of others together over the holiday rush, including an exceptionally long close where Manager Tom insisted on playing Irish ballads until 'The Rising of the Moon' was the final straw.

'Tom, stop!'

It is hard to watch her leave. Fionnuala takes off to Ireland for weeks or months at a time. Sometimes I say to her, 'Please don't go.'

'Michael, are you nuts? I have to go. I have to get out of this place. I'll go mad, otherwise. I'm not kidding.'

As things wind down in the afternoon, I am serving the steady but dwindling flow of customers and starting to allow myself to think, 'This is one of the last people I'm ever going to serve.' I'm sad.

Tom starts to move on the close as promised at 3 p.m. He made a solemn pledge at our big pre-Christmas meeting that he would get people on their way at 4 p.m. It was a thing he wanted to make happen as a point of honour.

And so it is. Borough Market begins to echo. For the last time, I am closing the stall with my colleagues, always a big moment of solidarity. Brushes are scrubbing tabletops, floors are being bleached, the bins are being taken out. I snap a couple of quick pictures of the close, me in my wellies, my final moments as a cheesemonger. One of them becomes my phone wallpaper that I look at every day of 2020 after I return to my job presenting the morning show.

The close is a badge of honour – and when I say the close, I mean all of them, my first close, the one the night of the Fishmongers' Hall Attack with Jon, the ones I finished alone, the one I first supervised with a new trainee, Cheesemonger Yasha (three times as long, my fault!), and every close where Tom or Cian and I were in complete, unspoken tandem: sweeping, washing, scrubbing, emptying, shoving, dragging, lifting everything to where it needed to be.

I am invited to the pub, this time the Wheatsheaf just at the end of our row. It's a final libation before Christmas with Daisy, Tom and Jon, who is buying the first round, Guinness all around. We sit outside under an umbrella – the roads are slick from an earlier rain but the temperature is warm enough. We talk, laugh and run through some of the customers of the day. We exchange our plans for the holidays. I get a little bit teary.

When Jon gets up to leave, he says: 'Michael, a word.'

I stand up to walk him out of the market. Jon rarely says anything if it's not in paragraphs. This time the message is simple. He puts his hand on my arm.

'Thank you for everything. Whenever you want to come back, the door will be open.'

'Thanks, Jon. Listen, there's something I've been meaning to tell you all day.'

'What's that?'

'It's about the Pérail.' I pause for effect, then give him a big smile. 'I sold four trays of it this week.'

He smiles back and chuckles. 'I knew you had it in you.'

In the end, Daisy leaves, too, and it is just Tom and me around the table outdoors. 'Well, it's been an absolute pleasure,' he says.

'Thank you. I have loved working with you. I've had so much fun and I've learned so much. I don't want to go.'

The market is hushed. Most people are headed to their homes for Christmas Eve meals. We finish our pints in quiet conversation and it's one of those blessed moments in a lifetime, moments where you are fully aware as they are occurring that you are profoundly happy, that you are both in sync. It's bittersweet as many of the best shared moments are – a religious person might call it a moment of grace. If only I could slow down time, stretch this moment out, stop it altogether.

I treasure my time with Tom and I think it's because I started from so close to zero, vulnerable in all the ways you know from reading this. We've achieved a kind of trust and mutual confidence that means there is nothing I can't count on him to fix or be there for. Even on the day of the attack, I knew how upset he was not to be present, and yet he was.

A week earlier, I sought out a book on teaching from one of the big booksellers on Piccadilly, bought it for him and inscribed a tribute to his patience and his skill in teaching me. A year later, Tom will leave the company to train in primary school education, something that turns out to be an interlude in his mongering career. He now holds a senior position at another cheesemongers. We created something special and precious together, something that concludes together on that Christmas Eve over pints of Guinness.

On the way back to the stall, 'Difficult moment,' he says. 'I need to ask you for your keys.'

'Of course.' I had them ready in my pocket. 'I've left the black fleece jacket hanging at the back – it needs laundering though.' The jacket carries the company logo across the chest. I'd worn it all through the autumn since finishing my probation.

'Oh, Michael. You can have it. You've earned it.'

There is nothing I wear with greater pride. We shake hands and say good-bye. The wet streets of London reflect head and taillights, red and white. I walk home with a heavy heart and a lump in my throat.

I leave Borough Market and London having filled in a part of me that had been hollowed out, maybe that had never been there in the first place. Thinking back to the day when I interviewed for the job, the day they asked why mongering would be a good fit for me and I blurted out what was in my gut – 'I think it will ground me' – it has done exactly that in ways I couldn't have imagined at the time.

The plane ride home to Montreal feels long, and like something is breaking.

Petit Blaja / Tarentais

'I want to go about like the light-footed goats.'

– Johanna Spyri, *Heidi*, 1880.

Origin: Petit Blaja originated seventy years ago. The recipe was handed down to the couple who took on the original farm where it was made, the current cheesemakers, Gabriel and Soizic Cattenoz.

Presentation: About 200g a piece and the size of a shrunken tea mug, Petit Blaja is a striking cheese that evolves from an ivory to an ochre hue as it matures. It has a *Geotrichum* rind, a handsome pattern that recalls Islamic art. The centre has a firm consistency. In the mouth, it resembles peanut butter in texture, though not in taste. When young, it has a pleasant, tart, citric acidity and a slight farmy flavour which evolves into a fuller, more animal taste. Highly recommend sampling both the younger and more mature versions of this cheese – they're surprisingly different and delicious each in their own way. Don't be put off as you see it develop different moulds and colourings as it matures.

How to serve: This is not your classic French goat's cheese, so a great addition to a summer goat's cheeseboard to demonstrate the range that's possible with goat's milk. Perfect to take for a summer picnic as it won't run all over the place. I prefer to eat it on its own, no cracker, no bread. Walnuts or dried fruits like apricots will accompany it nicely. This is one of those heftier goat's that would pair well with a fuller-bodied red.

Fun fact: Petit Blaja started out life as a Savoyard cheese, also known as Le Tarentais. Gabriel and Soizic then packed their bags and their herd of goats and moved 600km away to the hotter, drier climate of the Haute-Garonne in the Midi-Pyrénées. Then, years later, they moved production back to the Savoie, with the name reverting to Tarentais. This is one of my favourite French goat's cheeses.

26
A Cheesesome Threesome

AT ANOTHER MOMENT IN my mongering career, I am invited to a swanky party at a warehouse flat in Borough where bottomless Champagne is on offer, fancy canapés, and guests show up looking fabulous and recounting marvellous tales of their adventures. One is working at a new gallery, another has started a wine importing business, a third has won a grant to examine the influence of the Harlem Renaissance in Britain.

'And what do you do?' someone asks me.

Paul, the host, jumps in, 'Oh, Michael's my cheesemonger.' Paul is a long-time customer. We sometimes have pints at a nearby pub and talk about our lives and careers. Lovely guy. He splits his time between here and Australia, where he's from.

Yes, you get close to some of the customers and when they ask you to come by for a drink, why not? Proper Champagne is not often on this cheesemonger's menu and it's nice to see new people. The British value eccentricity: I'll be seen as a curiosity, make some small talk and leave early. In the event, that's how it plays out.

When Lasse and Naomi invite me over for dinner, just the three of us, I have some reservations.

As we begin to sample their very nice wine, Naomi turns to me and says, 'So, did your cheesemonger friends think we were inviting you here for a threesome?'

Cue the vivid recollection of a scene from our stall not four hours earlier:

Cheesemonger Fionnuala: 'Oh my God, Michael. They are inviting you over for a threesome!'

Manager Elle: 'I think you should be careful. What are you going to do?'

'Well, I'm not going to have a threesome with them. I was invited for fondue.'

I toy with the idea of an outright lie to Naomi – 'Oh goodness no, Naomi' – but decide if the evening is going to be fun, the tone needs to be set. 'Yes,' I answer. 'It's Nuala. She has a dirty mind. I can only apologise for her. We're not, are we?'

'No!' Laughter all around, only slightly uncomfortable. 'I always complain to Lasse that we don't meet new people. We both really enjoy being served by you at the market, and I said, "I bet he's fun. Let's invite him for dinner."' Years later, we're still friends, still having dinners together.

Timing is everything, goes the cliché. My invitation to fondue with Lasse and Naomi, and to that swanky party at Paul's, they're both the result of short interactions repeated over time, dozens of them. The time we have together is mostly spent over artisan cheese – hard not to be friendly when such a magical product is at the heart of it, something that's been bringing people together and nourishing relationships for centuries.

In Lasse's line of work, timing is literally everything. Lasse works in financial tech. He's developing software which delves into the universe of time and financial transactions, the carving up of seconds, even fractions of seconds to the advantage of traders. It's fascinating work, highly precise, and I enjoy hearing about it even if it boggles my brain.

Ironically, Lasse's favourite cheese is one of our most traditional Alpine cheeses, L'Étivaz. It takes so long to make and there are so few wheels available commercially that we often run out. Everything that's romantic about cheesemaking can be summed up in a wheel of Étivaz: cows with large bells grazing in high Alpine pastures, curds being cooked in a big, copper kettle over a wood fire, cheesemakers following on in the footsteps of their parents, making cheese the old-fashioned way, working at elevations where there are no roads – equipment needs to make the trip up via a contraption that resembles a ski lift!

L'Étivaz is also the big finish for one of our mongering magic tricks. For someone looking for Alpine cheese, we'll begin by tasting the Comté, nutty with a pleasant sweetness, move through the slightly herbaceous Maréchal with its flax and sage-like notes, then on to the meatier Beaufort and the crunchy, caramelly Gruyère, before ending up at L'Étivaz.

'Give it a bit of a sniff before putting it in your mouth.'

Customer sniffs, arches eyebrow.

'You should get a hint of tropical fruit.'

'Oh yes, I suppose you're right. I do.'

'Now, go ahead and taste it.' Pause. 'It should be giving you a tang from the higher acidity, and right about now you should get a blast of pineapple.'

'You're right! Honey, it tastes like pineapple, can you taste it?'

'Is there pineapple in it?'

Heaven forbid. It's a mystery, or magic as I said before. When you cut open a wheel, the sudden smell of pineapple bursts forth and if you close your eyes, you might even imagine yourself in a pineapple grove. It's that lush.

You would think a cheese like that would fly off the slate and you'd be right. It does. There is even a famous cheese writer, buyer at one of the most prestigious dairies in London, who comes to buy our Étivaz. We are one of the few who stock it and mature it.

Why, then, is there sometimes a sad quarter of Étivaz stuck languishing in our hard cheese cupboard, being brought back and forth to the display, no takers day after day? Once cut from the wheel, there's only so long a wedge of Alpine cheese can hold on to its zing, its pzazz.

L'Étivaz

'Aujourd'hui nos buts premiers c'est de faire vivre les 70 familles.'

– Pascal Guenat, Director of L'Étivaz Cooperative, explaining the importance L'Étivaz places on tradition and providing a livelihood to the seventy families who make it.

Origin: L'Étivaz is produced only in the milder months, 10 May to 10 October, when cattle feed on grasses and wildflowers in Alpine pastures in and around le Pays-d'Enhaut, in Switzerland. It's an entirely artisanal production, with the curds cooked shortly after milking, directly on the farm in great copper kettles, always over a roaring woodfire, giving it smoky notes. The first traces of cheesemaking in the area date back to the twelfth century. The name Étivaz derives from the word *estivage,* a reference to its production through summertime months, l'été being the French word for summer. L'Étivaz farmers organised in the 1930s, establishing the cooperative, maturing caves and production methods that make it unique, and so prized, today.

Presentation: These are substantial wheels of Alpine cheese, but smaller than Gruyère and can vary greatly in height and diameter. Some will weigh as much as 35kg, others are as light as 10kg.

How to serve: Such a rare and delicious product on its own, to appreciate it is to eat it without adornment, cube by luscious cube. L'Étivaz does not like the heat, so don't sit it out on a summer's day. Like its cousin, Gruyère, it melts wonderfully and will make an exceptional fondue, albeit a pricey one. For pairings, demi-sec or brut Champagne, aromatic whites, full-bodied reds, or try it with a whisky for a whole new experience.

Fun fact: No one has ever explained to me why a cheese with the most traditional of methods, made in Swiss Alpine valleys by families of dairy farmers, should smell so strongly of pineapple when you cut into a wheel. Chalk up another cheese mystery.

Part IV
Bi-continental

27
Back to the Microphone

B ACK FROM MY CHEESE cure and settled again in Montreal, I am no longer the same person. I went away a presenter. I am coming back a newly-trained cheesemonger. The team of the breakfast programme and I put our heads together to make changes to the way we work with a view to solving not only the overarching problems of the routine that was crushing me, but also to address things that were making their professional lives difficult. It turns out to be a rewarding process for everyone, one that includes a number of fresh, creative initiatives. We make structural changes and we take some easy wins in the name of lightening the collective burden. For example, we set some red lines for when meetings are to be held and when things are to be finished. Deadlines can be stressful but they are also releases.

Our re-imagined programme is a success. It is the best vintage we ever produce together. We manage to stick to our high-minded principles – we work hard but we have each other's backs, keeping everyone's workflow in mind. The audience responds, ratings are good and the listener feedback is plentiful and spontaneous. It is exactly what I value in morning radio: a powerful, daily communion that sets the agenda.

That leaves me to explain why my passion for it continues to wither. I have a couple of wise friends who say, 'There's no going back.' It's trite in its formulation, but that does not make it wrong. The expression recurs in my head over these weeks. It eats away at me because if there's no going back, where does that leave me? I can't go back to radio and now I can't go back to cheesemongering? How does that make any sense?

One thing is for sure, through all these months, my mind is frequently back at the cheese stall at Borough Market. One manifestation of that is that I am still subscribed to our cheesemongering group chat. I couldn't bring myself to drop out when I left. That means daily updates.

```
Cheesemonger Daisy: Has anyone got any
good info on the Lingot de St-Nicolas and
who makes them? Also I've heard they used
to be goats but are now sheep. Why's
that?
Manager Laurence: It's made in a monas-
tery. They used to have a herd of goats
but had to sell them in 2015. They kept
the creamery though and work with a local
supply of sheep's milk.
```

Lingot de St-Nicolas, now that's a name I've not heard in a long time. A long time. I have a major-league swoon at the thought of it, put the phone down and sit on the corner of my bed. The cheese is shaped like a small gold ingot, white with the *Geotrichum* that grows on its rind, giving it an intricate, patterned wrinkling on its surface. The sheep's milk makes for a buttery texture due to the higher fat content – a knife will almost slide through the paste. There is a line of thyme oil, nothing untoward. It's simple and smooth-tasting, with a decadent richness. What a cheese.

I made the mistake when I first tasted it of not reserving one to take home. The whole box sold out quickly and it's one of those cheeses that if you blink, you miss it. We only tend to carry it for a month – it constantly sells out. It only ends up in the hands of people with luck and impeccable timing.

I feel like messaging Daisy to tell her to hold some of it back for certain favourites from among our regulars and not to forget one for herself! But I am lurking in the group chat. I shouldn't even still be there. I could message her privately but I think that could come across as intense and strange and besides, I'm leery of messaging into the UK time zone where it's now much later and she might be asleep.

Clearly, I'm not finished with the Lingot de St-Nicolas, not finished with our cheese chats, our new cheese discoveries and old cheese friends, my colleagues, our regulars, the market. How can there not be any going back to that?

This whole period is one of intense confusion and uncertainty because the stakes are higher. We are no longer in the realm of a sabbatical with my job waiting for me on the other side. A return to cheesemongering would mean leaving the microphone definitively, leaving a high-profile, well-paying career for good.

I try to push these thoughts away and carry on through the icy early spring in Montreal. When the pandemic hits, all our worlds change. I am bound to our audience even more tightly as we try to figure out what's going on, how our governments should act and what we, as individuals, should be doing about it. I'm also keeping an eye across the cheese group chat, concerned for my colleagues and the health of the business.

In May, George Floyd is murdered on camera by police in Minneapolis. We cover race issues frequently and have for years. Now, with all the thoughts going through my mind about my future, how can I not focus on the fact that all our Montreal CBC weekday radio presenters are white? At some point, you have to look in the mirror. I believe I have earned my place but I also have the confidence to put the question out there: have I held that place long enough? Is it time to make way?

Also in the spring, a birth. Our Senior Producer, Sara, leaves to have her beautiful baby girl. It is thrilling. It fits into the theme of renewal of the programme, the renewal of my life, and is a reminder that time marches on, things change. I'm so happy for her, but not having Sara for a year ends up making things harder and inevitably places a greater burden on me.

Quitting my job with little idea of the economic consequences of the global pandemic scores highly as a bold move. That's why I leave the final decision to September, no longer than that, though. If I go for good, I want to give enough notice to the bosses. The sabbatical was priceless. Leaving the audience in the lurch again is a hard no. I want the next person to take up the morning show seamlessly, the Monday after I leave.

Leaving definitively is being made possible, should I choose to, by changes I make thanks to lessons learnt over the past year. Gone are many of the luxuries of my former life. Applying mongering budgetary rules now to my presenter's pay allows me to amass a war chest. It'll be enough to buy me a couple of years to figure out how to make everything work out. I eat out hardly at all. Coffees are made at home. I keep to my recent, voracious reading habit, meaning my entertainment bill is cut.

The summer becomes a time to reflect on the final decision, whether to make the jump or not. With Coronavirus infections on the wane as the weather turns drier and warmer,

I decide to test the cheese waters again – see how the pandemic has changed things – and take a flight to London. I drop Manager Laurence a note. 'Hey, do you need a hand at all this summer?'

Bleu de Termignon

'Je cherche les produits perdus – dans ces grands produits perdus, on a un concentré de nos valeurs.'

–Jacques Vernier, French cheese connoisseur and Mauriennais, explaining how he looks for exceedingly rare products such as Bleu de Termignon because 'in these great lost products, we have a concentration of our values'.

Origin: Savoyard blue-veined cheeses date back to the eighteenth century. This is not a protected origin cheese, so production is intimately connected to the lives and histories of the small group of people who make it and to the high mountain pastures where it originates. Termignon was once a commune in the Val-Cenis in Savoie, not far from Italy.

Presentation: Wheels will vary as production is entirely artisanal, but expect them to weigh 7 to 10kg, about 30cm in diameter and 15–20cm tall. This cheese is a beauty. The rind is mottled sandy brown to grey, not unlike the colour of pelts you would find on farm animals. Some say it resembles the cave walls where it matures. The miracle of Bleu de Termignon is that the blue moulds are entirely natural, not introduced, often by injection, as with most blue cheeses. That means there are no tell-tale puncture marks in the rind. When you cut a wheel open, you'll get a paste that is golden to ivory in colour with little or no hint of blueing. Wait. As the paste reacts to being opened up, blue moulds begin to appear in intricate patterns moving from the rind to the centre. This is one of the wonders of cheese.

How to serve: Bleu de Termignon is one of the most expensive French cheeses and is only available in the winter. Think carefully before losing it on a cheeseboard – it deserves pride of place, to be served on its own or with only one or two others. Reactions will vary. Depending upon its age and how it's been matured, this cheese can taste anywhere from floral, similar to a Parmigiano, to slightly anchovy, but always farmy. My appreciation for it was cemented when I took it for a date one night (by now, you'll gather, I do this a lot) – just the two of us and a glass of Pinot Noir. We read and nibbled and sipped for a glorious couple of hours. If the Pinot seems wrong to you, try a round or mountain white wine, something medium sweet, all great choices for a pairing. Why not try a Tokaji? The right pairing will depend on where the cheese has arrived in its life. The bluer it gets, the sweeter you may be tempted to go.

Fun fact: One of the rarest cheeses: there are only a handful of producers who make it. The milk comes from cattle who graze only in high Alpine pastures in the Haute Maurienne, in le Parc Nationale de la Vanoise. It's as close to natural cheesemaking as you get nowadays – there are no imported bacterial starter cultures used. Those come from its native environment, the cheesemakers' moulds and tools; the blue mould comes from the maturation caves.

28
Cheese in a Time of Corona

CHEESEMONGER LAURENCE TELLS ME he does need help that summer, but I would be working mostly in East Dulwich at the cheese shop. Am I interested? 'I'd love to. Thanks.'

I get a big Laurence grin from him on my first day back. 'Hi Michael, so good to see you!'

London's first lockdown has been lifted, but only a few weeks earlier. Exact numbers are difficult to obtain – at least 40,000 people have died across the UK and there is still among our customers, to my read anyway, a sense of shellshock. It is mixed together in a cocktail of emotions: relief that case numbers have plummeted and the wave subsided, a good deal of lingering wariness and some joy at the return of warm weather and smiles.

This is still the early phase of the pandemic, three months in, and there is a lot of trial and error, casting about for solutions. We are given plastic visors and a supply of face masks at the cheese shop. The visors go hilariously badly. They look alien, much more so than face masks. In fact, with their rectangular shape attached to our head we look a bit like Cybermen from *Doctor Who*. They also fog up easily as you do physical work and they make it hard to hear. The curvature of the plastic over the mouth means we hear our own voice and breathing, and less well the customer. Most importantly, they get smeared with cheese constantly. Mongering means tasting regularly to check on the cheese. Seven times out of ten when I go to put a piece of cheese in my mouth, I hit the visor. We give the visors a good go, but in the end it's the masks that make most sense.

Face masks present the same barrier to tasting, but you can't forget they're there. The bigger problem with them is a most unpleasant discovery. I guess you won't be surprised to hear that eating cheese gives you cheesy breath. Strangely, I was. I didn't expect it to smell quite like it does. Let's just say the masks are taking some getting used to.

The shop has not been kitted out with plexiglass to separate customers from cheesemongers. With the display changing every day and cleanliness so important, it's deemed the plexiglass would get dirty quickly and be tough to clean. The owners have decided instead to go with a line on the floor set out in thick white tape to keep people back and maintain a physical distance. Every few days the tape wears off, the remnants need to be peeled away and the tape re-applied in a more or less straight line.

The tape is one measure that's in place, the other is to limit the number of people in the store at any one time: two (plus a child if there is one, and there are a lot in East Dulwich!). We've stopped accepting cash – let's be honest, cash can be a bit dirty, but more important is the contact back and forth. In retrospect, it seems hard to believe that the mask mandate went into effect so late. They are such a staple of the pandemic, but it is only on 24 July that face masks become mandatory in indoor spaces in England.

A burden is placed on shop clerks and cheesemongers to enforce the new rules, not something I enjoy. There have always been strict hygiene rules in the cheese shop. We have cheese contact rules and we have been expert hand washers since day one of our employment, well before Covid-19. Now, here we are having to tell people not just 'Don't touch the cheese', but to go back outside if there are already two people in the shop, stand behind the white line once inside, and put on a mask. That's a lot of instructions. For the most part, prompting people to respect the rules goes well enough. The English know how to queue, one of their specialist subjects. The rest is taking some getting used to, however.

There is a woman, a regular, who comes into the shop with a man wearing a Christian religious collar. She is absolutely in the market for cheese and not browsing. One day, she begins to ask me questions about the cheeses but with each question she reaches up to her face, pinches her mask at the mouth and pulls it down before speaking.

'Remind me the difference between your Gruyère and L'Étivaz?' She then places the mask back over face and mouth.

'Er ... well, they're both Swiss. The Gruyère is rich and caramel in flavour. L'Étivaz is similar but with smoky notes, even specks of ash in the paste, and a strangely sweet finish like pineapple.'

I am saying these words but I am squinting my eyes a bit trying to compute what just happened. She says, 'I see, and with the Maréchal?'

She's once again pinched her mask and pulled it away from her face to speak! It's as though she has completely misunderstood why she's wearing the mask. It's not to sit on your mouth only when your mouth is closed and you're not using it. It's expressly intended to be kept on while you open your mouth to speak. It's about limiting aerosols. How do I go about saying something? 'I'm happy to answer any of your questions, but would you mind not removing your mask when you ask them?'

In the end, I don't say that and instead I tell her that the Maréchal is also Swiss but rubbed with flax flower and hay and has a sage-like finish. I chicken out – I am just dumbfounded. Also, mask enforcement is not proving comfortable for me.

Another woman walks in purposefully later in the day. I can see she is holding a mask but has forgotten to put it on. This can happen, I think, not a problem, I will politely remind her. She walks over to the fridge containing butters and yoghurts.

'Excuse me, I'm sorry. I have to ask you to wear your mask in the shop.' This is the stock phrase I settle on for future use. It reminds people that there is a law we are complying with.

She turns and fixes me with an annoyed stare. Two beats. Her eyes widen. 'I have one!' And she lifts the hand holding her mask into the air and gestures at me with it.

I look back at her. She doesn't put it on, turns around and continues to examine the contents of the fridge, mask still in hand.

Every once in a while at the shop, different tradespeople will call soliciting for business. A man enters the shop later in the week with a name tag and a uniform that indicates he works for a security and alarm service. He has a clipboard and a bunch of pamphlets in his hand.

He has a face mask. It's around his neck, settling just under his mouth like a chin strap. Mouth and nose are fully exposed.

'Hello, I've noticed that the security system you are using could be improved and I'm wondering if I could speak to you about what packages we offer.'

'I'm sorry. I have to ask you to wear your mask in the shop.'

He looks at me, seemingly not understanding. 'I am wearing a mask.'

Now to this man, I feel, really, it is fair game to be more blunt. He is, after all, in the security trade and I am wondering about his credentials. If he is having trouble understanding the mask/security concept during a pandemic, what other elements of our workplace security might he not fully be grasping?

'I'm sorry, but I need to ask you to wear the mask so it covers your mouth and your nose. It's because it's the law now; I have to ask people to comply or we could get fined.' Reluctantly, he puts the mask on. I go through the motions of listening through a bit of his spiel but, in the end, I just take his card and tell him I'm not the owner of the shop, but I'll let him know he called. He lost me at chinstrap. When Cheesemonger Laurence, the manager, emerges from downstairs I explain what happened and ask him if he'd like the card. No, I quite understand.

Then there are the people who forget a mask and instead pull their t-shirt collar over their mouths when they come into the shop. There are the people who ask if they can just run in 'ever so quickly' without a mask. There are those who want to be served at the door, maskless. Some people who are wearing a mask don't want to come in either but also want door service. In England, there are quite a few people who say, 'Oh, I have an exemption!' Those are the magic words. Everyone backs off and no one asks to see the exemption or enquires why it was awarded. There is a fear of embarrassing someone who might have a condition and the potential embarrassment seems to override everything else, pandemic and all.

The whole thing is distracting, sometimes befuddling and open to interpretation. Also, it takes so much attention away from the cheese. How am I supposed to reach my mongering élan when I need to police masks, white lines and store capacity?

As for the more forthright anti-maskers, I have asked Laurence for a guideline of how to respond to conscientious objectors because I watch online videos like everyone else and I would like to know what he thinks best practice is. Laurence doesn't believe this will happen. I am rolling my eyes inwardly as I nod and say, 'Okay.' I have lost some faith in human beings.

Cheesemonger Molly later tells me how a man came up to the stall we have at the Voyager Market in Bermondsey – it's attached to our Arch, our HQ. She says after being asked to wear a mask he unleashed a ferocious tirade that was so full of vitriol the actual contents just washed over her, then he turned on his heel and left. Thirty seconds later he returned, picked up the vitriolic tirade where he left off and made a second dramatic exit.

Quite honestly, I don't want to have to live that.

Much later in the pandemic, once the vaccines are out, a woman comes into the cheese shop served by Manager Elle. She is not wearing a face mask and she's touching the cheeses. Touching the cheeses is where I draw the line. I understand they are hard to resist but how do you think they feel? It's never been okay.

'I'm sorry, I'm going to have to ask you not to handle the cheeses. It's especially important during the pandemic,' says Elle.

'Oh. Have you had your vaccination?' she asks.

'Yes, I have,' answers a puzzled Elle.

'Not me. I don't think it's wise.'

It was a pandemic non-sequitur, not the first nor the last. She leaves without buying. Objectors end up being a minority, just enough to be an irritation, not too much to ruin a day.

The pandemic weighs on my decision-making. Of all the rules we cheesemongers are suddenly stuck with enforcing, the worst is that we stop tasting out the cheese. It's a huge part of what we do. Not sharing the cheeses with the customers is sad.

The pandemic also takes one of the most pleasurable things out of broadcasting. We are no longer allowed to have guests in the studio. Interviews are all done on phone lines, often poor. It's just not the same when you don't get to meet people and look in their eyes. Gradually, even regular contributors to our programme are staying out of the studio. Our set-up team no longer comes into the office.

At least with cheese, tasting out or no, you still deal with people face to face.

At Borough Market this summer, the stall is so different. Tom is at The Arch, Cian has left the company. He got a job at a school working with kids whom others find too difficult to handle. It seems like a perfect fit and I tell him so when I see him. We meet at the market when he hears I'm back. He gives me a big hug, pandemic be damned, and tells me we will always share a bond. I feel exactly the same way.

Staffing has gone down to one monger at our stall this summer, except over the weekend. Footfall is down significantly. The one monger on duty most days is Emily. We don't know each other but when I stop by to say hi, she immediately says, 'Michael! So nice to meet you! Of course, I've heard all about you. How's Canada?'

Emily is Owner Jon's sister. It's not obvious – Emily has long blonde hair which contrasts with Jon's darker features. Emily's career plans have hit a bump in the road due to the pandemic and she has taken up service at the market. It being slower, she puts speech radio on in the background at the stall. This is generally thought of as a no-no. It's Radio 4 and the BBC World Service, so that endears her to me.

'Canada is good! I mean, we have the pandemic, too, but at least it's summer now so people can breathe a little. Are you running the stall on your own?'

She sighs. 'Yes. There are just not enough customers to justify a second monger.'

'Yeah, I get it, but how are you managing? That's a tonne of work.'

'It is, but I don't mind. The days are a bit long, mind you. When I need the loo, Allan and Barbara watch the stall.'

'Well, I have no plans the next few days, so I'm coming at lunchtime to give you a proper break.'

'Don't be crazy. It's fine.'

I am a man of my word. I like popping up to the market to say hi to everyone (including the cheeses) and in the end, Emily enjoys having forty-five minutes to walk around, then sit down for some lunch. I start spending more time with Francesco, too, the skinny, curly-haired Italian who runs the stall across the alley. Francesco is also a musician – he plays in a band that's starting to do well. During the pandemic, that part of his life is on hold.

His is one of those stalls at the market that features little finds that you might not see anywhere else. These are products that the owner sources during his visits to Calabria, often limited editions. There are tins of lip-smacking tuna in olive oil and dried beans that will make you completely reconsider what a bean dish should taste like. There are wheels of Pecorino, anchovies, oils, dehydrated sliced oranges and strawberries, pasta, jams, 'nduja and cured meats. The strawberries in winter are madness.

Francesco stores a guitar just above his seat behind the main counter. The stall is festooned with dried peppers and wild oregano. Among the regulars is a woman named Maria. Maria must be about seventy-five years old. She wears a kerchief over her hair, a long brown coat and vintage leather shoes. She has a slight stoop. She comes weekly during the pandemic, and when she arrives, Francesco finds a chair for her to sit down. I always know when she arrives because I hear Francesco cry out, '*Maria! Come stai?*' They chat and laugh for a few minutes and on some visits he'll pull down his guitar and play a few chords of a favoured song, leading Maria to sing along.

One day I go over to record them. Happy I take such an interest, they are singing a song from after the war, they explain, sung to Italians who were getting on boats and heading to America to start a new life, a song full of melancholy.

One rainy day, one of Francesco's many younger female admirers stops by and the guitar comes down again. It is a quiet weekday – the pandemic has eliminated tourism. This time the song selection is vintage Rolling Stones, '(I can't get no) Satisfaction'. All the traders in the neighbouring stalls lean in to listen as he plays and she sings, and afterwards, our little row of stalls erupts in applause.

It inspires me to broach the topic of performance with Emily. 'You know, Emily, I feel you have potential West End chops. In my view, you are lead material.'

'Don't be so silly,' she says, busy cutting Roquefort into smaller wedges. 'What do you mean?'

'Well, you have bucketfuls of personality, twinkling eyes, energy that seems never to stop and you wear your emotions on your sleeve.'

'I don't sing well.' She is finishing a tricky Roquefort wrap. She looks up, 'I should get you to help me write my CV, though.'

'How long do you plan to stay at the stall?'

'I don't know. I'm just helping Jon out. I need to start looking around again. It's just not a great time for that.' She takes a long pause, puts her knife down and then sighs wistfully. 'Oh, maybe I'll never leave.'

As summer continues, I come by any day I can to relieve her for an hour, and I manage to pick up a few shifts at weekends with her. I develop an attachment to Emily and in my spare time I write a big West End solo number for her entitled 'Maybe I'll Never Leave'. The Borough Market cheese stall, that is. It's a plaintive ballad where the main character, pulled by the competing desires to move on or to stay, breaks into song before finally deciding to abandon cheese just before the interval. It's tense and sorrowful:

> *Oh, maybe I'll never leave!*
> *Maybe, maybe*
> *Maybe it's selling cheese*
> *That fills me*
> *Imbues me*
> *With a love of the land*
> *With a love of animal husbandry*
> *With a love of family!*
> *How could I forget my family?*

While we're working sometimes, I sing it for her, which makes her laugh. Me too. In truth, it's not sometimes. I sing it frequently that summer and I imagine her alone on the stage in the spotlight. I don't know what's got into me. Maybe it's the daily anxiety of pandemic life that demands a counterweight in song, like Francesco and his guitar across the way.

Emily thinks I've lost my mind, but I catch her humming the tune I wrote for 'Maybe I'll Never Leave' more than once, even singing it. 'Oh! Look what you've made me do, you nutter!'

As the nights begin to draw in, my surreal summer does, too, so I board the plane and head once again for Montreal. I've learned what I need in order to make my decision.

Reblochon

'Soit par les cornes, soit par les lunettes, soit par les couleurs.'

– Tristan, a dairy farmer from Savoie whose milk is used for Reblochon, explaining how he recognises each of his cows, 'either by the shape of their horns, the patches around their eyes, or the hue of their coats'.

Origin: The story goes like this: tenant farmers were taxed based on the amount of milk their cows produced. In order to keep that tax down, they milked their cows lightly. When the milk controller left, the farmers went back for a second milking, known as the *reblochon*. The verb *reblocher* means to milk for a second time. Reblochon is the cheese made traditionally from that second milking that escaped taxation.

Presentation: Each wheel is about 14cm in diameter and weighs between 450 and 550g. They're 2–3cm tall and tend to bulge slightly. They look chubby. The rind is ochre and the paste ivory.

How to serve: Reblochon is a soft mountain cheese, farmy, mildly fruity, slightly hazelnut. It's a solid addition to a cheeseboard and serves nicely with fruit and nuts. Its star turn is as part of a dish called tartiflette, where great chunks of it, rind-side up, bubble and crisp as it's baked atop a mix of cream, potatoes, onion, bacon lardons and more reblochon. For pairings, why not try a dark, Trappist ale, a bolder red such as Rioja, a Gewürztraminer or a wine that hails from where Reblochon does, the Savoie.

Fun fact: It has a historic reputation as a 'clandestine' cheese, secretly produced from those black-market second milkings, but in modern times, it was one of the first French cheeses to receive an AOC, in 1958. There is a point in its life where the paste begins to break down into goo and the rind erupts in places. Buy! Buy! Buy!

29
Decision Time

THAT AUTUMN, EMILY FINALLY does make up her mind to leave definitively. So do I.

One evening, on my own, it suddenly occurs to me to get out the computer and solve a mystery that's been niggling at me. How did my former CBC presenter colleague Sheila end up answering her own 'What the hell else can a radio presenter do' question?

It doesn't take long to find an archived story entitled, 'CBC Saskatchewan host to hang up her headset'. It's from three years prior. Much of the article is a tribute to her career and expressions of sadness from the audience. Then I find the money graph. 'It was the promise of an adventure – to live in the Galapagos Islands with her sister – that convinced her to leave what she always referred to as "the best job in journalism".'

Huh. The Galapagos Islands. If she'd said that at our presenters' meeting, we'd have been in awe. I wonder how long it took for her to figure that out.

I take a whisky glass out from the cabinet and place it on the bar. I find the bottle that my friend Alison gave me in Glasgow and pour a good dram. There's plenty left, as I've been saving it. The first notes are earthy, lightly peaty, and along with the oak, they conjure the spring, the land, the outdoors.

Alison's gift is a powerful souvenir from the sabbatical, which feels appropriate tonight. Staring into the burnished hues of the whisky in the evening light, I allow myself to imagine where I'd be today if I hadn't taken the path of change last year. Would I have got myself out of the monochrome rut I'd got stuck in? Would the Comté still be tasting flat and me just carrying on without bothering to stop and taste, ploughing through the days?

I spend a moment thinking about her and how precious those few days were in Scotland. I try to imagine what she might say to me if there was another glass on the bar and she was seated beside me.

Alison has the type of voice that sticks in your head forever. In her broad, Dundonian accent, I can hear her say exactly this: 'Aye, you started down a path and good on ya. Now ask yourself, are you finished walking it?' It's in that moment that I realise the answer to something that had been tormenting me, that returning to mongering is not going back, not at all. It's choosing to continue forward.

A few days later during a pandemic walk in Montreal's Jarry Park, I share all of this with my radio boss. There are tears, mostly mine. I tell her that for me, Borough Market, the cheese, the mongers, this new life of mine, they bring me too much joy. It's all become organic, connected and impossible to deny. They fill my life with colours. I must listen to my heart and in its own searing way, the pandemic has confirmed it: this cheesemongering journey has to continue.

Selles-sur-Cher

'Il va être plus riche en hiver. On va avoir un goût beaucoup plus crémeux en hiver qu'au moment du printemps ou de l'été.'

– Stéphanie Vignier, award-winning cheesemaker, explaining the difference between winter and spring/summer production. The winter Selles are richer and creamier.

Origin: The first written record of Selles-sur-Cher appears around the beginning of the twentieth century, in relation to a cheese 'said of Selles', a town on the Cher river. Selles-sur-Cher is a market town where cheeses have pride of place and these popular goat's cheeses were made by farm families in the area. They were (and are) commonplace and delicious. It became an AOC in 1975.

Presentation: Like chubby, cheesy grey pancakes, Selles-sur-Cher are ashed, natural rind goat's cheeses with a bright, white fudgy paste. They're never bigger than 9.5cm across and weigh around 150g. They can break down and become gooey around the rind and have a wonderful fresh feel in the mouth as they coat the palate and the tongue. They are an accessible goat's cheese for newbies, nothing very strong. They are more often vegetal and not particularly farmy. The texture is often the star.

How to serve: Great for snacking, chunk after chunk if no one's looking. I love them when they're still a bit plump and not too aged. They'll stand out nicely on an all-rounder cheeseboard and would be missing from any goat-only cheeseboard (try it!). They marry nicely with nuts, honey, fruits and jams. A dry sparkling rosé is a good bet in summer. Loire Valley whites and reds are a natural accompaniment, coming from the same region.

Fun fact: The Selles I'm used to aren't called Selles at all, even though they are, but rather Couffy, a close relative that isn't matured in the designated area for the AOP so must take a different name by law.

Part V
Cheesemonger's Choice

30
Changes

I N THE REALM OF not always getting what you expect, quitting my decades-long journalism career in the middle of a pandemic certainly delivered.

I should have known straight from the get-go, when I flew on a near-empty plane from Toronto to London, one of the few still making the crossing, and then quarantined for two weeks at my flat. I mean, I did expect things would be different when I returned to the cheese stall, but not this much. Emily is gone, Daisy, too, and Tom is now handling the burgeoning online arm of the company. Less dramatically, Cheesemonger Molly is no longer a vegetarian and has made a new market boyfriend at one of the butchers', meaning free sausages and intrigue. For the first time I meet Elle, short for Eleanor, who is destined to become a big figure and teach me about flat Comté.

When we first meet, she's new and we immediately strike up a rapport. Just turning thirty-one, she is a good complement to me. She cares passionately about the detail of making things work, which is not my strong suit. Specifically, she is steeped in shopkeeping basics like monitoring sell-by dates, stock rotation, making sure she's in touch with the warehouse and deliveries, all the paperwork, and all the surprise drudgery. She seems to have learned exactly how the operation works in a matter of weeks, including many things that are still somewhat mysterious to me after eighteen months.

Elle is dating a wiry English bloke with a dashing, mischievous side. They have two pet geckos. It's wonderful to see her in love. They get engaged outside a kebab shop late one night in Hammersmith, ring and all. I am embarrassed to say it takes three weeks and prompting from Cheesemonger Nuala for me to realise Elle is Welsh. In my defence, it's a light Welsh accent, but hey ho, it's funny how things get rusty when you're first back from Canada. It usually takes me that long to stop saying dollars instead of pounds and to stop riding the bike-share accidentally on the right-hand side of the road.

Within only a few hours of returning to the stall, however, my hands are moving over the till as though they'd never left it. I am wrapping cheeses, making intricate folds by muscle memory, and I can speak lovingly and in detail about how each of the cheeses tastes. I guess some things return to you more quickly than others.

'You told us you wanted to come back, and here you are. Welcome back, Michael.' Owner Jon is happy to see me, apron on, back at the market ready for the ramp up for the holiday season.

At our stall, we now sell cider, perry (cider made with pears, for the uninitiated), beer and wine. All wines are low-intervention, natural, organic and/or biodynamic. We sell crackers and chutneys and British Territorial cheeses. All of this is partly down to the pandemic and partly to Brexit. Not knowing how things will turn out, it makes sense to carry more British and Irish cheeses, even if there are others in the market who do the Brits well. Some of the market's restrictions on what we can sell have been lifted as part of measures to help everyone make enough money in the pandemic, and that includes allowing us to sell alcohol. It's a lot of product to get up to speed on and I worry about the consequences on my liver of having a staff discount on wine. Also, I've never sold wine before. Thankfully, Elle has worked at a wine bar.

There's another big change, of course: I've returned as a full-fledged cheesemonger, and not a trainee. After all Tom's training, my first Christmas, the day of the Fishmongers' Hall attack, plus my weeks during the pandemic summer, I have earned a pip. The apron feels good. What that means, beyond having a fuller picture of all the things I don't know, is that with Elle and with Cheesemonger Fionnuala, whom we are paired with at weekends, something seems to fall into place.

'Can I open one of these Camemberts yet?'

It's Saturday, 7.45 a.m. at Borough Market – we arrived exactly fifteen minutes ago, Manager Elle, Cheesemonger Nuala and me. I am no slouch in the tasting department, but I can't compete with Nuala's enthusiasm for cracking into cheeses and getting them tasted.

Nuala and I don't agree on everything. I am a resolute fan of a washed-rind goat's cheese called Barriquet. It has a funky peanut energy that I hanker after. Nuala thinks it sometimes veers over into damp dishcloth. She, meanwhile, is a solid stan for Crottin de Chavignol, which, she says, is the most dependable of the goat's week in and week out and remains under-rated.

Camembert, though, that is another level and a point of common accord. Alongside Brie, it is the classic French bloomy rind cheese, worthy of veneration. We're talking about good Camembert, of course, proper Camembert de Normandie. Like any fine, artisanal cheese, it has a lifespan, a window where it is at its prime. For those fleeting hours, Camembert can be celestial. It has a lot to tell you, if you will but taste, and asking it to reveal its secrets often sets the tone for the day.

Camembert comes pre-packaged in waxed paper, then they're placed in a round wooden box. It's a hurdle to tasting and enough to hold junior cheesemongers back. Not Nuala.

'Oh yeah, I am ready,' I answer to Nuala's invitation. I love how dependably she reminds us to pay attention to what really matters.

'Oh, me too. Ever ready!' Manager Elle is busy pulling out cut pieces of the Alpine cheeses from the hard cheese cupboard.

You don't want your Camembert to be an afterthought at a stall that specialises in French cheeses. You want it to blow minds, to be the star of the show. It can get overlooked because the only preparation it requires in the morning is to be pulled from the fridge and stacked nicely on to the display. I think that's a mistake. Nuala, too. She is keenly aware of Camembert's fire power.

Our standard Camembert de Normandie is made from raw milk – it has to be to carry the AOP – and comes from the homeland of Camembert, Normandy. The milk is sourced from a local cooperative and matured in the manner traditional to the region. We are in another universe here from an average supermarket Camembert – you can get dodgy ones.

Assessing a Camembert involves what might appear like theatre. It did to me when I first saw one of our most prized regulars, Selim, ask to do it. 'Can I?' He looked at me.

I was a bit nervous about what he was about to do. What was he about to do? How many of our rules might he break? Still, Selim is one of my all-time favourite customers. I've liked and respected him from day one, so I answered nervously: 'Sure.'

Selim took hold of a box, opened the lid, brought it close to his face and took a long, slow sniff in through his nose. I watched him closely, fascinated, while also looking out into the market with some concern, not knowing what was coming next and not wanting people to see what he was doing. It felt so intimate.

He then pressed his right thumb gently into the middle of the waxed paper wrapped cheese. He was deeply concentrated and it struck me there was something almost religious in the way he was proceeding. After a moment, Selim closed the box and set it back on the table. He took another. The exact same careful process was repeated. Sometimes, he will examine five Camemberts in this way until he's satisfied he's identified the right cheese for him.

Over time, I learned that Selim does not like his Camembert too ripe. He was hoping to discern through smell and resistance to his pressed thumb at what stage the paste had arrived. If it's resistant to pressure, it's younger and the paste will be springy, even chalky in the centre. If his thumb sinks into the cheese, the paste will have begun to break down, sometimes considerably, giving you a runny Camembert. Smelly, too. Only he knows exactly the right degree of resistance he's hoping for.

Of course, to get an accurate steer on a Camembert, it's much simpler just to open the package and have at it, as Cheesemonger Nuala, Manager Elle and I are about to do. As with so many of our artisan cheeses, each on their own living journey, Camembert is full of surprises. Two or three days is more than enough for it to cross a line, several lines even.

I feel Nuala, Selim and I are aligned on the subject of Camembert: we like them before they're too funky, while all the complexities are there to be enjoyed. We are always searching for the perfect one – to strike gold, again – because we've had it once before. We know, and we know we know. Perhaps it's folly ever to think you can recreate a uniquely sublime tasting experience, but chasing that high, or going one better, is a driving motivation. In my experience, that same desire inspires a lot of our customers' cheese purchases.

On this pre-dawn Saturday at Borough Market, with the sounds of market traders preparing their stalls all around us, I watch Nuala remove the wrapping of the boxed Camembert she's chosen, but not in the careful way Selim did. She does it vigorously. She sets it on the table, positions a small, black-handled knife and she presses through. I swear I can give you an educated first guess on what it will taste like just by seeing how much give there is as the knife sinks through the paste. A second cut produces the first wedge, then she cuts one for Elle and one for herself: the moment of truth.

'Thanks.' I take hold of mine. I've been next to her watching, but also quietly absorbed in plotting my strategy for the goat's cheese display while Nuala's been focused on the Camembert.

Elle is hoisting the big Alpine wheels effortlessly. 'Got it,' she says, after coming over to us and picking up her bit of Camembert. When we taste together, there is always silence, even if it's just a beat.

I tend to defer to Nuala and certainly on Camembert. She was with the company from Day One and has an astonishing palate. She's in her thirties, shoulder-length brown hair, shorter in stature, considerable in influence. Elle and I have big love and big respect for her.

Five full beats now, a low growl emerges from her. Then: 'Oh yeah.' Nuala smiles.

My verdict is also a wow. 'How can that taste so good?' It's an earnest question, though taken rhetorically.

This Camembert has a faint line of chalk running through the centre but it yields easily to pressure, like a medium-firm pillow. There is nothing in its aroma that pushes back in an untoward way. This Camembert is all about drawing you in, a seductive cheese that's got a lot going on.

'Wild garlic,' says Fionnuala.

Elle puts it simply but in her light Welsh accent each syllable gets emphasis: 'That is delicious.'

For me, a good Camembert gives you a breath of the sea, nothing too strong, mind you. Do the cheeses pick that up from cows feeding in the sea air near to the coast? Probably not, but I like to think so. There is a hint of mushroom, grassy notes absolutely, butter more than cream. I am also brought to imagine a freshly scrambled egg.

'Ah, I'll be taking one of these home,' says Nuala with satisfaction.

When you're against the clock on a Saturday morning, so many tasks take priority. If you thought this magical moment wasn't one, our Saturday apron-clad trio pausing as a group to taste the Camembert, you'd be wrong. This is how cheese gets sold, this exact moment before any customers arrive. In these initial hours, each of us is quietly staking out a position on the day's offerings. Our direction of travel is being set.

Sure, some people come to the stall knowing exactly what they want. However, most of our customers are looking to us for cues and counsel. The most common question I get asked about cheese is, 'What's your favourite?' The answer to that question emerges every morning – ask me around 10 a.m. I can tell you right now, we'll sell out of Camembert today.

'Guys?' says Nuala.

Elle: 'Yeah?'

'I love working with you.'

Elle looks at us both, 'It's gonna be a good day.'

Camembert de Normandie

'Tout le dessert défila devant lui, sans qu'il acceptât autre chose qu'un peu de camembert.'

– Émile Zola, 'All the desserts were paraded before him, though he accepted nothing but some Camembert.'

Origin: Local legend has it that Camembert was invented by a Normande farmer named Marie Harel in 1791, on advice from a visiting abbot, Charles-Jean Bonvoust, who specialised in Brie-making. Large-scale manufacturing of the wooden box began 100 years later, allowing it to be stacked and easily transported. It has since become a symbol of the country, *'the real, the only, the authentic taste of France'*. Camembert de Normandie can only be made from raw milk and received its AOC in 1983 and its AOP in 1996.

Presentation: Bloomy rind, small wheels about 8cm diameter, weighing around 250g. They are wrapped in waxed paper and boxed. Inside, the paste can be gooey or firm or a bit of both, depending on how mature it is.

How to serve: Curiously, wine pairings are tricky. Some cheeses just don't pair well with wine and end up tainting your appreciation of the wine. Camembert de Normandie is a good example – try beer or a dry cider instead; bitter is best.

Fun fact: Camembert de Normandie really isn't the same cheese as 'Camembert'. Choose carefully and read the label.

31
We Close at 5

SERVING A CUSTOMER IS an elastic affair. It's something we don't have metrics on, a shame because I'd love to see them. It takes the time it takes for people to choose their artisan cheese. Even Cheesemonger Cian, who didn't faff about, would spend fifteen minutes taking a good customer on a voyage through our cheeses. No one begrudges them, and maybe this is down to the thrill of working with exceptional cheese, but any annoyance with the customers is rare.

For the record, mind you, here's a thing that will drive most mongers bonkers, when after taking a customer on a journey through cheese, sometimes tasting as many as a dozen, using all our wiles to try to suss out what the right cheeses might be for them, they end up saying this:

'Okay, I've decided. I'll take seventy-five grams of Comté.'

'You know that's not a lot of cheese.' In Great British Pounds, it's around £2.50. I show them with the knife how thin the slice is going to be.

'Oh, actually, I'll take just a bit less than that.' I am so greedy that I cannot conceive of coming home with less than 100 grams of cheese. It feels like an amount you could easily eat all at once, almost like a mint.

'I can't make a clean cut that thin, I'm afraid. Also, 100 grams is the minimum we sell.'

'Okay then, 100 grams, please.'

So much time spent for such a meagre purchase, I move on, cut, wrap, collect payment, and send them on their way. We are, of course, happy to serve 100 grams of Comté to anyone at any time. The issue here was having become invested in an affair of the heart, pairing cheeses to a potential suitor, and coming up so short.

Did I say, 'happy to serve to anyone at any time'?

We close at 5 p.m.

That doesn't stop some people and closing time customers are a breed apart.

On the positive side, people who show up at the last minute are often so relieved you are still selling that they will buy, somewhat recklessly, large quantities of cheese. Alternately, you get people at the end of the day who are acquainted with European markets and their rhythms and come looking for closing time deals. They can walk away with all sorts of riches if they play their cards right.

It's hard to get upset with these folks, unless they are irritated that you're closing. That seldom happens; however, I once had someone come up to the stall forty-five minutes after the market closed. Our cheeses were all sound asleep in bed, the floors had been washed and the tables put away.

'Excuse me! Are you still open?'

'No, sorry, the tills are off and we are just about to shut off the lights.' The rest of the market stalls are already dark. We are one of the last ones on site because there is so much cleaning to do.

'Seriously?' He asks.

''Fraid so! Open again tomorrow at 9 a.m.'

'But it's for tonight!'

Well, at least it isn't for next week, right? That would be annoying. 'For tonight, I'll sell you a Camembert or a Mont d'Or, which are awesome cheeses and don't need me to do any cutting, weighing or wrapping. You'll be a hero.'

'I wanted some Brie.'

'Okay, that's a hard no. The Brie is tucked up in bed. Final offer, Camembert de Normandie or Vacherin Mont d'Or, two of our finest, take it or leave it.'

'I'll take it.'

We got there but it doesn't have to be like this, because serving after close can be a delight. I hold in great esteem one customer in particular, a French woman in her late forties and a mum, who came right up to me as I was getting ready to cash off the till, half past five on a Thursday.

There is not a single cheese anywhere to be seen, all put away. The first thing she says to me, in English, is: 'Do you speak French?'

Now that is a question that means something completely different.

She doesn't need to speak French – her English is fine. What she wants is a cultural ally, someone who will understand that her late purchase of cheese that evening is a) an oversight that a busy French mother can be forgiven as she runs from shop to shop to prepare a crucial meal; b) a sign of respect for our product: French cheese is this important to her, she can't miss out stopping at our stall even after close; and c) a signal that she is serious about purchasing a significant quantity of cheese, sight unseen, provided she is going to be dealing with someone equally as serious as she.

All of the above will require someone who knows French, even if they aren't a passport holder. I make a split-second decision to serve her and answer: 'Oui, je parle français.'

Who am I kidding? She has me in the palm of her hand. She switches immediately into French and gets down to business.

She is throwing together a last-minute raclette for some unexpected guests.

Raclettes are a hearty, convivial treat, a meal where people cook seated all together while chatting away and having a glass or two of wine or beer. With the classic home raclette appliance, you choose a bit of cheese and place it in a small implement that in French is called *une pelle* (a shovel, a word that feels somehow crude in translation), which slots underneath a heating element. You wait for the cheese to bubble up, sip your drink, listen to the conversation, and watch other people compose their own raclette creations. Once your cheese portion is ready, you're the boss – you slide it on to, well, on to whatever you fancy: little new potatoes, cornichons, pickled onions, cured meats, crusty bread, there are lots of options.

For the cheese, you need a good melter, to state the obvious. Some people are happy with just basic cheesiness – it's enough for them and that's fine – so they're not picky. However, if you want to take your raclette to a higher gustatory plane, you'll want something that's got a bit of kick and character. The eponymous Raclette cheese is the go-to cheese for a raclette dinner, and there are plenty. You can also go off-piste. Morbier works well, has a buttery, farmy taste and a tell-tale line of ash through the middle of its paste. It melts wonderfully. We have a goat's cheese called Tomme de Chambrouze – I've mentioned it before – also a great melter, if a bit pricey. Those will all step up your raclette. There are goat raclettes and smoked raclettes, raclettes of many varieties which we don't carry, but in France, you'd find them with relative ease even in supermarkets. You can get adventurous and go for a blue cheese, though they can come out a bit salt-forward. Fourme d'Ambert is a great choice. Melted, it's lovely and oozy.

My late-in-the-day emergency French customer is going classic – she wants a solid raclette, and she's in the right place. We normally have two, they are both raw milk and have plenty of flavour. Our French raclette is cheaper, less interesting as well. I am a huge fan of it – it's outrageously gooey when melted, but if I'm being honest, it's more texture than taste. When I get some trimmings of it, I will toast up some sour-dough bread, spread on some Dijon mustard and slice up an avocado, then pop the raclette trimmings on top of the avocado and under the grill it all goes. Heaven. It's thanks in no small part to the mustard, though.

Our star raclette is the Raclette d'Alpage, made in Switzer-land. Alpage indicates the milk is from cows that graze in Alpine pastures. These ladies get all the mountain treats at 1,600 metres altitude during the summer, and you can taste it. The cheese is made at the Au de Morge chalet, brined and washed every two days as the wheels mature. This gives them a handsome ochre rind and big-time *fromunda*. The wheels are about thirty-five centimetres in diameter. This is what you'd call a 'stinky' cheese if you were to use the term. The rind is sometimes tacky and as soon as you unwrap a wheel, everyone in the stall will know what you're up to. It can be a lot of cheese. Having said that, cut it up and melt it and what was (for me, anyway) slightly too big a cheese becomes succu-lently on point for a raclette. It delivers all the gooey texture of its French cousin, but also packs rich, meaty, umami flavours and a hint of artichoke. It's another level. Oh, and don't remove the rind. You'll see what I mean.

Our French mother immediately settles on the Swiss Raclette d'Alpage, so off I go to pull out the wheel that I had wrapped and put to bed half an hour ago. Cheesemonger Fionnuala is looking at me curiously, albeit with something like a grin. She carries on with the close and makes no effort to stop the late sale. Our French mum breaks into a wide smile and a look of delight as I take it out of its paper and ask her how much she'd like. She's buying about £40 worth of cheese here.

'Nuala, can you bring me a wire, please?' Everything has been put away and she's just finished the washing up.

'Coming right up!'

After the Raclette is wrapped, our customer looks at me with a glint in her eye and says, 'Do you have anything else really special?'

My respect for her levels up. I talk to her about a couple of the goat's cheeses that are on particularly good form, and specifically the Lingot des Causses. When they are at their peak, they should carry a pleasure-overload warning: cakey consistency, slight lactic acidity, gorgeously goaty. 'Oh. I'll have one of those please.' Again, she chooses sight unseen but when I bring it out to her, her eyes light up in satisfaction.

'Make that two,' she says. I am now bursting with affection.

Finally she asks, 'Avez-vous du Saint-Nectaire?'

She also leaves with a piece of Saint-Nectaire, which rounds things out nicely in that it's not our best cheese on the day, but what it demonstrates is that she has her favourites, comforting cheeses like Tomme de Savoie for me, and you can but admire that.

Cheesemonger Nuala is a Francophile of the highest order. 'Wow Michael, she had us both from "Do you speak French?" – am I right? I enjoyed every second of that.'

Raclette

'Un goût franc, pur, comme l'eau de source.'

– Eddie Baillifard, Raclette du Valais AOP Ambassador,
describing the taste of a fine Raclette as a 'clean, pure taste, like
spring water'.

Origin: There's a legend (there often is), of a Swiss farmer and
cheesemaker named Léon who wanted a warm meal to eat
but had no utensils, so he heated his cheese directly over the
fire. Raclette was born. There is some confusion between the
meal and the cheese. Both originated in Switzerland,
probably around the twelfth century in the Valais. Today,
you'll find Raclette du Valais AOP, Raclette d'Alpage, and
scores of declinations.

Presentation: Most raclettes tend to be fairly hefty wheels,
around 30cm in diameter and 6cm high. They'll have a
pink-ish rind with a smooth, supple paste inside. Definitely
eat the rind when heated, it can be the highlight.

How to serve: Raclettes are made to be melted by approaching
an element and scraping the melted cheese on to a plate filled
with potatoes, pickles and meats, or by putting them in little
shovels under an element. There are other ways of doing it,
including the legendary Léon and his open fire. Some people
seek out the finer raclettes as a table cheese. Depending on
where it's produced, it will have variations in taste, but
principally, a lovely, farmy creaminess. It can be strong.
Aromatic white wines with higher acidity make for good
pairings, and why not seek out a mountain white. For reds, go

light- to medium-bodied with some good acidity to cut through the fat – Pinot Noirs and Gamays are good bets. For beer, try something cleaner and lighter so as not to overwhelm everything on the plate.

Fun fact: Down at the end of our alley in Borough Market, people queue up for raclette made in Bermondsey, called London Raclette. I know it's huge in France, Switzerland and Montreal, but I'll always associate raclette first and foremost with a chilly winter's day in Borough Market, where dozens are sat on concrete blocks eating up heaped, steaming plates of it. Yum.

32
New Cheese on the Block

'NEW CHEESE, GUYS!' THE delivery's come in and Elle has pulled something out of a grey crate that neither Cheesemonger Fionnuala nor I have seen before.

'What's it called now?' asks Nuala, squinting at the label. 'Jesus, that's a mouthful.'

'Tommette de la Croix Lucas,' I read out loud.

Matter of factly, Nuala says, 'That's about the Frenchiest French name you could possibly make up.'

'They're so high!' says Elle, pointing to how the wheels are a good seven centimetres in height, although each one's slightly different. Across, they're about twelve centimetres.

'I love the colour. Like an ochre, close to orange.' Nuala is weighing one in her hand. 'They're washed rind then?'

'Lightly,' says Elle. 'Cow's milk. Ben says they're not particularly punchy but with solid character, recent addition to the stable.'

'Can we try one already?' I love new cheese day. It's like Christmas.

Nuala grabs a tomme knife and halves one. The cheese is semi-soft, very much on the firm side.

We each get a piece, hold it to our noses almost in unison and take a sniff. Then we have a good chew, but it's not a magic moment.

'Meh,' says Nuala.

'Let's see how we get on with it,' says Elle. 'I think they sent us a sign as well.' She looks in the admin box to see if she can find it.

I don't say a word at the time because there's not a lot to say. It's proper artisan cheese and it's got character but nothing is standing out for me. Nothing is standing out for anyone, from what I can see. The paste is wound up so tight, it's not giving anything away.

Hang on a minute. There is a sweet and sour tang in there somewhere, and some good funk, it's just faint.

'The jury is decidedly out,' I end up saying. 'I reckon we can do something with this but it's going to have to be a two-way street.'

I pick up the cut half wheel, hold it up dramatically and look at it right in the paste.

'*Alors,* Monsieur Tommette de la Croix Lucas? I hope I've got that right.'

I bring out my European French now, sternly. '*Écoutez, Monsieur.* We are going to need a bit more effort from you, *n'est-ce pas*?' Then back into Canadian English: 'Relax a little, will ya?'

Ten days later, same Borough Market cheese stall, same cheesemongers, same cheese.

Cheesemonger Nuala: 'Holy, Michael! Have you had a taste of the Tommette lately?'

'I have not. I felt spurned by it the other day. Update?'

'Taste for yourself.'

'What's going on?' asks Elle. 'Whoa, what's happened here?'

Nuala has cut into a wheel of Tommette and the paste, instead of being tight, is bulging, starting to ooze from the centre. What's happened is that over ten days, the mysteries of cheese ripening have worked a miracle, beating stubborn casein proteins down until they relent and produce a gooey elixir.

'Let's get tasting some of that pronto.' I reach in for a piece that you almost have to scoop off the knife, pop it in my mouth and ... it's a creamy, umami, *fromunda* onslaught.

'Oh, my stars.' I take a step back and begin to clap. 'Ladies and Gentlemen, Monsieur Tommette de la Croix Lucas has entered the building.'

We're always told never to think we can know someone from the first time we're introduced to them. For cheeses that holds tenfold. That Tommette made its appearance only recently and is now a firm favourite among the mongers.

Saint-Nectaire

'Si l'on veut vous y régaler, c'est toujours du saint-nectaire que l'on vous annonce.'

– Pierre Jean-Baptiste Legrand d'Aussy, writing about his trip to l'Auvergne in 1768, telling his readers that 'If people there really want to treat you, they'll always bring out the Saint-Nectaire'.

Origin: Geographically, Saint-Nectaire comes from one of the smallest AOP areas, a patch of the Auvergne between Cantal and Puy-de-Dôme. The cheese has a rich history, first appearing in texts as Saint-Nectaire in 1651. Before that, dating back to the Middle Ages, the cheese was known as 'rye cheese' for having been matured on stalks of rye. These *fromages de seigle* were one way peasants settled their accounts with landowners. Once Saint-Nectaire was served to the Sun King, Louis XIV, it became a royal favourite. The first production syndicate was established in 1947, and its AOC was awarded in 1955.

Presentation: A cheese with a handsome moleskin rind, wheels are about 22cm wide and 3 to 5cm thick. Weights vary but the upper end is 1.8kg. The paste can be ivory to golden and should be on the softer end of semi-soft, as though it wants to ooze. If your Saint-Nectaire is too firm, it is likely to have been kept without the proper humidity or is possibly over-matured. It's still tasty with a firmer paste, but a proper Saint-Nectaire head-rush comes from luscious, yielding paste with just the right amount of farmy, hazelnut flavours. Eat the rind.

How to serve: A beauty on a cheeseboard, it can happily be eaten on its own, no bread or crackers necessary. One of my ideal lunch plates is a wedge of Saint-Nectaire next to a fresh salad with a light, Dijon vinaigrette. Wine pairings, try a Cabernet Franc or a Merlot, say a Chinon Rouge from the Loire Valley or a Pomerol from Bordeaux. This is a cheese that works well with beer, something more substantial even, a wheat beer or a porter.

Fun fact: There are two varieties of AOP Saint-Nectaire: fermier and laitier. Aim for a Saint-Nectaire fermier – a farm-produced cheese that's made from raw milk. More taste. The laitier version is made from milk that's been heated close to or at pasteurisation. It has a more lactic flavour, still tasty, and will age less aggressively. One of my few cheese aversions is to Saint-Nectaire that's been matured too long – it can exude an ammoniated odour that I won't spend any time describing in detail, but that I can't erase from my olfactory memory.

33
Tier Four

IN OUR AGE OF mass-produced food sold in supermarkets, we expect things to taste the same as they did the last time we bought them. If they don't, we are not best pleased. If I buy a product that disappoints me compared to my last purchase of it, I can get radical. 'I won't buy that again.' No second chances.

I am such a hypocrite, because that's not at all the way it is with artisan cheeses. They taste different every day – sometimes they taste different in the afternoon to how they did in the morning – and I love them for that! In fact, I'm suspiciously curious to know what's been done to shrink-wrapped, mass market cheeses so that they taste identical to the last piece I bought months ago.

One of our more variable cheeses is a Basque-country beauty called Ossau Iraty. It's an AOP, named after the Ossau Valley and the Iraty forests in France, south of Pau. It's a sheep's cheese and comes in wheels about twenty-five centimetres in diameter, weighing around five kilograms, which makes for a smaller wheel compared to other hard cheeses, but it's sizable enough. The rind reminds me of the colour of a butternut squash on the outside. You often get bright ochre spots on it. In my head, the more ochre spots there are, the nicer it will taste, but that is based on absolutely nothing except my own experience from having worked with it. Most often it's spotless.

A good wheel of Ossau is tough to stop eating. I get a sweet warmth from it, almost a biscuit flavour close to toasted caramel. It's not unlike Manchego, which more people are familiar with, smoother tasting though. The higher fat content means it has a melting quality on the tongue. People swoon for it.

I have also had wheels of Ossau that have the same butternut squash rind but taste like tuna and cucumber sandwiches. I know that's an odd tasting note, but Cheesemonger Llewi, who works in the warehouse, came up with it out of the blue and it was a light bulb moment. 'It does taste like tuna and cucumber sandwiches, Llewi!' When you get two such different wheels – caramel biscuit v tuna cucumber – in a blind taste test you might think it was a different cheese altogether. It's a wonder how a cheese can swing so wildly.

Ossau Iraty is made at cooperative scale, a significant production. It's popular enough in France that some big food companies make savoury biscuits that come in an Ossau Iraty flavour. Ours is thermised, meaning that the milk is warmed during production, not to the point of pasteurisation; nevertheless, it's a method of sanitising raw milk.

At Borough Market, there's a French gentleman in his seventies who comes round and makes a beeline for the Ossau Iraty, usually on Fridays.

'Here we go again,' mutters Cheesemonger Fionnuala. 'Do you want to handle this, or shall I?'

'I feel you normally do, so I'll have a go today.'

'It's all yours.'

'Good afternoon, sir. Do you fancy trying some cheese? I have some Ossau Iraty here on the knife.'

He looks up, 'Is this a raw milk Ossau Iraty?' By raw milk, he's asking if it's unpasteurised. We specialise in raw milk cheeses and many customers seek us out for them. They believe strongly that raw milk enhances flavour. So do I. Many people also believe it's healthier – they don't like how pasteurisation kills off good bacteria along with potentially harmful ones. Cheesemakers who don't pasteurise take special care with their production for safety's sake. There is, however, a heightened risk with raw milk cheeses, and people with immune deficiencies and pregnant women are told to avoid them. In my time as a cheesemonger, there has never been a problem with any of our raw milk cheeses.

'Sir, our Ossau Iraty is thermised, not raw milk. There is a raw milk version of the cheese called Ossau Fermier, but I'm afraid we don't stock it currently.'

'Last time I was here, the sign for your Ossau Iraty indicated it was a raw milk cheese. It was wrong.'

'Do you remember when that was, sir? Our sign hasn't changed in some time.'

He thinks it was a year ago. 'You can't label thermised cheeses as raw milk. That's not ethical and it's terribly misleading.' He makes the same protest – exactly the same protest – every time he comes to the stall.

I could just nod and let him finish, but on this occasion, I switch suddenly from English into my best Parisian French. This gives me licence to be more pointed with him. You can be far more direct with customers in French than in English, especially European French. It's expected. I tell him that the sign has not changed in my time cheesemongering. I agree with him, emphatically, that selling a thermised cheese as a raw milk cheese would be unethical and I say, with a hint of Gallic affront in my voice, that it is something we would never do.

He looks at me straight in the eye, nods, and not another word is spoken of it.

'I think he just misses going to the shops in France,' says Nuala after he leaves, meaning he misses the robust repartee in France. When people complain about Parisian waiters being direct (rude), I respond that I've always considered that to be part of a mutually agreed-upon contract with Parisian customers, who are just as direct.

We've all had this exchange with him in our own way. Manager Elle one day gets into an extended discussion with him, including about the merits of raw milk Ossau Fermier, and as a result, a few weeks later, we get a wheel of it in to sell. Excitement! It has a wild, pockmarked rind, and the paste, too, is a bit bonkers, mottled with the occasional bruise. To me, it tastes strongly of black olive. On other occasions it has tasted strongly of mangoes. Yes, mangoes – go figure!

Our French gentleman returns and gladly purchases a wedge. There is something beguiling about it, he is right.

Just as I'm getting acquainted with all the changes at the stall and only a couple of weeks after leaving my radio job definitively, something disturbing happens that reminds me of that dark day in November of the year previous. One afternoon, despite the day starting off normally, things start to feel very wrong at Borough Market.

It's the Saturday before Christmas 2020, one of our busiest days of the year, but the crowds are thinning, and people are visibly on edge. There's a febrility in the air. It's something you can't quite put your finger on, nothing like the sudden panic of the Fishmongers' Hall attack, but it's real and it's contagious.

I can see it in our cheesemongers' faces as well, furrowed brows, constant straightening of face masks. We are still busy filling Christmas orders, but from our jumpy, jittery customers things begin to emerge. I am catching snippets of conversation between them and other cheesemongers about a 'Tier Four'.

That can't be, I think, with my journalist's hat on. There are only three Coronavirus tiers in England. People get the news wrong all the time. Initially, I chalk the whole thing up to just another example of Covid weirdness. Tiers have been introduced in Britain as an alert system – medium, high, and very high – each with its own rules and guidelines. As much as I try to push the worrying talk aside and get on with things, the bad vibes continue and Cheesemonger Nuala finally grabs a moment with me as we are each wrapping an order in the same part of the stall.

'Tier Four now, Michael, I don't like it,' she says.

'Tier what now? I thought there were three?'

'There were, now that fool Boris Johnson has added another. After all that talk just last week about it being inhuman to cancel Christmas! He should have been more cautious from the start.'

We don't have time to talk, so I return to my customers. The next people in the queue are regulars, a sensible retired couple who live in the Barbican. I greet them warmly.

'Hello, hello! Lovely to see you two. How are things?'

'Well, when we heard about the new restrictions, we decided to come right over and finish our Christmas purchases so we can stay low for a while.'

'What have you heard?'

'The numbers look bad. Handbrake turn, Boris is calling it. No other choice. We think it's going to be a long winter.'

Deep breath. If there's a rise in infections, things have been getting worse for a while and it's only showing up now. We're outdoors, we're masked, I've decided I want to be working as much as possible and not locked up at home. I've made my peace with this level of risk. There's no point being any more worried than I was three hours ago. Besides, it is Christmas at the cheese stall, a magical time.

'Right, let's get you hooked up with some of these beauties and on your way then, shall we?'

Elle laments the timing to me between customers. 'Great to have this happen on our busiest Saturday of the year, isn't it? But what can we do?'

'Stick to the plan and remain calm, I reckon. We already have our Covid rules. Some people are feeling scared though, I think.'

The new Tier Four rules come into effect at midnight, so some of the customers we might get on a day like today have clearly decided to bolt to the non-essential shops to finish their Christmas shopping – after today, those shops will be closed until the numbers drop. Others are staying at home, staying safe. We are a bit less busy and customers are impatient. They are trying urgently to tick things off their list and move on. People want to get home. When the market shifts into closing gear, the happy buzz of traders cleaning up is nowhere to be heard. We are looking to get home as fast as possible, too.

In the end, our Corona Christmas is different from the year before, but also familiar. We are extremely busy and we sell a lot of cheese. Last year, we maximised the number of people in our space in a way we simply could not this time around. Then, people crowded into the stall like you might into a pub. This time, the market sets up a single file queuing system with tapes.

My Christmas duties have changed. On top of selling, I'm in charge of the end-of-day delivery and stay in the market past closing time, on my own, waiting for the white van to come by with tomorrow's cheese. While I wait, I lay lining paper on top of all the newly Topaxed surfaces and empty the fridge completely. Every box, every piece of cheese comes out, so that the newest, the younger batches go in first.

It feels a bit lonely and not in the spirit of comrades in arms from last Christmas. Sometimes, after having emptied the fridge completely, I sit at the back of the stall, alone with a low-alcohol Table Beer and a pack of the dark rye digestives we sell now and listen to BBC Radio 6 Music while I wait for the delivery. 6 Music has a feature they call the 'People's Playlist'. To honour the sacrifices key workers are making, they are allowing them to make requests and doing shout-outs to them. Alone on my stool, I type in a message. 'Don't forget the cheesemongers lol, key workering away.' They read it out. I feel a rush of solidarity. Radio, bruv.

It's not until January that the scary part of this second wave of infections and its new variant begin really to hit home. One of the iconic figures of Borough Market is taken ill. It's Maria, owner of the café at the heart of the market. She's in hospital and we hear has been put on a ventilator. That news spreads around the market like wildfire. At the stall, we learn that one of our drivers has come down with Covid, a lovely guy, sturdy and dependable. We are worried for him and for his family. The news is unnerving.

Then, suddenly, a number of staff who work at Cheese HQ get an evening phone call asking them to report to Leicester Square, where there's a rapid testing operation. There's a concern over one of the cheesemonger's flatmates having taken ill. With people working indoors in a refrigerated environment, albeit with lots of space, there can be no taking chances. Everyone comes back negative, another collective shiver. At the shop, one of the cheesemongers' housemates tests positive and now he has to stay home to avoid any chance of contamination. Another player down, this one key to our functioning and our morale.

At that point, some big decisions are made that set the tone for the rest of the winter and the lockdown. We set up bubbles at the different sites. Normally, we would work where needed, no more. Our Borough Market bubble is to be Manager Elle, Cheesemonger Nuala, and me. Deliveries come when we're not there for the most part, so contact is reduced to a minimum.

In the weeks following, our market lives settle into a surreal routine. Every fifteen minutes, a taped message is played over the tinny market public address system, 'At this time, we kindly ask customers not to consume food or drink on site. If there's a queue forming, come back later. Stay calm. We are all in this together.' The recording is in a 1950s style, with cut-glass vowels. It has a *Doctor Who* feel to it. The market hires a dozen security guards and sets up barriers to control any crowds.

In a month, the news turns better for Maria. She is off the ventilator. Our driver has recovered, as well. We see him one afternoon from a distance and have a good talk. The company has managed to avoid any other positive test results. We are a group of people in whom sanitary regulations are ingrained from day one – we are doing well under the circumstances. On top of all that, the pandemic has transformed the market from what had become a tourist destination to, well, a market, its original vocation.

It becomes a time I will treasure, despite being aware of how much strain and suffering are going on hidden from view. Treasure, because we become a destination for comfort and a chat. People still want their cheese. Not only do they have to eat, but treats make nervous times feel better: a fondue, a Reblochon-stacked tartiflette, or a baked Vacherin make for an excellent 'Big Night In' on a cold, pandemic winter's evening.

The market is located about 500 metres away from Guy's Hospital, so a number of NHS staff come to see us. They are weary, determined people looking for little points of light in their day, a cheesy treat, some stolen time for a quick chat.

I find myself drawn to them, saying: 'Listen, this is going to sound strange coming from a cheesemonger but just thank you for everything you're doing. We are so grateful to you.' In these disconcerting pandemic days, I find emotions have the power to rush me, suddenly.

Our special attentions have an impact on them, despite the fact they almost seem like they're sleepwalking by the time they see us. We give a small discount and a free treat when we have one. They come back and tell us how much they enjoyed their last order. We fuss over them, always happy to see them back. It makes us feel like we're doing our part in a time where we mostly feel powerless.

In normal times, with so many tourists, you make connections where and when you can at the cheese stall. Now, things are completely different. Everyone becomes a regular, or a potential regular. People who live in the neighbourhood start coming to see us, partly because the crowds are gone, partly because they say they like that we're outside. It makes them feel safer.

One of our regulars is named Ellen. She comes on Fridays and spends up to fifteen minutes choosing her cheese and recounting her week's adventures: walks across London, things she's never seen or noticed before, new recipes she's trying at home. It's like a friend popping by who just happens to be picking up cheese.

Plenty of regular customers are French, Belgian or Swiss. There's one woman in particular who I think comes just to have a conversation in French. She buys only a single goat's cheese but stays for a lengthy chat. I become her one-on-one, her non-Zoom chat with a flesh and blood human being. For people like her, the visit feels like an almost stolen, forbidden pleasure. For us, too.

We get a lot of questers, people who are looking to make a recipe or to find a cheese they tasted once on a holiday. A guy in his twenties comes up to us wanting to recreate a French recipe for cheesy, garlicky mashed potatoes, aligot. It's part of a pandemic project instead of travelling: to cook dishes from around the world, post them and describe them, one per week. We don't carry the Tomme Fraîche he is looking for, it's hard to source from London, but we take some time coming up with a combination of cheeses that would make a plausible substitute. It's a fun half-hour of talking and laughing, filled with the pandemic thirst for interaction and contact. We get a big shout out in his aligot post, and the final product looks awesome.

With these humanity seekers, we share smiles and little jokes about the routine and monotony of our pandemic lives. Cheesemonger Nuala tells everyone who will listen that they absolutely must start bingeing *Call My Agent* (*Dix Pour Cent*), the French dramedy about a Parisian casting agency, and *Spiral* (*Engrenages*) the Parisian police procedural. There is a customer who takes two tubs of plain organic yoghurt early every Saturday morning who is about to become a grandfather. We get updates every week, until one day.

'The baby's here!'

'What! That's fantastic,' says Elle. Nuala and I join at the front of the stall to coo over the first photos. They haven't met their grandchild yet, of course, and who knows when they will, so that pleasure is still to come.

Elle, Nuala and I become tight, each other's saviour. I look forward to working partly because it means seeing them, real human beings. And the cheeses, of course. We keep each other on an even keel. We swap stories about our pandemic home lives, laugh a lot about silly things and bring in baking and treats. Nuala wants me to try all the strange British things I've managed to avoid in my years here, like Soreen. I believe part of this project is to watch my face as I eat them. The Soreen goes down badly as she laughs and laughs.

With the other traders at the market, we build stronger ties. Pietro, the big, handsome, curly-haired Italian from the cheese toastie and raclette stall, starts stopping by. Every so often he brings along a piping hot toastie that beats any I've made myself. It turns out his mother is French, so we have chats in French that remind him of her.

One day I ask him, 'How did you end up in London, Pietro?'

'I was drugged by an Englishwoman and brought here tied up in the back of a car.'

Next door at the Italian ham and Mozzarella stall, Phil's three adult children have started to take over the daily running of the stall. More often than not it's Benjamin, Jonathan and the glorious Esther who are on duty. Esther is a gorgeous, pixie-faced young woman whose hair changes colour every few weeks. Hot pink is my personal favourite. She and Elle are inseparable. The three kids are hard-working, but also silly and rambunctious whenever there's time. It's infectious for all of us.

Phil is still present, of course, in fact more present than I ever suspected. He loves to tease us, good-naturedly, about how long his queues are and how large his sales are. If we go particularly big on a display on what is likely to be a slow day, he will rib us, 'My, that's a hubristic display of cheese.'

One day I arrive at the stall and to my horror there are muddy tracks and dirt all around one of the front corners inside our stall near the drain. In the strange way your brain works early in the morning, I start thinking I messed up the close, forgot to clean the floor. How could that be?

Phil is around the corner as I am WTFing, and says, 'Oh, there were workers in your stall cleaning out the drains. Did they not tell you about it?'

'Wait, what? When? While you were still here?'

'No, I was watching at home on the CCTV.' It turns out there's a camera near the stall and Phil watches it on his mobile phone from home. That morning Nuala and I spend the first half hour scrubbing and bleaching to clean up the mess and get everything in order.

Every day begins with 'Buongiorno Francesco! Hello Allan! Hello Barbara!' We share goodies with each other. Francesco will sometimes make a plate of pasta on the small burner he has at the back of the stall. Barbara will pop by: 'Michael, here's some of those olives I know you like so much, the green ones, gordal, with the guindilla peppers.' We become a second family to each other. I make her cheese lunch plates with our trimmings to share with Allan.

The winter lockdown weeks pass by like this, and along with the increasing light and the emergence of spring flowers, the quick progress of the vaccination effort lifts everyone's spirits. Whenever I speak with friends and family back in Canada, stuck in lockdown, I say to them, 'I'm so lucky to be working at the market through this.'

Ossau Iraty

'This is just very different from both. It's not as gritty, it's not as aged ... it's very flavourful.'

– Afrim Pristine, author and cheesemonger, discussing how Ossau Iraty compares to its Spanish and Italian sheep's milk cousins, Manchego and Pecorino.

Origin: This cheese is eponymous with the mountains, valleys and forests of the Pyrenees, its name derived from local geography. Cheesemaking in the area goes back centuries, and there's written evidence of it as early as the first century. Could this be one of the first cheeses ever made? Some think so. Notarised evidence of sheep's milk cheesemaking in the area dates to the fifteenth century. Ossau Iraty received its AOC in 1980 and its AOP in 1996.

Presentation: I love the description of Ossau as 'the shape of a small millstone'. They are much easier to handle than an Alpine wheel, 20 or 25cm in diameter, 11 to 13cm high with a convex heel. They weigh no more than 7kg. Their rind reminds me of the colour of a butternut squash and can be covered in bright orange spots of mould. Inside, the paste is off-white. Taste before you purchase – the taste profile of any given wheel can be vastly different. When you get a good one, you know it.

How to serve: This is a luscious ewe's milk cheese that melts in the mouth, so it's great for snacking on its own and will also complement any cheeseboard. Quince paste is a natural accompaniment, as are figs and apricots, fresh or dried.

Basques are known to eat it with black cherry jam or conserve. Try it in pasta as you would a Pecorino. You can make creative canapés with Ossau: so many possibilities. In France, you'll find several savoury biscuits flavoured with it on grocery shelves. For pairings, be careful with reds – tannic wines tend to do it no favours and that goes both ways. Seek out a rounder red, or instead go white with some nice fruitiness, or a Jurançon sec with round, honey notes, for example.

Fun fact: Farm-produced Ossau Fermier tastes like a different cheese altogether from Ossau Iraty, funkier and with strong black olive energy, sometimes mango, whereas Ossau Iraty tends towards a biscuity sweetness. Both are fantastic cheeses, just don't expect them to taste the same.

34
Good Friday

I HAVE BEEN DREADING TELLING you this part of the story, but here goes. Let's start way back in time to when I was a freshly trained cheesemonger. The delightful Susan came in for a shift – Susan is the former manager I once told you about. She's the one who used to have a market boyfriend, the Ukrainian raw milk stall guy.

Susan hasn't worked with us for a long time – she teaches primary school now and loves it. When she drops in to help us out and fill a shift, she works in the assured way of the manager she was. This leads to something horribly cringe-making for me.

At this point, I have recently overcome a mental block with a goat's cheese called Crottin de Chavignol. I couldn't figure out how to sell it, probably because it just didn't stand out for me among the many enticing, creamier, magical-looking goat's cheeses. I would always steer people elsewhere.

Crottins are sturdy little numbers, about five centimetres in diameter and three centimetres high. As they mature, they lose moisture and become more compact. The cheese inside is firm with a gentle aroma. They are one of the most reliable cheeses we carry, one reason they are a favourite of Chee-semonger Fionnuala.

I guess I was held at bay by Crottins based on appearances, possibly as well by the name.

Une crotte, in French, is a poop. There's some confusion whether Crottins are named after goat poops, which is sort of cute but a little disturbing, or from a patois word, *crot*, which means hole, as in the hole in the clay that was used originally as a mould to make a Crottin. It's the latter that's the true origin.

Whatever it's called, once you cut off a piece and pop it into your mouth, it has loads of rich, full, yeasty flavour. I sometimes say a Crottin has the taste of good sourdough bread, toasted and buttered. No matter how many times I eat one, I am always surprised by how deeply cheesy and rewarding it is. Also, sliced and placed on a crouton under the grill, it can be the winning part of a warm goat's cheese salad. Yum. I am won over.

When you open a new box of Crottins, they are often covered with an insane amount of mould. In French they call it *poil de chat* or cat fur. The cat fur will cover an entire box in a pattern, reaching beyond each individual Crottin to try to connect up all its other little brothers and sisters. Individual rinds at this stage are mottled light blue, grey or green; the pastes are moist as well as firm. They become firmer, darker and greyer as they mature, and they lose the cat fur completely. I prefer them more mature, and that's where we get to the cringe in this story.

On the day Former Manager Susan comes in for a shift, she decides to reduce the price of two mature Crottins. She wants to shift them. I take this personally, both on my behalf and on the Crottins'. I have been snacking away at these older Crottins all week and I know they are popping, possibly the best cheese at the stall this week. Then Susan swings in, declares them past it and deep discounts them.

'You know, they're tasting awesome,' I protest.

'Maybe, but they're the last of a batch – they need to go. The new ones make them look so hard and tired.'

Hard and tired. I stew in silence. Customers come and go, I get on with the day, but I am dwelling. 'So they are making the other Crottins look bad, bringing down the side, are they? Maybe it's the new ones who look funny next to them, did you ever think of it that way?' I think to myself.

Then the inevitable happens. While I am at the other end of the counter, Susan sells them to a nice enough looking man who likes a bargain.

'I'll give you these, two for a fiver,' Susan says to the customer. I don't look up, but gasp, audibly.

'Oh yeah? I'll give it a go, sure, why not?' He answers, ignoring me.

Before I can stop myself, this comes out of my mouth: 'You're lucky to have them at that price, you know.'

Awkward silence. Susan is completing his order. It's not really the done thing to comment on anyone else's sales while they're with the customer, unless it's for a smile or a laugh.

Swept away by righteous indignation, I add: 'Actually, I'm a little upset she's sold them to you. I was going to take them.' It has the ring of an ultimatum.

Susan looks over at me with a puzzled but clearly irritated expression that reads, 'Get back in your box, weirdo. What's wrong with you?'

So convinced am I of being right, and that defending those Crottins' virtue puts me in the right, that it is not until I get home, shower and change that the full embarrassment of that moment, the inappropriateness of it, floods in. My cheeks turn red. Meet my dark side. Alone, I say to myself, 'Christ almighty.'

Which brings us to Good Friday 2021, the darkest day of my cheesemongering career, when I convince myself that I have reached the end of the road and that it is time to leave the market and take off my apron for the final time.

There is a build-up. On the heels of the lockdown time in our bubble that I have treasured, and as the pandemic eases up, I begin to feel a pressure weighing down on me, threatening to turn me back into someone I do not like. At all costs, I do not want to return to the overburdened, overtired days of radio presenting. I only realise looking back, the idea scared me.

Part of it is coming from Cheese HQ and is totally understandable. The backdrop is that public health restrictions are being lifted one by one, in phases. The number of Britons vaccinated is approaching 50 per cent and a government public health survey suggests the number who have antibody protection against the virus is nearing 60 per cent. Combined with Brexit, full effects not likely to be known for months or years, only a brave soul would predict what business might look like for the rest of the year. However, you can be forgiven for making some pessimistic assumptions. This virus is stubborn, mutating. Equally mysterious are people's changes in behaviour after months of lockdown. Some have more disposable income, some less and the prospect of much less. Also, when the restaurants and pubs re-open, how much of our business will be redirected there? Then there's the question of cheese as indoor, pandemic comfort food. That imperative will fade. We are at an inflection point and it puts Cheese HQ into a defensive crouch, even as retail sales rise and continue to surprise. The bosses are intent on keeping costs in check so that any sudden downturn in sales can be compensated for in advance.

What this means for the cheesemongers is that we are being asked to revise our productivity and reduce labour costs. We begin to work alone, often. Whether you're two people or one, it's still the same amount of work to set up the stall from scratch, then put things back, clean and close for the evening.

Elle begins to lean on me to take more responsibility. I am more often given the complicated job of assessing our stock of cheeses and ordering, something I don't mind doing now, but it was not part of my original training and I don't have much confidence in myself to do it well. Things occasionally go un-done as a result of the extra responsibilities and working alone; stress builds up. I begin to have feverish dreams of things going wrong at work.

It all culminates in the week leading into Easter as Manager Elle has to leave town to be with her father in Wales, who has taken ill. Suddenly, all the balls she has in the air become mine, and I don't have me, a sturdy lieutenant to lean on. Adding to the burdens, we do not realise that with the mood brightening in the country thanks to the vaccination programme, people are primed to come out and buy a lot of cheese for the Easter holiday weekend. Staffing levels have not taken that into account.

On the Thursday before Easter, I end up on my own in the afternoon. Sales are through the roof and I make a personal best, but much of the fun of it is gone. There is no extra time to spend with any of the customers, little opportunity to share my enthusiasm for the cheeses, and with all the volume, I am keenly aware of making bigger messes, messes that only I will be there to clean up. With two more big days ahead, short-staffed, I don't want to be bleaching and scrubbing long into the evening after a full day's selling.

There is something in the sharing of effort when you are more than one that makes closing not just bearable but enjoyable. We spur each other on. As one picks up steam, the other feeds off it and the jobs are ticked off surprisingly quickly. When you're on your own, that energy is gone. There is still a drive to the finish line, but it is demoralising when you realise that it's you who will need to get through the entire, lengthy checklist. There will be no surprise assist that speeds you across the line. I begin to feel sorry for myself.

On Good Friday 2021, I wake up early and go for a run in Battersea Park to try to shake it off. I'm surprised by how much energy I have despite how busy I was the night before. Much of the fatigue, I calculate, is not physical but down to the burden I'm carrying being in charge. Overnight, I dreamt of stocks that had run low, awkward interactions that cropped up with customers or colleagues, cheeses that have now come to a point in their maturation that they need to be sold with a deft hand or prepared just so in order to present well. Arriving at the cheese stall, there is a feeling slightly akin to dread.

I arrive just two minutes early on that day, which is pushing it to the limit. Cheesemonger Nuala arrives moments before. Then Cheesemonger Cameron shows up with the weekend delivery, which throws up two problems. First, we have been bubbled for so long and we miss Cameron so much that we want to chat and catch up. I am the worst offender here. Even though I know it's going to cause a problem, I press pause. Cameron and I even decide to give each other a hug. I know, gasp! Despite the fact that I've had my first vaccination, this is strongly discouraged by the government. Many people think it's illegal and it's against company policy, but it feels great.

The second problem with Cameron's appearance is a slight screw-up with our urgent top-up delivery of cheeses and yoghurts so that we have enough for the weekend. Some goat's cheese we would dearly love to have is not there, some cheeses we have plenty of have come instead. It turns out this is down to crossed wires because I didn't pick up the phone while running that morning. Instead, Cheesemonger Nuala fielded the call and made a guess. Clearly, this is my mistake, but I think to myself, can I not have an hour to go for a run?

Then at 9.30 a.m., customers begin to arrive. The stall does not open until 10 a.m! They are thirty minutes before opening, and the stall looks sparse at best. I have put out a few wheels of hard cheese. Nuala has started on the bloomy rind cow's milk cheeses, but most of the slates are bare. We were not early when we needed to be, then we talked to Cameron, and now we are in a right pickle, a *cornichon* even.

Something even worse happens then. Faced with a huge problem, Nuala and I de-couple in our approach. Nuala feels the stall needs to be at the very least in a good functioning order before we serve, otherwise it will be chaos the entire day. She also believes that opening hours should hold sway and that customers who turn up early should be politely told to come back in half an hour so that we can focus. At the shop in East Dulwich, all is closed and locked while setting up, although sometimes a tap comes at the door.

My view differs from Nuala's. We are working in a market and the idea of opening and closing hours is a bit fuzzy. Some vendors are open to sell at 8 a.m. A baker will sell you bread even earlier. In a market, customers learn that early is no bad thing and they may as well try to buy earlier than at advertised hours.

It's a public holiday. Thinking it would be rude, I can't bear not to serve or tell people to come back in half an hour. It's Easter! People have come early to buy something special, a treat during the pandemic, and some of them are our regular customers who make bigger purchases. There is also a substantial subset of customers wary of the midday and afternoon crowds due to the virus. There will be consequences to turning them away, even for half an hour.

When all these people approach the stand, and even though I know we are in a tough spot, I can't help but smile and make them feel welcome. It's instinctual, kind of my thing. Nuala feels that I am making a crucial error, laying waste to the organisation that must be in place so that we can tackle the busy part of the day still to come. She is emanating negative energy, some of it for the entitled early birds and some of it for me. It doesn't help that some customers are making snide comments, such as: 'This is not your usual display.' No kidding, and 'So what exactly is the problem this morning?'

With nerves frayed, differing positions, and a whiff of panic, we decide that I will carry on serving while Nuala keeps her head down and gets the cheeses out on to the display. It doesn't really work and we never stop chasing our tails. What a horrible feeling. At times like these, if you are in tandem, you get by through solidarity and singular focus, but we are pulling in different directions. It's awful.

I am not proud of myself today. At all. I have been re-introduced to a person I do not like, myself, under stress and in charge. I start to snap at Nuala.

Her: 'Where are the small bags?'

Me: 'Where they always are.'

Her: 'We could use another bucket of alco-wipes up front.'

Me: 'Go ahead and get them.'

Why am I the one in charge? I am plunged into a negative feedback loop. I can't seem to stop myself from being cranky, then my own crankiness makes me more cranky. Worse, I am aware it's happening and I can't seem to stop it – it's making me not like myself, which makes me miserable.

There are some good moments even during the struggle and one hilarious, unexpected one that stands out. One of our early customers is a woman named Sylvie who used to manage the stall some time ago. When we hear her voice, Nuala's mind and mine go to exactly the same place: *deus ex machina*, we are saved!

'Sylvie!' We smile and sing out in tandem. 'How are you? What would you say to coming back here and putting on an apron?'

Sylvie says she absolutely can't – she has commitments.

We don't give up. As we work, we make friendly, flattering small talk to her. She's a few back in a slow queue. Twenty years of being a journalist persuading people to speak publicly when they aren't sure has made me, if anything, persistent. Tiresome, you might say.

No, no, no, she says, I'd love to, but the bosses never call me any more.

'I'm sure that's an oversight!' we say. 'We love working with you.' This has the added bonus of being true.

Nuala tells me later that in her time as manager, a thing Sylvie could never bear were cheesemongers who didn't open well. I can just imagine what she must have been thinking waiting in that queue. In the end, practicalities win out, and it all happens suddenly.

Sylvie realises that not only has she been standing and waiting for a long time, but the orders are also bigger than normal and she will end up standing for some considerable time more. It is always true, on top of that, that when you fill your own order, you get the best cheeses. There is a French saying, *On n'est jamais mieux servi que par soi-même.* 'One is never better served than by oneself.'

Next thing we know, Sylvie is behind the counter. She has found herself an apron and is tying the knot in front, pulling out a series of knives and wires. Hallelujah. We share a big laugh.

In my years working as a journalist, many of them have been as an editor and manager as well as being a presenter. I know how to lead, how to make an operation work and I can do it well, but it requires a certain amount of friction. I recognise that now and I don't want it. It was never something I sought out as a cheesemonger. Mongering is the cure, and was never meant to entail that kind of a burden.

The problem here and now is that I have shown I can manage the stall, and I am being asked to do it again and again. Once you've arrived at that stage of the job, of any job, part of the magic dies. It feels like this Easter is the weekend the cheesemongering magic has come to an end.

What a mess and what sadness. A voice inside me from the past rises up in alarm.

Crottins de Chavignol

'Leur lait n'est pas propre à faire du beurre, mais on en fait de très bons fromages: ceux du Sancerrois sont connus sous le nom de Crotins de Chavignolles.'

– *Statistiques du Cher*, 1829. In this departmental administrative tome, the author notes of local goat-keeping: 'Their milk is not suitable for making butter, but they make very good cheeses: those from the Sancerrois region are known as *Crotins de Chavignolles*.'

Origin: The name comes from Chavignol, a village in the Loire Valley. Back as far as the sixteenth century, goats were a fixture in the area. Husbands tended the vines, wives often kept goats, which were easy to feed and produced excellent milk for cheese. *Crot* refers to the original mould for the cheese, the word means a hole in the clay in regional dialect. The first Crottins de Chavignol began to make their way to Paris, and fame, in the 1900s. AOC from 1976, AOP from 1996.

Presentation: Make an O with your thumb and index finger, and you've got roughly the size of a Crottin. When they arrive young, they are mottled blue and grey and covered in cat fur mould. At this point, the pastes are bouncy and white. They firm up and begin to break down around the rind, which you must eat, by the way. As they age and lose moisture, they become greyer and develop a deep, rich yeastiness.

How to serve: Drop a few around your cheeseboard to the delight of everyone, or just snack away on one, one small wedge at a time. These work tremendously well in salads and are my go-to for *salade de chèvre chaud.* Slice them in discs and place them on similarly sized, lightly toasted rounds of bread or crouton, then under the grill for a few minutes – monitor closely so as not to burn the crouton, or just use the regular oven element to play it safe. When done, place them on top of your salad. They marry nicely with beetroot and will work in most recipes that call for goat's cheese. For pairings, the most obvious is a Sancerre, white, red or rosé, where Chavignol hails from.

Fun fact: Top friend-making tip: If you, like me, get a kick out of giving cheese as a gift, this is such a great option. A Crottin fits neatly into a larger pocket or a handbag, it's sturdy, travels well and is packed with flavour.

35
Tying the Knot

IT'S JUST NOT ENOUGH to know the cheeses well if you want to be an expert monger. There's a simple reason for this that ties back to our number one fan of Mrs Kirkham's Lancashire: we all experience them differently.

That's why you need to know yourself, to understand your own cheesy dispositions, and also try to know your customer's. No, I will never fully empathise with our Kirkham fan's deeply felt connection to Lancashire, but at the very least I can be open to imagining it. He radiates it, after all.

The other day, a young French woman came to the stall with an English friend. The French woman was talking her through the cheeses. I love it when that happens because I am so used to explaining them, it's good to hear someone else's perspective, particularly someone who grew up surrounded by them.

She had arrived at the bloomy rind cheeses and said that the Coulommiers was strong, much stronger than the Brie. I would jump in to ask her why she thought that, but on the day, she was spot on. Sometimes, it's milder than Brie, mind you. Depends.

Perhaps she grew up with a father who loved strong Coulommiers, or next to a cheese shop that had a different supplier of Brie de Meaux? Difficult to say. The point is her perception of those cheeses is at variance with mine, meaning that my capacity to sell her cheese will be competing with her childhood food associations. For me to open her eyes to a popping batch of Coulommiers will take a bit of guile. Know the cheeses, know your customers, know yourself.

I have read a French food writer refer to Époisses not as a cheese, but as 'a dream, a gourmet ritornello; a lingering taste, an olfactory imprint; a gustatory apostolate'.* (One can go too far with the cheeses, you don't need to tell me that.) Clearly, that writer and I don't share the same dreams – and who does exactly? That's my point. I need to be in the right mood for Époisses, and likewise, it has to be in the right mood for me. If it is riding a wave of creamy, bacon-y richness, I shall embark. Too much washed rind testosterone, too mature and I'm out.

I once had a customer butt in front of another – yes, that rudely – to say he was in a rush and needed to purchase one specific Époisses from the display. It was clear to me that it was a ripe Époisses, you could tell from looking at it, but so determined was he for that particular wheel and so rushed, I sold it to him without warning him how ripe it was. He returned the week after to complain it was too strong, a thing that happens so rarely, you remember each case. I misjudged that moment. I misjudged him. It was a good reminder that some folks come at selecting a cheese from a perspective that can be hard to suss out at first.

There is a type of customer who swaggers up to the cheese stall and asks in an over-loud register: 'What is your BEST cheese?'

Me: 'Well, it's hard to declare any one cheese better than all the others by its nature. Would you like to know what's best today? These little Castillon Frais are sublime. First of the season, fresh sheep's cheese. They're unusual, currently with a hint of sesame, low salt with a mousse-y texture.'

* Jacky Durand, *Libération*, 17 June 2010.

'Show this cheese to me.'

'It's right over here.'

'That cheese is small and costing £6.'

'Yes, indeed, sir. Quite reasonable. And versatile, lovely on its own, with a cracker, in salads or even with fruit.'

'No, no, no, no, no, no. This is not what I'm looking for. Not at all.'

'What are you looking for?'

'I am looking for premium.'

'Ah, I see.' He's looking for status cheese, a Rolex, a Porsche, or the Louis Vuitton of cheeses. I might have clicked to it if I'd paid more attention initially to his dress and the swagger.

'Do you like Alpine cheeses or blue cheese?'

'Which is the best?'

'Well, it's hard to … (never mind). Our Roquefort over here is produced by the smallest of only seven Roquefort producers. It's an exclusive affinage, done especially for us. This half wheel will be £72.'

'Wrap this up for me, please. I am travelling with it.'

'Would you like to taste it?'

'Not necessary. What else do you have?'

'Well, our Gruyère Suisse AOP, you won't find another like it in London. One kilo about £55, sir.'

'Give me three pieces of one kilogram.'

'Of course. Right away.'

Four guys from Serbia came to the stall one summer, dripping expensive male jewellery, shirts unfastened past the third buttonhole, hairy chests, the whole nine yards. They explained they were staying in a hotel and wanted to drink single malt whisky and eat fine cheese. They ended up buying a quarter-wheel of L'Étivaz and it cost them £250. I'll admit there was a part of me thinking primarily of the cheese as I prepared their order: 'Do I really want to send you home with these guys? Will they treat you properly, respect you and appreciate you?' In the end, I think they were all happy to be going back to the hotel together.

Know them, know the cheeses, know yourself. If you are out of balance on any of these fronts, you are not going to be an exceptional cheesemonger.

On that Awful Good Friday, how had I allowed myself to get so far out of kilter that I was mean to Cheesemonger Fionnuala, of all people?

'Nuala, can I talk to you a minute?'

'Of course, Michael. What is it?'

'I need to apologise to you for Good Friday.'

'God, what an awful day that was.'

'I know, but that doesn't matter. I shouldn't have snapped at you and become disrespectful. I'm sorry. Really, I'm kicking myself.'

'Oh Michael, thanks, but we all have bad days. I don't ever want to have a day like that again in my life. You know that was the worst day I have ever had here? That's saying something.'

'Me too, but I think I'm partly to blame for that.'

'You are, are you? Yes, maybe. Maybe the pandemic was partly to blame. Maybe the staffing was all wrong, the shifts were badly timed, the delivery got screwed up and came too late, maybe the customers weren't at their most excellent. Maybe a lot of things. Give yourself a break. But thanks. Let's not do it again.'

'Let's not. Maybe I'm doing too many shifts.'

'Maybe you are. Do you need the money that badly?'

'I'm trying to help out while Elle's in Wales.'

'I know and that's great. So when she gets back, maybe take some time off. I haven't been to Ireland in so long it's killing me.'

'How long?'

'Don't ask me! I'll start blubbering. All I know is this summer, if the restrictions are all lifted, I'm going for a couple of months.'

In that moment, something big happens. Not only has Fionnuala granted me absolution for my Good Friday behaviour, she's given me one of the keys to understanding how she keeps herself grounded, balancing her big, competing loves: home, and being among us, selling our awesome cheeses. Nuala has always been more adept at cheesecare than I am, she has a wickedly sharp palate and an eye for when a cheese is in distress. It seems that talent extends to herself, that she's aware enough to take out the metaphorical cheese iron and *carotte* herself regularly. Not me, or not yet anyway. My Comté had been souring for weeks before I was ready to stop, taste, evaluate, and choose a course of action. In fairness, this is a substantial improvement over having gone years living as Flat Comté without taking stock. Nevertheless, now here I am, knowing something is wrong.

If there was ever a time for a dram or two of Alison's whisky, it was after we closed up on the last evening of that Easter weekend. Sadly, the whisky was in Montreal. A pandemic pleasure of mine those days was to go for a takeaway pint of Guinness from my local. I would often order one, walk it round the corner to my flat, drink it, then return the glass. Sometimes rinse and repeat.

So it's plain that I have let myself veer off into the edges of that same sort of territory that led to my cinematic epiphany two years earlier. It crept up on me and I'm kicking myself. Now what?

Some uncomfortable questions follow: was it really cheese that acted as a cure for me, brought me to a better place, from flat to technicolour? Maybe you can get just as tired of cheesemongering as you can from the grind of breakfast radio presenting. Thankfully, mongering has delivered a lot of insight over the last two years, not least my axiom: Know the cheeses, know yourself, know the customers.

When I close my eyes to reset and reflect – deep breath – the magic of becoming a cheesemonger fills me almost to bursting, not just the cheeses, although that's already a lot, the whole thing: the learning, the skills, the market, the customers, and my colleagues, the other mongers, all in one big, glorious package. I think back to what Fionnuala said about returning to Ireland, how she needs it to stay balanced. This resonates with me, and I wonder how exactly Montreal will need to slot into my life.

Above all, when I reflect on the last few months, I realise that after decades of producing, editing and presenting in journalism, my tolerance for being in charge is nothing like it was. I now crave the energy of the cheeses and everything they represent – joy, sustenance, history, environment, humanity. I also crave the dynamic I get with our regulars and with the mongers. It's on another plane entirely. What I don't want to do is manage the operation.

Recently, two of our favourite regulars came to the stall, a handsome couple, great chemistry, who are always so happy to taste through things and choose together. What a delight when they approach the stall. She's French, he's English. They certainly know each other, have different tastes, one from the other, and are perfectly aware of it.

I give her a taste of a newly washed batch of Langres, and she says to him: 'This one's going to be so good for you!'

'Oh, you're right. I love it,' he tells me.

'Great, would you like one? I happen to have a half here, or a whole.'

'Oh, a half will do. It's just for me, right, honey?'

'Yep, I'm going to take a goat's cheese myself, so the half will do nicely,' she says.

We find her a goat's cheese, I pack their order up and we are saying good-bye when suddenly they seem to be lingering before taking their leave.

'Listen, there's something we'd like to tell you,' he says finally to me, looking serious but with a glint in his eye.

I get that slightly tingly, slightly trepidatious feeling you have when you anticipate an announcement is about to be made. 'What is it?'

She holds up her hand: an engagement ring.

'Oh. My. God. You guys are engaged! Congratulations! This is such fantastic news. Elle! Fionnuala! Come over here.'

'We wanted to make sure we told you, because we feel like our whole relationship has played out here at the cheese stall,' she says.

He jumps in. 'It's true. We always tell our friends that our cheesemongers knew before we did that we fancied each other.'

That is absolutely true, by the way, and good on them for owning it. Later, as we are closing, Elle says, 'Oh, come on. I mean, who didn't know those two fancied each other?'

'It's funny the things you realise and the things you don't,' I say. 'Thank God for cheesemongers knowing their customers.'

'I'll drink to that,' says Nuala. 'Hey, you guys up for a proper pint of Guinness this week in town?'

Many pints are shared among the three of us, and often with Esther from next door to boot. Sometimes around the corner at The Rake pub, sometimes on a mission for a good pint in the West End. During the pandemic, we sit for an hour on the kerbside with a big bottle of cider. After close on a Saturday, we often crack open a bottle, or two, of wine. One

night, epically, we find a hidden Soho speak-easy that Fionnuala knows about.

When I get the invitation for Elle's wedding, a year after
that awful Easter weekend that knocked me back so brutally, I
can't believe my eyes. I am both honoured and excited. I
planned to be in Canada at the time, but when I find out she
wants Nuala, Esther and me to come to Swansea to watch her
tie the knot, I change all my plans.

I remain a monger to this day – it's who I am – and there's
not much stress about my comings and goings with Cheese
HQ. I give them plenty of notice. I make sure I'm in London
for the busy times because I know that's good for them. They
like having someone they know and trust come to monger – I
love being back with the cheeses, the other mongers, and the
market. They're also happy to have one less employee in
slower times. I cannot resist the call of winter in London, an
enchanted time when the cheeses taste sublime and when
cheesemongers work, furiously but joyously, to keep up with
all the cheese love from our customers.

I dare to think I may have cracked it, the secret to my bright
Comté. When I'm back with the cheeses, I monger and don't
manage, even though I am happy to be left in charge on any
given day. I split my time between London and Montreal.
Montreal is in my blood, just as Ireland is in Fionnuala's. I've
even gone back to the radio to do a weekly column in French,
so I have the highs of live broadcasting and communion with
the audience, but none of the grind and little of the burden
involved in daily presenting. I've found a good balance. I know
broadcasting. I know myself. I know the people I work for. I
can thank the cheese cure for that.

There's something more. Cheesemongers are in the business of delight, feeding people with beguiling pleasures. What

a wonder to be part of that, and what a balm for the soul. Journalists are mongers of morosity, though it pains me to admit it – it prompts uncomfortable introspection. Yes, there is a trend towards what's called 'solutions journalism' and the sharing of 'good news'; however, the fact remains that a big part of a journalist's job is to deliver bad news, of wars, dictatorships, looming problems, natural disasters, human tragedies, crime, loss, bankruptcies, and so on. I've always been entertained in the company of journalists, but there is a good measure of gallows humour – it takes a toll. The fellowship of cheesemongers is fundamentally of a different nature. Becoming a monger has brought a measure of peace to my life I hadn't known, and a different, shinier happiness.

The day Elle gets married, everything is perfect. Well, almost everything. Certainly, the weather couldn't be better: brilliant blue sky, sunshine, and just enough wind to catch her veil, drawing it up to the heavens but not pulling it from her hair. We spend hours drinking, dancing, eating fish and chips, and playing games in the arcade on the pier. Later that night, plus ones elsewhere, Elle, Fionnuala and I sit in a booth beside the tray of cheese Owner Jon had laid on as a gift.

'No one is going to eat these cheeses.' Elle takes a forkful of Langres, somewhat glumly. At this point she is drooping a bit, we all are, like the cheeses before us.

'They have cut into all the Langres. It's a massacre.' Nuala laments.

'Wha-aat?' I am searching the platter for a Langres that has not been eviscerated.

'And they've baked all the Camemberts. Every wheel!' Elle can't believe it.

'They're Camembert de Normandie, not clubcard specials,' I protest, taking the full measure of the situation. 'How could they do that?' I ask Elle.

'Oh, I don't know. They're ruined. Don't tell Jon.' She looks like she might cry. We have all had a fair few drinks at this point.

'Well, the fish and chips were excellent.' It's true. I feel it needs to be mentioned as a mitigating factor.

'Guys,' Nuala says. 'We are such fucking snobs with these cheeses. We got what we deserved.' She starts to laugh and laugh and laugh pointing at all the sad, untouched baked Camembert de Normandie and the Langres pieces collapsing into piles of orange and ivory.

Are we snobs? I don't see it that way. We are damn good mongers, is what we are – bonded with cheese – and I love everything we are together.

Roquefort

'Roquefort is essential—a foundational product. Roquefort has the particularity of combining force and elegance. The sheep's milk gives it gentleness, and the mould gives it power and character.'

– Laurent Dubois, Maître Fromager, Meilleur Ouvrier de France

Origin: The origin story of Roquefort is a legend (yes, another one) and centres on a shepherd and his sheep cheese sandwich which he is about to tuck into when a beautiful woman distracts him. He places the cheese sandwich out of sight in a cave to pursue the woman and returns some time later to find the cheese in his sandwich has become mouldy

(*Penicillium roqueforti* at work). Hungry, he eats it anyway. Boom – the amazing taste of Roquefort cheese is discovered in that instant and the rest is history. Question, where did that delicious *Penicillium roqueforti* originate? From the cave or the bread? Some new research suggests the mould which produces the blueing in Roquefort comes from a plant pathogen of rye and not from cave air. This is one of several Roquefort rabbit holes you may want to dive into. One of the amusing ones is whether Charlemagne, the Holy Roman Emperor, fell in love with Roquefort after a monk persuaded him to stop picking out the blue mouldy bits with the sharp point of his knife. Certainly one of the key moments in Roquefort history (books have been written!) was on 26 July 1925, when it was granted the first ever *appellation d'origine*. Roquefort is always made from raw sheep's milk (only the Lacaune breed), always from sheep that feed in pastures in and around the Aveyron region, and always matured in the caves of Roquefort-sur-Soulzon with French *Penicillium roqueforti* moulds.

Presentation: About 20cm across and weighing around 3kg, Roquefort arrives in half wheels wrapped in foil. The paste is a wonder – such a pure white, spotted with blue moulds – a thing of beauty. Its high fat content means that it melts on the tongue like butter. Using a lyre, we cut wedges on demand. Roquefort can be a bit goopy, which is no bad thing, except when it's –5°C and you have several to wrap. Simply take the blade of a knife and give it a scrape for a clean appearance.

How to serve: Try it straight out of the refrigerator in summer – cold Roquefort melting in your mouth on a hot day is a wonder. Recognise that not all Roquefort is the same, some are sweeter, some are stronger. Get to know your palate and seek out the affinage that's right for you – there are only a handful of Roquefort producers and they produce different affinages that vary in strength and taste profile. For me, Roquefort is heavenly when it's sweet and salty at the same time, fruity, too, producing a headrush. It is delicious straight off the knife, unaccompanied. Popular food pairings include nuts like almonds or walnuts, breads and crackers, dried fruits and salads. Some swear on buttering bread before applying the Roquefort. For pairings, Sauternes is a classic. Try ice cider or ice wine. Peaty Islay whisky or bourbon, stouts or porters are also possible, so play around and trust your own taste buds.

Fun fact: In China, it's been a struggle to convert people to Roquefort because blue cheese is so alien to most folks there. A trick French Roquefort ambassadors use to make converts is to offer a slice of banana to calm the effect without completely masking the taste. It's not a bad pairing if you want to give it a try.

36
Cheese Daemons

AN UNINTENDED CONSEQUENCE OF my later-in-life career change-up was a brief tussle with my identity, mostly in other people's eyes, but in my own, as well, if I'm being honest. It took me several months to answer the oft-asked question as cleanly as this: I am at a bar in London, being introduced to someone I've never met.

'Are you working in London?'

'Yes. I'm a cheesemonger.'

'A cheesemonger? Cool! What is that, exactly?'

That's the reaction I hope for, but presenting myself as a cheesemonger came belatedly. For most of my first summer, when strangers asked, I answered, 'I'm a journalist.'

Thinking back, I suppose my hesitancy coincided with the imposter syndrome I felt wearing the apron. This was back when I believed I could never be a cheesemonger like Laurence or Tom or Emma. It was just beyond my reach. That meant that when I put on all the kit it felt like it was wearing me and not the other way around.

That first summer, the choices I was making made me sometimes feel less than. At an end-of-summer barbecue in South East London with a group of friends from Brazil, heaping plates of grilled meat and salad but no cheese, people come up to me and say, 'I hear you've got a new job?' They look happy enough for me, I mean, they are smiling, aren't they? Then as I start to describe cheesemongering and how much I am enjoying it, I can see their faces falling somewhat, looking puzzled with maybe a hint of disappointment, or is that sympathy?

'But aren't you a broadcast journalist?'

'I mean, I still am, but I'm loving cheesemongering and I'm learning so much.'

After a few caipirinhas, when I announce to a new arrival that I am learning to be a cheesemonger, a chorus of friends shouts out 'Part-time!', and everyone bursts out laughing.

This is a battle I am not going to win in this particular venue. Most of the people at the party went to extraordinary lengths to end up in London and fought their way to getting good, or just decent jobs. They cannot understand why a well-paid journalist would take up a service sector position by choice, working weekends, making less money. One of them tells the story of coming to meet me as I was closing one evening only to find me scrubbing tables and cleaning the floor in a pair of wellington boots. The story has now gone beyond laughter and a look of concern ripples through the faces listening. This is not what success looks like to them, and it is definitely not glamorous. It is a puzzling evolution to a privileged life, eccentric to say the least, possibly unstable.

What a contrast that same month when I am invited to a dinner party hosted by a friend I worked with at the BBC, just off the Holloway Road in North London. It is a dinner for ten, and I volunteer to bring the cheese course. At the stall on my break, I pick the best selection of the moment, the cheeses that are on fleek: a slice of Maréchal that smells of warm butter, celery and sage and a Gour Noir, goat's cheese with a bright white paste and dark grey rind that tastes of both the sweetness of goat's milk and the flintiness of wet stone. I choose a Langres with its rich, slightly boozy aroma and otherworldly pockmarked surface, and a slice of Cantal, a Cheddar-like cheese from the Auvergne that looks like something you might see on a medieval feast table. The Coulommiers is perfectly gooey and tastes lightly of garlic flower, the perfect complement to a wedge of Fourme d'Ambert, a blue cheese with a pink-ish hue, creamy with a taste similar to pan drippings and plenty of *fromunda*.

My audience is in cheese heaven and by extension, so am I, watching them. The platter goes round and round, people taking seconds and thirds, holding forth on which one is their favourite. Opinions are happily divided, challenges are tossed out. 'You must try this one! Give it a chance.' Someone mentions a convention that states you must not take a bit from every cheese on to your plate or it appears unseemly. Nonsense, I say. You have to taste them all.

When they ask me to talk them through each and every cheese, I have never seen people more rapt. My anecdotes from years as a broadcaster and journalist – watching George W. Bush and Vladimir Putin meet for the first time in Ljubljana, say – they never kill like this! These are successful Londoners – professionals, doctors, authors – people who were first acquainted with me as a journalist, for whom I have now been elevated to star status via cheese.

My new life that is mongering, writing and some broadcasting has required sacrifices. I'm no longer on a presenter's wage and while I may be a full-fledged monger, I'm not a manager, meaning I've had to downsize some projects I'd had for my future to fit my lifestyle into my more modest means. Honestly, the choice wasn't a hard one and thinking about it makes me smile because those former projects hold considerably less appeal than what I'm doing now. A simpler life agrees with me. When I'm in Montreal, it's a thrill and a comfort to know I retain the keys to the magical cheese kingdom back in London, and yes, keeping those keys requires the same amount of hard graft as it always has when I'm back at it, but the reward in kind is immense. It's all part of the package.

There is a swagger to cheesemongering as there is in almost every job, an energy, when you come to know what you're doing with enough confidence you radiate it. At this point, the apron no longer wears you, it rests over your shoulders with pride. When a customer asks for a difficult cut, you nod and proceed with confidence. You break open new wheels of cheese with flair and ceremony. You talk about the cheeses with deep knowledge and affection and customers take your counsel. Your wrapping is done efficiently and beautifully. Fewer things really surprise you in the life of your cheeses. You can even name the moulds that you see on them.

People want to be impressed by their cheesemonger – anything less is suspicious, diminishes the experience. What you want is for them to watch you with fascination as you pass the wire through a wheel of cheese and remark, 'Wow' or 'That's impressive' or 'I love watching this part.' You want them to have that look of satisfaction in their eye that shows they know they are in the hands of a professional.

I experienced the first suggestions of my cheesemonger swagger only in the autumn of 2019, after four solid months of training with Manager Tom. One day, a regular, a chef no less, asked if he could film me while I cut into a new wheel of Comté. I was surprised and thrilled, and when he sent me the video: I could barely recognise myself. Much later, a well-known author of cheese books came by the stall to place an order, and I pulled off a difficult cut. She exclaimed, 'That's some impressive mongering there.' I felt like a million pounds.

I will never stop wanting to observe my colleagues work, the other cheesemongers and their swagger: how they approach customers, how they break the ice, how they offer cheese for tasting, how they anticipate needs and desires, how much they direct their customers, how they describe the cheeses, whether they small talk and about what, whether they flirt and with whom, how they react to rejection or disrespect, how they close sales.

I remember Tom telling me when I was training that it's important to watch and to try to understand how our colleagues operate, to find out what kind of salesperson they are as you develop your style. The tills let you know how sales are going by a number of metrics. Whether and how often you check the 'Operator Totals' or 'Average Basket' says something about you, not always flattering. I check fairly often. When I say, 'I am whupping your arse today,' Manager Elle tends to answer with a smile, 'Go for it, Michael.' It's seldom a fair fight with Elle because she's busy being the manager, but in one-on-one battles, she often leaves me coughing up the dust from her wake.

An esprit de corps is in place throughout serving so that if there's an experience with a customer that is unusual, you have the sense your colleagues are right there for the assist when necessary, or silently supporting you, or whispering encouragement into your ear. 'You handled that well,' 'That was hard work,' or 'She kept you on your toes.'

On one of the days when a CBC Radio fan comes on a pilgrimage to the stall in Borough Market to meet me (yes, this happens), I am filling the blue towel dispenser. Blue towel is used to mop up spills. Something former Cheesemonger Manager Susan once taught me is that if you write 'Weeeeeeee!' in big, descending letters in black marker on the plastic film surrounding the blue towel before inserting it into the dispenser, you will delight the monger who does the next refill when they, in turn, go to change it. On opening the dispenser, the empty plastic will glide to the floor. You'll see the 'Weeeeeee!' as it floats downward and there'll be smiles all around. How can you not enjoy that? I wonder what that starry-eyed Montrealer thinks, catching me engaged in such frivolity.

At closing time, someone on shift will select a soundtrack. Many of our cheesemongers are in their late twenties and have a university arts education, so pop is normally off the menu, unless it's vintage or ironic. There's good new British music about, the kind you might hear on BBC 6 Music or on university radio, so there's a lot of that. Cameron is always a popular cheesemonger to end up with because he will gaily throw on ABBA. If I close on my own, I will often pick ABBA and pretend that Cameron is scrubbing alongside me but just out of sight. Tom has eclectic tastes. One time, early on, when it was my turn to choose, I put up a Shania Twain play-list, a bit of Canadiana that to my surprise delighted him. 'We listened to this all the time when I was a boy.' In the chorus to one of her best-known hits, I'd shout out while laughing, 'Oh so you're a cheesemonger? That don't impress me much.'

One day at the stall, the mongers and I have a discussion about what cheese comes closest to defining our true nature. In Philip Pullman's trilogy *His Dark Materials*, he imagines animal daemons. They are living manifestations of the inner selves of his characters – they both represent and comple-ment the spirit. His main character Lyra's daemon, Pantalai-mon, shapeshifts at first before finally settling on becoming a pine marten. Why can't cheesemongers have cheese daemons? It feels appropriate given the time we spend together.

I was going to call mine 'Maréchal', but Tom said it first. I find it a fitting tribute to him and his excellent training that I should have aspired to harbouring the same cheese spirit in my soul as he did. Why did we both want to be Maréchal? It's certainly a handsome cheese, a medium-wheeled Swiss Alpine, less forward than Gruyère or L'Étivaz. It has a habit of surprising the punters with its warm sage-like notes. I find it conjures a Sunday roast and all the comfort that goes with it because it can taste like a roast chicken dinner with stuffing. It is dependable and, occasionally, totally wow.

Cheesemonger Daisy is on that day. We all agree our cheese daemon is not Munster. In fact, we go further and say that Munster is simply not sexy. Goat's cheese is sexy. Although recently on Saturday, a really hot couple bought Munster and we felt a bit stumped by that. Maybe we are being a bit prudish with Munster.

Cheesemonger Susan loves Langres. Great fit for her. Premium, creamy and a bit punchy.

Daisy, I think, could do worse than having Cantal as the cheesy manifestation of her spirit, because it has a wonderful fizzy tang and a soul that goes back through the ages.

Cian's would be something with real flair, maybe Roquefort because it's bold, salty and sweet, and compared to its blue siblings, it is the boss. It can also be a bit tricky to handle.

Cheesemonger Molly has a passion for Mrs Kirkham's Lancashire. I have heard her advocate for it many times to the customers, going into detail about the cheesemakers and their process. As one of only two raw milk Lancashires left in England, it is exceptional, not prepared to compromise on its principles. It's versatile, you can have a lot of fun cooking with it, and it's the type of cheese you hanker after: big, rich and rewarding. As demonstrated by our number one Kirkham's fan, it forms solid attachments.

I see Cheesemonger Fionnuala's cheese sprite as some-thing approachable, warm and moreish, with notes that surprise. Our raw milk Camembert de Normandie really fits the bill, and she loves it. What a wonderful, smooth but complex flavour, a bit seashell, slightly garlicky. I associate it with the sea, as I do Nuala with the Irish Sea.

I can't help but hook Cheesemonger Manager Elle up with Selles-sur-Couffy, her favourite goat's cheese. When you cut it open, you get a gorgeous, fudgy, white paste that's not what you might expect from the exterior, and it's absolutely packed with depth and flavour. It's a cheese many customers get attached to.

I have always associated Owner Jon with Bleu de Termi-gnon, a rare cheese to find in London, or indeed in France. On display, it makes a big impression, much oohing and awing. As an unpierced blue – the blue moulds come natural-ly, not as a result of injection – it doesn't achieve its full beauty until you have cracked it open and spent some time with it. It is fussy. The blueing spreads gradually in from the rind towards the centre. Ours has a wild backstory, made by a female farmer and ski instructor with a smaller herd of cattle in the high alpine pastures of France.

Cheesemonger Manager Laurence is a nice fit for L'Étivaz, an Alpine AOP cheese from Switzerland that uses raw, summer milk. I've seen it described as 'an important cheese, boldly carrying the torch of tradition'. It is impressively complex, with all those warm Gruyère flavours of salted caramel, a real sense of terroir, plus smoky notes from the woodfire and even a tropical fruit zing which hits you unex-pectedly right in the nose when you cut into it.

I wonder if my cheese daemon isn't Saint-Félicien. It looks slightly unassuming in its wooden barquette with its golden rind, *Geotrichum candidum*, and patches of white. When you finally taste, there is a creamy richness to it with a hint of lactic sweetness, some solid *fromunda*, and a pillowy texture. It has devoted fans. Saint-Félicien is fortified with cream – sometimes it's a bit much, actually – and it's not unusual to find some bitterness. It's dependable, good value for money and a bit of patience with it will pay off. It's a cheese that can present a bit tight at first, but as it gently matures, it begins to break down into a gooey creaminess. At this point, strap yourself in and enjoy. Saint-Félicien is also served well, like me, with a chilled Sancerre or a light, fruity red.

Saint-Félicien

'Lorsqu'il devient en crème, c'est une petite merveille de fromage.'

– Didier Lassagne, fromager et affineur, Meilleur Ouvrier de France, calling the Saint-Félicien a 'little wonder of a cheese once it gets proper creamy'.

Origin: A Lyonnais cheesemaker came up with the recipe towards the beginning of the last century as a way to make the most of his unsold cream, so a fairly recent creation. It was inspired by a goat's cheese by the same name from the Ardèche, but it's made using exclusively cow's milk and cream. The first written mention of it dates to 1956.

Presentation: Each wheel is about 10cm in diameter and 2cm high. Because they're soft and creamy inside – so soft they can run away – they're often sold in little terracotta dishes or in paper trays set into a wooden barquette.

How to serve: Never straight out of the fridge. Lashings of
Saint-Félicien over crusty bread, tough to beat. Pair with a
white Sancerre or a lighter, fruity red.

Fun fact: The fact Saint-Félicien is enriched with cream doesn't
always endear it to the more serious cheesemongers.
However, when it's on point, it packs a creamy cheese wallop
that's hard to resist.

Acknowledgements

BRINGING THIS BOOK TO life has been a joy and an education. During the many pandemic weeks, writing at my desk looking out over the Borough, the Shard poking out from amidst the trees, it all came gushing out indulgently. Long-form writing was a novelty for me and if it weren't for Claire Bolderson and Bridgette Kam reigning me in and nudging me forward, I think the whole enterprise might have come to a screeching halt. I'm grateful for Claire's wisdom, insight, and generosity at that tender, formative stage. Initially, it was Bill Richardson who helped light the fire.

I owe a great debt to my French sister, Catherine Roux, for her constant enquiries about my progress during the many family meals she hosted in North London as the years went by and my writing advanced in fits and starts. To the entire Roux clan who adopted me into their family at the awkward age of sixteen, I am not only grateful but forever changed. This book would certainly not exist if it weren't for you.

The Arvon Foundation's memoir workshop in the Shropshire springtime provided a key breakthrough. Thanks to Alexander Masters, Ciaran Thapar and my writing cohort for their community and support. The grounds bursting into flower were a powerful metaphor; the sheep and cattle grazing nearby provided the ideal touchstone for a writing cheesemonger.

I am indebted to all my readers for bringing their perspectives to bear: Andie Bennett, David Ferguson, Heather Harris,

Tom Richardson, Naomi Drummond. Helen Evans was that midterm reader who got me over a big hurdle with resolute backing and crucial notes. She has walked with me every step of the way, good times and bad, and is this book's godmother alongside my extraordinary friend, Claire. This book would never have been what I wanted it to be if it weren't for Andrew Wilson asking whether she'd mind him having a look at the manuscript on her night table and then proceeding to bring not just conviction, but a clear vision to the final product. Thank you so much.

I owe another debt of gratitude altogether to my crew at CBC Daybreak in Montreal, and especially Sara DuBreuil, Rebecca Ugolini, Shari Okeke, Julie Chamberlain, Claudia Sanchez, Laura Marchand, Jessica Rusnak, Jennifer Yoon, Leta Poulson and Meredith Dellandrea. All those crazy mornings together! Radio does not just disappear into the ether. To Pascale Lévesque and Pénélope McQuaide, in whose company I am currently continuing my romance with the wireless, thank you for your priceless solidarity. My thanks as well to the many listeners who shared so much time with me over the years, and in particular to all those who made a point of coming to see me from Canada to the cheese stall at Borough Market.

Thanks to Jean-Louis Klingel for the smaller box, to Sal Fierro for skin the cat, to Mike Guzzo for his prodding, and Fay Jagger for all the snatches and her boundless cheese excitement. They taught me I could exceed physical expectations which, as it turns out, was a big part of all of this. Graham Griffiths and Rainey Tisdale have always thought big thoughts and inspired me to do likewise. Thanks to Leandro Sudario for his indomitable spirit, affection and backing. I am lucky to have two powerful journalist-artists in my orbit, Rachel Reid and Leslie Knott, around whose creative fires I have been warmed and recharged. Speaking of light and warmth, my dear friends Melissa Calaresu and Mark Kilfoyle have been constantly supportive companions in this enterprise.

My cheesemongering crew, how massive are you. Thanks for welcoming me into the society, with special mention to Jon Thrupp and Jane Hastings for embracing me, imparting so much knowledge and for putting up with my comings and goings. Likewise to Laurence Lindars and to Emma Young for your faith from the start. For their unmatched fellowship and mongering *esprit de corps*, thanks to Elle Lovell, Victoria Stewart-Liberty, Tom Richardson, Molly Powell, Cian Holland, Daisy MacDonald, Emily Thrupp, Llewi Roberts, Taylor Lyttleton, Cameron Abery, Martha May, Laurie Pike, Yasha Muraben, Thomas Cary, Jake Egelnick, Daniel Benson, Andrew Postlethwaite, Anne Hastings, Samuel Moore, and to Emily Wright, who came on stage after the events of this book and who has delivered so much camaraderie and so many wonderful moments that I could fill another tome. Marika Pincigher has been a key, cheesy booster and is a force of nature, understanding without reading a single word what this project was all about. At Borough Market, I have had endless good vibes, companionship and inspiration from the Crouches, Phil, Esther, Benjamin and Jonathan, from Francesco Buffone, John Trindle, Pietro Alberti, and Bill Oglethorpe and others too numerous to mention. To our glorious, cheese-loving customers, I really don't think you know how much your passion and energy fuel our days and our spirits.

My agent, Rachel Mills, popped into my life like a bolt of irrepressible belief and enthusiasm. She seemed instantly to get everything as I'd intended, honing into the heart of what I'd written. I wish everyone could have a champion the size of her. To the team at HarperCollins UK, so much gratitude and respect to my editor Joel Simons for his faith in this book, to

Iker Ayesteran for the lush illustration, Annie Lee for her red pencil, Kara Nielsen for her magical spark, Christopher Kwok and Gaurika Kumar for making things happen. Thanks to Fuchsia Dunlop and James Read for their encouragement and generous insights into the world of food writing and publishing.

To the cheesemakers and the cheeses, I am in awe of what you do, which is nothing short of miraculous. This journey of discovery is because of you, and the road ahead exciting.

Finally to Dom Prigent, for the perfect desk, the lush garden, your steadfast love. You are my Breton lighthouse.